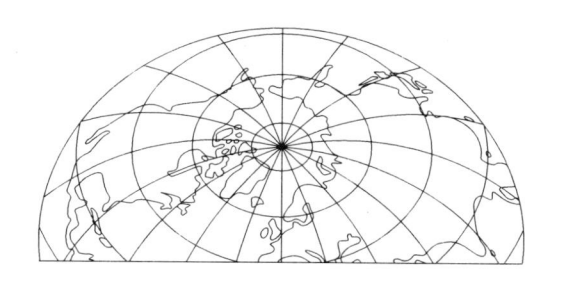

資料で読む
欧米の社会と文化

菊池 重雄 編著
佐藤 成男

大学教育出版

from THE GREAT GATZBY by F. Scott Fitzgerald
Copyright © 1925 by Charles Scribner's Sons.
Copyright renewed © 1953 by Frances Scott Fitzgerald Lanahan.

Used by permission of Harold Ober Associates Incorporated, New York
through Tuttle-Mori Agency, Inc., Tokyo

A TESTAMENT OF HOPE (Page 497-504) by Martin Luther King, Jr.
Reprinted by arrangement with The Heirs to the Estate of Martin Luther King, Jr.,
c/o Writers House Inc., as agent for the proprietor
through Tuttle-Mori Agency, Inc., Tokyo

Copyright © 1968 by Martin Luther King Jr.,
copyright renewed by Coretta Scott King

まえがき

　欧米、とりわけ、英語文化圏を構成する主要国である、イギリスとアメリカ合衆国について学ぼうとする場合に、英語で書かれた文書資料をとおして研究することは当然のことと言えます。翻訳書を利用して研究することも可能ですが、訳者によって生じる微妙な言い回しや行間のニュアンスの差異など、原典と照らし合わせて読めば、翻訳という行為もまた、訳者による原典資料の一解釈であることがわかります。たとえば、現在ではシェイクスピアの戯曲を数種類の翻訳で読むことができますが、同じ作品でも翻訳者が異なることで、異なった印象を読者に与えます。また、ハリウッド映画などでも、字幕なしで見た後、改めて字幕スーパー付きのものを見直すと、まるで違った印象を受けることがあります。映画字幕の場合はスクリーン内の字数制限の問題もありますが、それにしても、登場人物の印象が、台詞のちょっとした翻訳の違いで見事に変わってしまいます。

　こうしたことを念頭に、本書では、読者が原典資料をベースにして、各ジャンルを学べるように配慮しました。読者は各章の英文資料を原典資料として、辞書を片手に、自力で読む必要があります。各執筆者の邦文を英文資料の前に読むか、後から読むかは、章ごとに異なりますが、いずれにしても邦文部分は英文資料の説明・解説・分析・評価として機能しています。邦文部分は英文資料の読み方の方向性（のひとつ）を示唆したものと考えていただくとよいと思います。また、それぞれの英文資料から、どのような問題提起が可能かということを示したのが邦文部分と考えていただいても差し支えありません。

　本書は4章で構成されています。最初に、英語そのものがどのような言語なのかということを歴史的文脈の中で学びます（第1章）。次に、言語および言語体系の意味や、社会の中で言語の果たす役割について英語の側面から学びます（第2章）。その上で、読む対象としての言語を代表する立場から、文学作品の考察を行い（第3章）、さらに、聴く対象としての言語を代表する立場から、教

会説教について考察します（第4章）。周知のように、言語とはその言語が使用される文化圏のアイデンティティの源、もしくはアイデンティティそのものであります。そのようなわけで、社会から切り離された言語文化は成り立ち得ません。執筆にあたっては、いずれの章でも、特にそのことに留意しました。

本書の出版に際して、新聞記事や公文書、書簡や日記など、多くのジャンル、文書が候補に挙がりました。今回とりあげることのできなかったジャンルに関しては、次の機会に譲りたいと思います。

大学教育出版の佐藤守氏には英文資料の版権取得にかかわるさまざまな問題を解決していただきました。心からの感謝を申し上げる次第です。

資料で読む欧米の社会と文化

目　次

第1章　アングロサクソン時代の言語 …………………………… 1

1. 英語のルーツ ………………………………………………… 1
2. 「英語をブリテン島に持ち込んだ民族とは？」 ………………… 8
3. 英語の言語名の起源について ……………………………… 12
4. テキストについて …………………………………………… 15
5. テキスト ……………………………………………………… 18
6. Appendix …………………………………………………… 48

第2章　言語と文化──社会文化的なアプローチを中心に …… 51

はじめに ………………………………………………………… 51
1. テキスト1── Language and the environment …………… 52
2. 記号体系としての言語とそのはたらき …………………… 58
   (1) 言語と人間と社会　58
   (2) 言語研究のパラダイム　59
   (3) 体系としての言語（language as system）　59
   (4) 内在化された知識としての言語（language as knowledge）　61
   (5) 社会的行為としての言語（language as behaviour）　61
   (6) 芸術としての言語（language as art）　62

3. テキスト2 ── Inter-organism and intra-organism perspectives … 62
　　4. 人間の社会化へのプロセス ……………………………………………… 67
　　　　社会化のプロセスにおける言語の役割（social perspectives）　68
　　　　　（1）個人（individual）と集団（group）　68
　　　　　（2）社会（society）と社会的役割（social roles）　69
　　5. テキスト3 ── Language and social structure ……………………… 70
　　6. 言語とその社会文化的な役割……………………………………………… 80
　　　　社会的─記号的視点に立った言語へのアプローチ　80
　　　　　（1）M.A.K. Halliday の機能的な言語分析　80
　　　　　（2）状況コンテクスト　82
　　　　　（3）文化のコンテクスト　84
　　　　言語と文化のコンテクスト　85
　　おわりに ………………………………………………………………………… 85

第3章　フィッツジェラルドの『偉大なギャツビー』を読む …… 88

　　1. ……………………………………………………………………………… 88
　　2. ……………………………………………………………………………… 98
　　3. ……………………………………………………………………………… 109

第4章　公民権運動とキング牧師の説教 …………………………… 122

1. A Knock at Midnight …………………………………………… 122
2. "A Knock at Midnight" を読む ……………………………… 133
　はじめに　133
　Ⅰ　133
　Ⅱ　136
　Ⅲ　140
3. Antidotes for Fear ……………………………………………… 145
　Ⅰ　147
　Ⅱ　148
　Ⅲ　149
　Ⅳ　152
4. "Antidotes for Fear" を読む ………………………………… 157
　はじめに　157
　Ⅰ　158
　Ⅱ　162
5. "Paul's Letter to American Christian" を読む …………… 169
　はじめに　169
　Ⅰ　170
　Ⅱ　172

資料で読む欧米の社会と文化

第1章　アングロサクソン時代の言語

1. 英語のルーツ

　まず英語のルーツについて説明してゆきたいと思う。英語の究極の先祖はインド・ヨーロッパ祖語（Proto-Indo-European）であり、英語はインド・ヨーロッパ語族（Indo-European family of languages）の中に入る。インド・ヨーロッパ語族という名前は地理的な呼び名から来ており、東はインドから西はヨーロッパのアイスランドに到る地域で話されている言語を意味する。今日、世界の言語の総数は、約3,000と言われている。その中で、系統的（genealogical）に確立されている主要な語族は、約10語族である。その中で一番有名なものが、インド・ヨーロッパ語族（Indo-European family of languages）である。インド・ヨーロッパ語族は、9つの語派に分類される。(1) インド語派（Indian）、(2) イラン語派（Iranian）、(3) アルメニア語派（Armenian）、(4) ギリシア語派（Hellenic or Greek）、(5) アルバニア語派（Albanian）、(6) イタリック語派（Italic）、(7) バルト・スラブ語派（Balto-Slavic）、(8) ケルト語派（Celtic）、(9) ゲルマン語派（Germanic）である。また、今世紀になって、今日のトルコで発見されたヒッタイト語は、アナトリア語派（Anatolian）に属す。また、同じく20世紀になって中国のトルキスタンで発見されたトカラ語は、トカラ語派（Tocharian）に属しやはりインド・ヨーロッパ語族の中に入る。

　しかし、同じインド・ヨーロッパ語族の領域内に入ると思われる言語でも、例えばフィンランド語（Finnish）やハンガリー語（Hungarian）は、ウラル語族（Uralic）に属す。また、旧約聖書の言語として知られるヘブライ語（Hebrew）や、アラビア語（Arabic）などは、セム語族（Semitic）に属す。インド・ヨーロッパ語族の個々のメンバーが解明されるようになったのは、18世紀後半以降のことである。

18世紀以前、中世のヨーロッパの人たちは、旧約聖書の言語がヘブライ語（Hebrew）であるということから、世界で一番古い言語はヘブライ語であると考えていた。「創世記」（Genesis）の中に描かれているバベルの塔の事件で神の逆鱗（げきりん）に触れ、人々は色々な地域に分散して行き、それぞれの地域で個別の言語が発達したと考えていた。

Authorized King James Version の『創世記』（Genesis）第11章の中でバベルの塔の事件は次のように書き記されている。

"And the whole earth was of one language, and of one speech. And it came to pass, as they journeyed from the east, that they found a plain in the land of Shinar; and they dwell there. And they said one to another, Go to, let us make brick, and burn them throughly. And they had brick for stone, and slime had they for morter. And they said, Go to, let us build us a city and a tower, whose top *may reach* unto heaven; and let us make us a name, lest we be scattered abroad upon the face of the whole earth. And the Lord came down to see the city and the tower, which the children of men builded. And the Lord said, Behold, the people *is* one, and they have all one language; and this they begin to do: and now nothing will be restrained from them, which they have imagined to do. Go to, let us go down, and there confound their language, that they may not understand one another's speech. So the Lord scattered them abroad from thence upon the face of all the earth: and they left off to build the city. Therefore is the name of it called Babel; because the Lord did there confound the language of all the earth: and from thence did the Lord scatter them abroad upon the face of all the earth."

世界中は同じ言葉を使って、同じように話していた。東の方から移動してきた人々は、シンアルの地に平野を見つけ、そこに住み着いた。彼らは、「れんがを作り、それをよく焼こう」と話し合った。石の代わりにれんがを、しっくいの代わりにアスファルトを用いた。彼らは、「さあ、天まで届く塔のある町を建て、有名になろう。そして、全地に散らされることのないようにしよう」と言った。主は降って来て、人の子らが建てた、塔のあ

るこの町を見て、言われた。「彼らは一つの民で、皆一つの言葉を話しているから、このようなことをし始めたのだ。これでは、彼らが何を企てても、妨げることはできない。我々は降って行って、直ちに彼らの言葉を混乱させ、互いの言葉を混乱させ、互いの言葉が聞き分けられぬようにしてしまおう。」主は、彼らをそこから全地に散らされたので、彼らはこの町の建設をやめた。こういうわけで、この町の名はバベルと呼ばれた。主がそこで全地の言葉を混乱（バラル）させ、また、主がそこから彼らを全地に散らされたからである。（新共同訳）

ところが1786年のジョーンズ卿（Sir William Jones）の講演がきっかけとなり、中世ヨーロッパの人々の言語認識は一掃されることになった。ジョーンズ卿は、1783年インドのカルカッタで裁判官となったが、インドの古い文語であるサンスクリット語に強い関心を示し研究した結果、サンスクリット語は、ギリシャ語、ラテン語、古ペルシャ語と多くの点で類似点を持っていることに気づき、このことを"ヒンズー語について（On the Hindus）"という講演の中で発表した。ジョーンズ卿は、サンスクリット語、ギリシア語、ラテン語、古ペルシア語は、1つの共通の祖語（common ancestor language / proto-language or primitive language / parent language）から進化したのではないかと考えた。次の文章は、ジョーンズ卿（1746-1794）の *The Works of Sir William Jones* I-VI.（London : Robinson & Evans, 1799, 6 vols.）からの引用である。

" The Sanskrit language, whatever be its antiquity, is of a wonderful structure ; more perfect than the Greek, more copious than the Latin and more exquisitely refined than either ; yet bearing to both of them a stronger affinity, both in the roots of verbs and in the forms of grammar, than could possibly have been produced by accident ; so strong, indeed, that no philologer could examine them all three without believing them to have sprung from some common source, which, perhaps, no longer exists : there is a similar reason, though not quite so forcible, for supposing that both the Gothic and Celtic, though blended with a very different idiom, had the same origin with the Sanskrit ; and the Old Persian might be added to the same family."

(Vol.I pp.19-34)

　サンスクリット語は、その古さがどのようなものであっても、すばらしい構造から出来ている。ギリシャ語よりも完全で、ラテン語よりも豊かであり、ギリシャ語及びラテン語よりも非常に洗練されている。しかし、サンスクリット語は、ギリシャ語及びラテン語に対して動詞の語根においても、文法の形態においても恐らく偶然に作りだされたものではないだろうかと考えないではいられないくらいの類似性を持っている。その類似性は、実際非常に強いので、学者は3つの言語を調査すれば、必ずこの3つの言語がある共通の源から生じたものではないかと思ってしまう。おそらくこの共通の源は、もはや存在しない。また、それほど強い根拠ではないが、ゴート語とケルト語には非常に異なった言い回しが混じり合ってはいるけれど、ゴート語とケルト語もサンスクリット語と起源が同じではないだろうかと考えるだけの理由がある。さらに古ペルシャ語も同じ語族に加えてもよいかもしれない。

　彼のこの1786年の講演によって、サンスクリット語とヨーロッパの諸言語との関連性が確立されることになった。

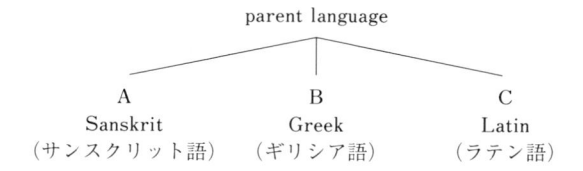

```
              parent language
         ┌─────────┼─────────┐
         A         B         C
      Sanskrit   Greek     Latin
   （サンスクリット語）（ギリシア語）（ラテン語）
```

　Jones の講演が契機となり、比較言語学（comparative linguistics）の歴史が始まり、諸言語間の比較研究が飛躍的進歩を遂げることになった。やがてこの共通の源（common source = common ancestor language / proto-language or primitive language / parent language）は、インド・ヨーロッパ祖語（Proto-Indo-European / Primitive Indo-European）として確立されていくことになる。

　ジョーンズ卿以降、古ノルド語（Old Norse）とドイツ語との関連を明らかにしたラスムス・ラスク（Rasmus Rask：1787〜1832）、グリムの法則（Grimm's Law）を発見したヤコブ・グリム（Jacob Grimm：1785〜1863）、ラテン語や

ギリシア語の形態を解明するためにサンスクリット語の形態を用いて説明したフランツ・ボップ（Frants Bopp：1791～1867）、そして、チャールズ・ダーウィン（Charles Darwin）の進化論の影響を受けてその考え方を言語に適用し、言語を生物学的有機体とみなし系統樹説（family tree theory）を提唱したシュライヒャー（August Schleicher：1821～1868）、波紋説（wave theory）を提唱したヨハネス・シュミット（Johannes Schmidt：1843～1901）、青年文法家と呼ばれるカール・ブルグマン（Karl Burgmann）等が現れ、比較言語学の領域で多いに貢献することになった。

　英語という言語は、ゲルマン語（Germanic）に属す。ゲルマン語はさらに3つのグループに分れる。即ち、北ゲルマン語（North Germanic）、東ゲルマン語（East Germanic）、西ゲルマン語（West Germanic）である。O.W. Robinson（1992, p.12）に基づいてゲルマン語（以降 Gmc と略記）の系統を示すと図1の通りになる。

　伝統的な解釈では、図1のゲルマン語の語系図から明らかなように、ゲルマン祖語（Proto-Gmc or Primitive Gmc）は、東ゲルマン語（East Gmc）、北ゲルマン語（North Gmc）、西ゲルマン語（West Gmc）に分かれたとする。West Gmc は、アングロ・フリジア語（Anglo-Frisian）とドイツ語祖語（Proto-German）に分れ、アングロ・フリジア語は、さらに古英語（Old English）と古フリジア語（Old Frisian）に分かれ、英語は Old English を通して現在に、フリジア諸島の言語であるフリジア語は、Old Frisian を通して現在に到る。ドイツ語祖語は、古高地ドイツ語（Old High German）と古低地ドイツ語（Old Low German）に分かれ、Old High German の系統から現代のドイツ語およびイディッシュ語（Yiddish）が誕生する。また、Old Low German（古サクソン語（Old Saxon）や古オランダ語（Old Dutch）が含まれる）の系統を継いでいる言語が低地ドイツ語（Low German）とオランダ語（Dutch）、アフリカーンス語（Afrikaans）である。アイスランド語（Icelandic）、アイスランドとシェトランド諸島の中間にあるフェロー諸島の言語であるフェロー語（Faeroese）、ノルウェー語（Norwegian）、デンマーク語（Danish）、スウェーデン語（Swedish）は、北ゲルマン語に属す。また、17世紀に死語となってしまったが、4世紀に

ウルフィラ（Wulfila）が四福音書をギリシャ語から翻訳した文献が残っているゴート語（Gothic）は、東ゲルマン語に属す。また、R. Rass（1987, p.17）は、Primitive Gmc は最初 North-West Gmc と East Gmc の2つに分かれ、次の段階で North-West Gmc は、North Gmc と West Gmc に分かれたと指摘しており Robinson の解釈とは少々異なっている。また、Rass は、West Gmc は、イングヴェオーニック（Ingvaeonic）と古高地ドイツ語（High German）に分裂、イングヴェオーニックは、さらにアングロ・フリジア語と低地ドイツ語に分かれたとしている。低地ドイツ語は、古サクソン語と古低地フランコニア語に分裂し、それぞれ近代低地ドイツ語（Modern Low German）と近代オランダ語（Modern Dutch）へと発達したと考える。高地ドイツ語（High German）は、古高地ドイツ語（Old High German）を経て近代高地ドイツ語（Modern High German）と近代イデイッシュ語（Modern Yiddish）へと個別の発達を遂げたと考えている。

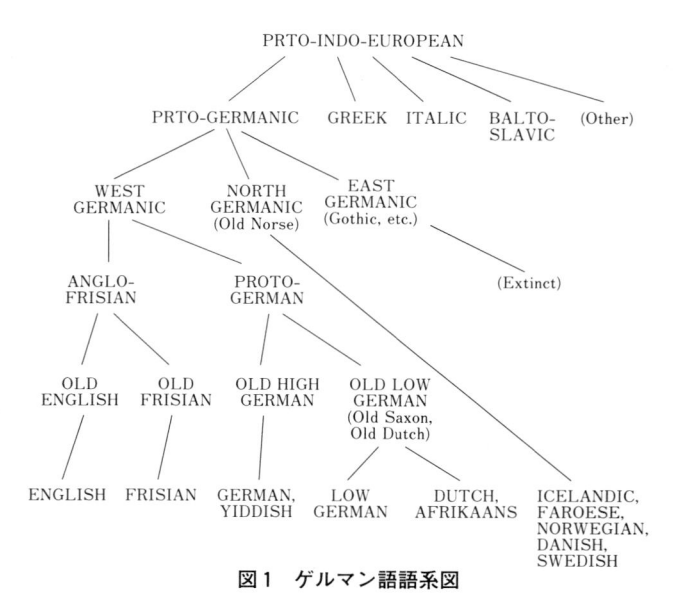

```
                      PRTO-INDO-EUROPEAN
                    /        |      |       |         \
          PRTO-GERMANIC   GREEK  ITALIC  BALTO-    (Other)
         /      |      \                 SLAVIC
      WEST    NORTH    EAST
   GERMANIC  GERMANIC GERMANIC
             (Old Norse)(Gothic, etc.)
     /    \       |                         (Extinct)
  ANGLO-  PROTO-
  FRISIAN GERMAN
   /  \    /   \
  OLD  OLD  OLD HIGH  OLD LOW
 ENGLISH FRISIAN GERMAN GERMAN
                        (Old Saxon,
                        Old Dutch)
   |    |     |       |      |       ICELANDIC,
ENGLISH FRISIAN GERMAN, LOW   DUTCH,  FAROESE,
                YIDDISH GERMAN AFRIKAANS NORWEGIAN,
                                        DANISH,
                                        SWEDISH
```

図1 ゲルマン語語系図
Fig. I. The traditional English family tree.
(O.W. Robinson 1992 : 12)

また、インド・ヨーロッパ語族の分類法に関するもう1つの説を紹介することにする。F. von Bradke は、Proto-Indo-European（インド・ヨーロッパ祖語）が、2つの方言、ケンテゥムグループ（Centum group）とサテムグループ（Satem group）に分かれて、そこから色々な語派に分かれていったという説を1890年提唱した。彼は、「百」を表す単語の語頭子音に着目し、「百」を表す単語の語頭子音が/k/音であるものを Centum group とし、また、「百」を表す単語の語頭子音が/s/音で始まる言語を Satem group に分類した。Centum および Satem は、それぞれラテン語とアヴエスタ語で「百」を意味する。「百」を表す単語の語頭子音によってインド・ヨーロッパ語族を Centum group と Satem group に分けた。ギリシア語派（Greek）／イタリック語派（Italic）／ケルト語派（Celtic）／ゲルマン語派（Germanic）は、Centum group に属し、インド語派（Indian）／イラン語派（Iranian）／アルメニア語派（Armenian）／バルトスラブ語派（Balto-Slavic）／アルバニア語派（Albanian）は、Satem group に属すと考えた。Centum group に属す言語で「百」を意味する単語は次のようになる。

Latin：*centum* / Greek：*(he)katón* / Old Irish：*cét* / Welsh：*cant* / Gothic：*hund*（Germanic では、Grimm's Law（グリムの法則）より k > h となる）

Satem group に属す言語で、「百」を意味する単語は次に示す通りである。

Sanskrit：*śatam* / Avestern：*satem*：Old Church Slavic (= Old Bulgarian)：*sŭto* / Lithuanian：*šim̃tas*

以上、彼の考え方を図示すると、次の様になる。

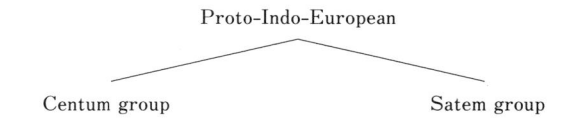

```
            Proto-Indo-European
           ╱                  ╲
    Centum group          Satem group
```

しかし、20世紀初頭中国のトルキスタンで発見されたトカラ語（Tocharian）では、「百」を表す単語の語頭子音は känt or kante で Centum group の特徴を示

している。地理的には Satem group に属すにもかかわらず、語頭子音の対応（k > s への子音交替を示さず、k のままである）に関しては、Centum group の特徴を示していることになる。東群（Satem group）にありながら西群（Centum group）の特徴を示しているということは、Bradke が主張しているようにインド・ヨーロッパ祖語が 2 つの方言に分かれていないことになる。

2.「英語をブリテン島に持ち込んだ民族とは？」

英語の歴史の初期の時代に起こった様々な出来事を知る上で欠かせない言語資料として「アングロ・サクソン年代記」（*Anglo-Saxon Chronicle*）とイギリスのノーサンブリア出身の修道僧であり歴史家のビード（Bede）が 731 年頃書いた「英国国民教会史」（*Historia Ecclesiastica Gentis Anglorum*）を挙げることが出来る。ビードの「英国国民教会史」と「アングロ・サクソン年代記」によれば、ブリテン島はかつて約 350 年間ローマ帝国の属州となっていた時代があった。しかし、ローマ帝国はゲルマン民族であるフン族の侵入を受け、当時ブリテン島に駐屯していたローマ軍は 410 年、全軍ローマに撤退することとなった。その後の経緯は次に示すとおりである。

当時、神のキリストにおける顕現後 423 年であった。テオドシウス II 世が、ホノリウスの後を継ぎ皇帝の地位に就いた。テオドシウスは、26 年間帝国を治めた。彼は、アウグストゥスから王位を継承して 45 代目であった。セレスティヌスと呼ばれるローマ教皇により、キリスト教を信じるスコット人のもとにパラディウス司教が派遣されたのは、テオドシウスの治世 8 年目のことであった。また、彼の治世 23 年目のことであるがアエティウスと呼ばれる有名な人がおり、彼は以前元老院議員の地位にあって、また 3 度ローマの将軍の地位に就いた人であった。そんな彼のもとに、ブリトン人の生存者たちから 1 通の手紙が届き、その手紙の初めにはこんな風に書き記されていた。

「3 度将軍の地位に就いたアエティウス様へ、ここにブリトン人のうめき声と悲しみが書き記されております。」彼等は、手紙の中で彼らの惨めな様子を述べた。「野蛮人により我々は海へと追いやられ、また海が我々を野蛮人のもとへと

押し戻す。野蛮人と海の狭間で我々はかくして二重の死に苦しんでいるのです。我々は、突き刺されて殺されるか、海の中で溺れ死ぬしかありません。」彼らはこのように嘆願したにもかかわらず、彼から何の手助けも得ることが出来なかった。というのは、彼等は当時フン族の王、ブレッドラとアッティラとの戦闘にあけくれていたからである。

　過去においては、援軍を派遣してもらうことは出来たが、結局彼らの願いは聞き入れてはもらえなかった。ブリトン人は北部のピクト人やスコット人の攻撃を受け、どこか他に助けを求めざるを得なかった。ブリトン人は、ピクト人やスコット人の度重なる侵入を食い止めるために何をなすべきか、どこに助けを求めるべきかを相談し、海の向こうのサクソン人を呼び寄せて救ってもらうことで、彼らの王であるボーティガンと意見が一致した。

　449年アングロ・サクソン人がボーティガンに招聘されて三隻の長い船に乗りブリテン島にやって来た。彼等はブリテン島の東部にあるサネット島に定住地を与えられた。最初は彼等と戦ってブリテン島を守護するためではあったが、彼らの真意はブリテン島の征服であった。それゆえに、アングロ・サクソン人は北部からやって来た敵と戦って勝利を収めた。やがて、この勝利は本国においてこの国の肥沃さと、ブリトン人の臆病さを示すものとして知られることとなり、以前にもましてかなりの艦隊が派遣された。この艦隊は、先にブリテン島にやって来た艦隊と一緒になり無敵の艦隊となった。

　ブリテン島にやって来たこれらの侵略者たちは、サクソン人、アングル人、およびジュート人の3民族である。最初にブリテン島にやって来た民族は、ヘンゲストとホルサ兄弟率いるユトランド半島の北部に住むジュート人であった。彼らはサネット島のエップスフリートに上陸して、今日のケント、ワイト島、およびハンプシャーの地域に住みつきケント王国を築いた。アングル人は、ジュート人よりかなり遅れてユトランド半島の南部からやって来て、ブリテン島の東部沿岸沿いに定住し、マーシャ王国、ハンバー川の北部のノーサンブリア王国および東アングリア王国を築いた。サクソン人は、ユトランド半島の南部および西部から北海の沿岸沿いに沿ってやって来て、477年からブリテン島の南部および南東部地域に定住した。そして、ウエセックス王国、サセックス王国、エセックス王国を築いた。これらのアングロ・サクソン人の3民族が築い

た王国をアングロ・サクソン七王国（Anglo-Saxon Heptarchy）と言う。

　最初アングロ・サクソン人はピクト人やスコット人を駆逐するために、ブリトン人の王ボーティガンに招聘されてブリテン島にやって来た。やがて次から次にこれらの民族はブリテン島にやって来て突然ピクト人と同盟を結び、矛先を彼らの同盟者であるブリトン人に向けることになった。アングロ・サクソン人とブリトン人の戦いは数10年間におよび、アングロ・サクソン人の優位は揺るぎないものとなった。さらに100年間にわたって、アングロ・サクソン人の移民がブリテン島にやって来て、北部や西部の高地地方は別にして、彼らの居留地は拡大し、英語の出現の土台が築かれることとなった。

　597年アウグスティヌス率いる約40名のローマの宣教師たちが、ケント王国のサネット島に上陸しアングロ・サクソン人をキリスト教に改宗させる仕事に着手し始めたが、6世紀のブリテン島で一番繁栄していた王国が、ケント王国であった。7世紀から8世紀前半にかけて隆盛を極めた王国がノーサンブリア

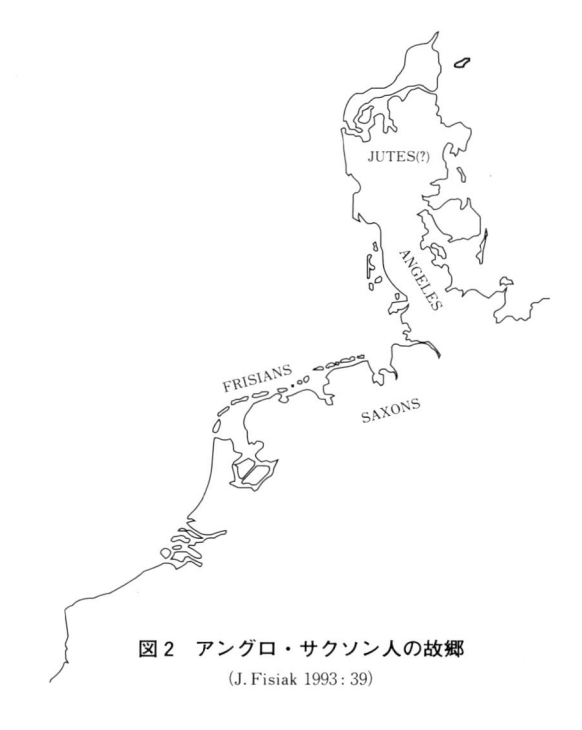

図2　アングロ・サクソン人の故郷
(J. Fisiak 1993 : 39)

王国であり、『英国国民教会史』の著者ビードはこのノーサンブリアの出身である。そして、次第に政治・文化の中心が北部から南部へと移った。8世紀後半から9世紀前半にかけてはマーシャ王国が栄え、オファ王の治世下で有名な叙事詩「ベオウルフ」(ca. 730) が書かれた。続いて9世紀後半からはアルフレッド大王が現れ、ウエセックス王国が繁栄することになった。

　サクソン人が築いた王国の中で一番優勢になった言葉が、ウエスト・サクソン方言と呼ばれる。今日伝わっている大部分の文献はウエスト・サクソン方言で書かれている。ケント王国で話されていた言葉は、ケント方言と呼ばれる。アングル人が築いたマーシャ王国・ノーサンブリア王国で話されていた言葉が、それぞれマーシャ方言、ノーサンブリア方言である。マーシャ方言とノーサン

図3　アングロ・サクソン七王国
(B.A. Fennell 2001: 57)

ブリア方言は、一括してアングリア方言と呼ばれる。

3. 英語の言語名の起源について

English の語源は下記に示すとおりである。

*Angli (= Angles) + isc (adj. suffix) > Englisc (= (originally) of or belonging to the Angles)

Klein's Comprehensive Etymological Dictionary of the English Language で Angle の項目には次のように出ている。

Angle, n., member of a Teutonic tribe that came in the 5th century from what is now known as Schleswig-Holstein to Britain and conquered it. — L. *Angulus*, pl. *Angli*, of Teut. origin. Cp. OE. *Angle*, *Engle*, prop. 'the people coming from *Angul* (= ON. *Ongull*), 'a hook-shaped district in Schleswig', fr. *angul* (= ON. *ongull*), 'fishhook, angle', which is rel. to *anga*, OHG. *ango*, 'hook'.

アングル人とは、5世紀にシュレースウィッヒ・ホルシュタインという地域からブリテン島にやって来て、ブリテン島を征服したゲルマン人の1部族——ラテン語では、*Anglus*（単数）、*Angli*（複数）で元来がゲルマン語起源。古英語（OE）では *Angle*、*Engle*、古高地ドイツ語（OHG）の *ango* '鉤' と同族語の *angul*（古ノルド語 *ongull*）'釣り針' に由来する *Angul*（＝古ノルド語 *Ongull*）'シュレースウィッヒ地方の鉤の形をした地域' からやって来た人々

つまり英語の語源は、ラテン語のアングル人の複数形 Angli に形容詞を作る語尾である -isc が添えられて、ウムラウトを受けた形ということになる。文字どおりには「アングル人の、アングル人に属す」という意味である。端的に言

えば、言語名は、ブリテン島にやって来たゲルマン人の1部族、アングル人に由来する。また、イングランドも同様にアングル人に由来する。

Engla (Gen. pl.) + land > England (land of the Angles)

すなわち、文字通りには「アングル人の土地」を意味する。しかし、*Englaland* という単語が文献に登場するのは、およそ1000年以降でありそれ以前は *Angelcynn* (= nation of the Angles) という単語が用いられていた。

英語の語源の他に、Wales と Welsh の語源について言及することにする。Wales および Welsh の単語が文献に登場するまでに、次のような史的発達を遂げた考えられる。

Welsh の項目をそれぞれ *Oxford English Dictionary* および *Klein's Comprehensive Etymological Dictionary of the English Language* で調べると次の様に書き記されている。

[OE. (West Saxon) *Wilish*, *Wylisc*, (Anglian and Kentish) *Welsc*, *Wælisc*, from *Wealh*, *Walh*, Celt, Briton, = OHG *Walh*, *Walah*...]

In OE the final *h* of the stem normally disappeared before the adjectival ending. The West Saxon type **Wielisc* (from *Wealh*) did not survive beyond the OE period; the two Anglian and Kentish types (from *Walh*) existed concurrently till the 16th cent., after which *Welsh* became the sole form in general use. (*Oxford English Dictionary*)

Welsh, adj., — ME. *walisch*, *welish* from OE. *wælisc*, *welisc*, ' foreign ' from *walh*, *wealh*, ' a foreigner ' (i.e. not of Saxon origin), hence ' a Celt ', especially ' a Briton, a Welshman ' related to Old High German *Walah*, *Walh*...
(*Klein's Comprehensive Etymological Dictionary of the English Language*)

West Saxon

*walh-as (-as: nominative plural ending) > *wælh-as > *wealh-as > wealas
a > æ: Anglo-Frisian Brightrning（アングロフリージア明音化）
æ > ea: Breaking（割れ）
h[x] > ø / m, n, l, r, ___vowel（鼻音あるいは流音と母音間の無声軟口蓋摩擦音の消失）
*walh-isc (-isc: adjectival ending) > *wælh-isc > *wealh-isc > *wielh-isc > wielisc
a > æ: Anglo-Frisian Brightrning（アングロフリージア明音化）
æ > ea: Breaking（割れ）
ea > ie: Umlaut（ウムラウト）
h[x] > ø / m, n, l, r, ___vowel（鼻音あるいは流音と母音間の無声軟口蓋摩擦音の消失）

Anglian

*walh-as > *wælh-as > *walh-as > walas（> wales）
a > æ: Anglo-Frisian Brightrning（アングロフリージア明音化）
æ > a: Retraction（後退）
h[x] > ø / m, n, l, r, ___vowel（鼻音あるいは流音と母音間の無声軟口蓋摩擦音の消失）

*walh-isc > *wælh-isc > *welh-isc > welisc（> welsh）
a > æ: Anglo-Frisian Brightrning（アングロフリージア明音化）
æ > e: Umlaut（ウムラウト）
h[x] > ø / m, n, l, r, ___vowel（鼻音あるいは流音と母音間の無声軟口蓋摩擦音の消失）

4. テキストについて

　ここで扱われるテキストの時代について、簡単に言及することにする。英語の歴史は大きく3つの時代に区分できる。700〜1100年頃の英語を古英語（Old English）、1100〜1500年頃の英語を中英語（Middle English）、1500年以降の英語を近代英語と呼ぶ。もう少し時代を細かく区分したい場合には、700〜900年頃の英語は、初期古英語（Early Old English）、900〜1100年頃の英語は後期古英語（Late Old English）、1100〜1300年頃の英語は初期中英語（Early Middle English）、1300〜1500年頃の英語は後期中英語（Late Middle English）、1500〜1700年頃の英語は初期近代英語（Early Modern English），1700年以降の英語は後期近代英語（Late Modern English）と呼ばれて区分される。また、古英語は、その特徴あるいは性質が後の時代の英語の特徴とかなりかけ離れているという理由で、アングロ・サクソン語と呼ばれることもある。

　ここで扱われているテキストは、アングロ・サクソン時代の「マタイ伝」である。言うまでもなく「マタイ伝」は新約聖書の中に収められている四福音書の1つである。

　アングロ・サクソン時代に使用された聖書は、ラテン語訳聖書の「ウルガーター」（Vulgata）であった。後にローマ・カトリック教会の公認聖書となったVulgataは、聖ヒエロニムス（St. Jerome：c. 347〜419 or 420）が、4世紀末から5世紀初頭に完成させた聖書である。ヒエロニムスは、新約聖書をギリシア語から、旧約聖書をヘブライ語からラテン語に翻訳した。

　中英語（Middle English：1100〜1500）の時代になってこのVulgataを基にして旧約聖書および新約聖書全体の英訳聖書を完成させたのは、ウィクリフ（John Wycliffe：c. 1330〜1384）である。ウィクリフ訳聖書には、前期訳（the Earlier Version：c. 1384）と後期訳（the Later Version：c. 1395）がある。

　近代英語（Modern English：1500〜）の時代に入って、ようやくW. Tyndale（c. 1494〜1536）が原典のヘブライ語・ギリシャ語から英訳聖書を完成させた。

　ここで扱われる作品は、マタイ伝のみである。マタイ伝は、ヨハネ伝、マルコ伝、ルカ伝と合わせて四福音書と呼ばれ、新約聖書（New Testament）の中

に収められている。旧約聖書（Old Testament）の言語はヘブライ語（Hebrew）であるが、新約聖書はギリシア語、ギリシア語でもアッティカ方言を基礎にイオニア方言などが混交したギリシア語であるコイネー（Koine or Hellenic Greek：標準ギリシャ語）で書かれている。ここでは下記に示すアングロ・サクソン時代（700年～1100年）の4種類のマタイ伝のテキストが掲載されている。

　Skeat（1970b）は、PREFACE（pp.i～xxxii）の中で、4種類の写本について次の様に説明している。

A．ページの左側の欄に掲載されているテキストは、コーパス写本（Corpus MS.）［ケンブリッジ大学コーパスクリスティー学寮図書館所蔵］に基づく福音書で、年代的には一番早くに書かれたものである。写字生（scribe）のÆlfricが、1000年頃にイングランド南西部のエイボン州（Avon）のバス（Bath）の修道院でウエスト・サクソン方言で書いた写本であると推定されている。マタイ伝の最後の部分に次のように書き記されている。

　　Ego Aelfricus scripsi hunc librum in Monasterio Ba∂ponio et dedi Brihtwoldo preposito — I, AElfric, wrote this book in the monastery at Bath, and gave it to Brihtwold the prior.

このウエスト・サクソン方言で書かれている福音書は、ラテン語のリンディスファン福音書およびラシュワース福音書とは異なる原典に基づいて書かれたものであると推定されている。残念なことに、このラテン語で書かれている原典は今日伝わっていない。

B．右側の欄に掲載されているテキストは、ハットン写本（Hatton MS.）［オックスフォード大学ボドレアン図書館所蔵］で、ヘンリー二世（HenryⅡ：1154～1189）の時代に書かれた写本に基づくもので、コーパス写本とは対照的に年代的には一番遅くに書かれたものである。上記のコーパス写本と同様に、今日伝わっていない原典を基に書き写された写本にボドレイ写本がある。このボドレイ写本（Bodley MS.）を基に書き写された写本がローイアル写本

（Royal MS.）であり、このローイアル写本に基づいて書き写された写本が、ハットン写本（Hatton MS.）であると今日考えられている。Skeat（1970b）は、写本の系図に関して次のように指摘している。

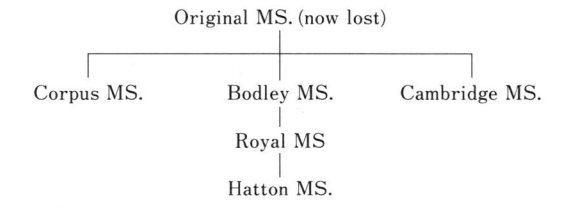

```
              Original MS. (now lost)
       ┌──────────────┼──────────────┐
   Corpus MS.     Bodley MS.     Cambridge MS.
                      │
                  Royal MS
                      │
                  Hatton MS.
```

C．3番目のテキストは、ダラム写本（Durham Book）として知られているリンディスファン写本（Lindisfarne MS.）[大英博物館所蔵]に基づくリンディスファン福音書である。このラテン語の福音書は、リンディスファンの司教エアドフリス（Eadfrith：698〜721）によって700年頃書かれたものである。このラテン語の福音書の行間註解（Interlinear gloss）は、250年後の950年頃に司祭のアルフレッド（Alfred）によってノーサンブリアン方言を用いて書き加えられた。

D．4番目のテキストは、オックスフフォード大学ボドレー図書館所蔵のラシュワース写本（Rushworth MS.）に基づくラシュワース福音書である。ラテン語の福音書は、写本の最後に名前が書き記されていることから明らかなように、8世紀頃に写字生のマクレゴル（Macregol）によって書かれたものと考えられている。行間註解は、ヨークシャー（Yorkshire）の西ライディング（West Riding）にあるヘアウッド（Harewood）の司祭ファーマン（Farman）とオーウン（Owun）の2人の手で10世紀後半に書き加えられた。ファーマンとオーウンの2人もまた自分たちの名前を、ヨハネ伝の最後の部分に書き添えている。また、ラシュワース福音書のマタイ伝のみがマーシャ方言で行間註解が書かれているが、残りの福音書の行間註解はリンディスファン福音書の註解に基づくものでノーサンブリア方言で書かれている。ただし、ここではラテン語のテキストは省略されており、行間註解のみの福音書となっている。

5. テキスト

CHAPTER VII.

1 Nellen ge deman ꝥ ge ne syn fordémede;

2 Witodlice ðam ylcan dome þe ge demað eow byð gedémed. ꝛ on ðam ylcan gemete þe ge metaþ. eow byþ gemeten;

3 To hwi gesihst þu ꝥ mot on þines broþor egan. ꝛ þú ne ge-syhst þone beam on þinum agenum eagan;

4 Oþþe humeta cwystiþu (sic) to þinum breþer broþur þafa ꝥ ic ut ado ꝥ mot of þinum eagan þonne se beam biþ on þinum agenum eagan;

5 La þu liccetere adó ærest ut þone beam of þinum agenum eagan. ꝛ be-hawa þonne ꝥ þu út adó ꝥ mot of þines broður eagan;

6 Nellen ge syllan ꝥ halige hundum. ne ge ne wurpen eowre mere-grotu toforan eowrum swynon. þe læs hig mid hyra fotum hig fortredon. ꝛ hig þonne ongean gewende eow toslyton;

7 Biddaþ ꝛ eow bið gesealo. seceaþ ꝛ ge hit findaþ. cnuciað. ꝛ eow biþ ontyned;

8 Witodlice ælc þæra þe bit he onfehþ. ꝛ se þe secð he hyt fint ꝛ þam cnuciendum bið ontyned;

Various Readings.

34. A. beon. A. ymbe. A. morgenlican (*twice*). A. ymbe. A. ymbe-.
Cap. vii. 3. A. broðer; B. broður. A. B. eagan.
4. A. cwyst ðu; B. cwyst þu. A. broðor (*for* broþur).
5. A. broðer. 6. A. Nellon. A. ꝥ halige syllan.
A. worpen. A. mere-grota. A. swynum. A. þy. 7.
A. secað. A. cnyssað (*for* cnuciað). 8. A. seceð.
A. fyndeð. A. cnyssendum (*for* cnuciendum).

CHAPTER VII.

1 Nellen ge demen. þæt ge ne syen fordemde.

2 Witodlice þam ilcan dome. þe ge demeð. eow beoð ge-demed. ꝛ on þam ylcan gemette þe ge meteð. eow beð ge-meten.

3 To hwi gesihst þu þæt mot on þines broðer eagen. ꝛ þu ne ge-sihst þanne beam on þinen agenen eagen.

4 Oððe hu-mæte cwæðst þu to þine breðer. broðer þafe þæt ic ut do þæt mot of þinen eagen. þonne se beam beoð on þinen agenen eagen.

5 Læt þu liketere. á-do ærest ut þanne beam of þinen agenen eagen. ꝛ be-hawe þanne þæt þu ut do þæt mot of þines broðer eagen.

6 Nellen ge syl þæt hilige (*sic*) hunden. ne ge-wurpen eowre mere-groten to-foren eowren swinen. þy læs hye mid hyra fotan hyo tofortredan. ꝛ hyo þanne ne on-gean ne wend eow to-slyton.

7 Byddeð. ꝛ eow beoð ge-seald. secheð. ꝛ ge hit findeð. cnokieð. ꝛ eow beoð untynd.

8 Witodliche ælch þare þe bit he on-fehð. ꝛ se þe sechð. he hyt fint. ꝛ þan cnokienden beoð un-tyned.

Various Readings.

34. hogiende; morgendlice; morgenlica daig careð; sylfne; Æghwylc; hæfð; eagan ymb-hugan.
Cap. vii. 1. deman; syn. 2. þan (*2nd time*). 3. broðor eagan; sihst þonne; þine agenum eagan. 4. cweðst; broður þafa; þinum eagum; bið; þinum agenum.
5. licetere; þonne; þinum agenum ægen; behawa þonne; broðor eagun. 6. halige hundum ne ge ne wurpen; eowrum swinum; þe; hyo; heora; -fortredon; þonne; toslyton. 7. byð; seceð; cnocieð; bið untyned. 8. Witodlice ælc þara; secð; þam cnuciendum bið.

CAP. VII.

         nellað ge   doeme   ꝥ   ge ne se gedoemed   in   ðæm   forðon   dome   gie doemes
       1 *Nolite   iudicare   ut   non iudicemini   2 in   quo   enim   iudicio iudicaberitis

       ge bið on gedoemed   ꓶ   in sua huelc   woegas   hripes   ge bið on gewegen bið   iuh   huæt   ðonne
         iudicabimini   et in qua   mensura   mensi   fueritis metietur   uobis   3 *Quid   autem

       gesiistu strē ꝉ mot in   ego   broðres ðines   ꓶ   ðone beam   in   ego   ðin   ne   gesiistu   ꝉ
         uides   festucam in oculo   fratris   tui   et   trabem   in oculo   tuo non   uides   4 aut

           hu   cueðestu broeðer   ðinum   buta ic worpe mot ꝉ stre of   ego   ðin ꓶ   heonu beam   is   in
       quomodo   dicis   fratri   tuo   sine   eiciam festucam   de   oculo   tuo et   ecce trabes est   in

        ego   ðin   ðu esuica   worp   ærest   ðone beam   of   ego   ðin ꓶ ðonne   ðu gesiist   geworpe
       oculo   tuo   5   hypocrita   eice   primum   trabem   de oculo   tuo et tunc   uidebis   eicere

       ðone mot   of   ego   broðres ðines   nellas ge sella꠷ halig꠸   hundum   ne   sendas ge   meregrotta§
       festucam   de oculo fratris tui   6 *Nolite   dare sanctum   canibus neque mittatis   margaritas

         iurre before berg   ðy læs   hia getrede   ða ilco mið fotum   hiora   ꓶ gewoendo ꝉ gecerdo   toslitas
       uestras ante   porcos   ne forte   conculcent   eas   pedibus   suis   et   conuersi   disrumpant

       iuh   giwias ꝉ gebiddas ge   ꓶ   gesald bið   iuh   soecað ge   ꓶ   ge infindes ꝉ ge begeattas cnysað ꝉ cnyllas ge
       uos   7 *Petite   et   dabitur   uobis   quærite   et   inuenietis   pulsate

         ꓶ   un-tyned bið   iuh   eghuelc forðon seðe giuæð ꝉ biddes onfoeð   ꓶ   seðe soecas infindes   ꓶ
        et   áperietur   uobis   8 omnis   enim   qui   petit   accipit et qui quærit   inuenit et

       ðæm cnysende ꝉ cnyllende   untuned bið
            pulsanti   áperietur

---

34. ne forþon sorgigaþ ge in morgen se morgen forþon dæg sorgaþ (sic) beoþ selfa him genoh weotudlice dæge
wea his
    Cap. VII. 1. ne doemeþ ge þy les ge sien doemed   2. in ðæm weotudlice dome þe ge doemeþ ge beoþ
doemde ꓶ in ðæm gemete þe ge metaþ bið eow meten   3. forhwon þonne gesihstu streu in ege broþer þine
ꓶ beam in ege þinum ne geseeȝ ꝉ sis   4. oþþa hu cweþestu broþer þinum broþer abíd ꝥ ic ofdo ꝥ streu of
ege þinum ꓶ sihþe beam in ege þinum is   5. þu licettere geþo (sic) æræst þone beam of ege þinum ꓶ þonne
gesihst þu awearpe ꝥ streu of þines broþer ege   6. ne sellað ge halig hundum ne gewearpaþ ercnan-stanas
eowre beforan swinum þyles hiæ tredan ða heora fotum ꓶ gehwerfæþ to slite eowic   7. biddaþ ꓶ eow biþ sald
soecaþ ꓶ ge gemoetaþ cnyssaþ ꓶ eow biþ ontyned   8. æghwilc wiotudlice seþe bit he onfoeþ ꓶ seþe soeceþ he
findeð ꓶ cnyssande him bið ontyned

9 Hwylc man is of eow gyf his sunu hyne bit hlafes sylst þu him stan
10 oððe gyf he bytt fisces sylst þu him næddran;
11 Eornustlice nu ge þe yfle synt cunnun gode sylena eowrum bearnum syllan. mycle má eower fæder þe on heofenum ys sylep gód þam þe hyne biddað;
12 Eornustlice ealle þa þing ðe ge wyllen ꝥ men eow don. doþ ge him ꝥ sylfe. ꝥ ys soþlice ǽ. ꞇ witegena bebod;
13 Gangað inn þurh ꝥ nearwe geat. forþon þe ꝥ geat is swyþe wíd. ꞇ se weg is swiþe rum þe to for-spillednesse gelæt ꞇ swyþe manega synt þe þurh þone weg farað;
14 Eala hu neara ꞇ hú angsum is ꝥ geat ꞇ se weg þe to life gelædt ꞇ swyþe feawa synt þe þone weg findon;
15 Warniað eow fram leasum witegum. þa cumað to eow on sceapa gegyrelum. ac hig beoð innane reafigende wulfas.
16 fram hyra wæstmun gé hi undergytað; Cwyst þu gaderað man winberian of þornum oððe fic-æppla of þyrncinum;
17 Swa ælc gód treow byrþ gode wæstmas ꞇ ælc yfel treow byrþ yfele wæstmas.
18 ne mæg ꝥ gode treow beran yfle wæstmas. ne ꝥ yfele treow gode wæstmas;

9 Hwilc man is of eow gyf his sune hym bit hlafes. selst þu him stan.
10 Oððe gyf he him bit fissces. sylst þu him næddren.
11 Eornestlice nu ge þe yfele synt cunnan god eowre bearnen syllen. mycele ma eowre fæder þe on heofene ys sylleð god þan þe hine biddað.
12 Eornestlice ealle þa þing þe ge willen þæt men eow don. doð ge heom þæt sylfe. þæt ys soðlice lage. ꞇ witegena be-bod.
13 Ganged enn (sic) þurh þæt narewe geat. for-þan þæt geat ys swiðe wid. ꞇ se weig is swiðe rum þe to for-spillendnysse gelæt. ꞇ swiðe manige synde þe þurh þane weig fareð.
14 Eala hu nara ꞇ hu angsum ys þæt geat. ꞇ se weig. þe to lyfe ge-læt. ꞇ swiðe feawe synde þe þanne weig findeð.
15 Warnieð eow wið leasan witegen þe cumeð to eow on sceapene kertlen. ac hyo beoð innenan reafiende wulfas.
16 Fram heora wæstman ge hyo undergyteð. Cwest þu. gadered man winberian of þornen. oððe fíc-epple of þyrncinum.
17 Swa ælch god treow byrð gode wæstmes. ꞇ ælch efel treow byrað yfele wæstmes.
18 Ne [mæg] þæt gode treo beren yfele wæstmes. ne þæt yfele treo gode wæstmas.

Various Readings.

9. A. sylest. 10. A. byt; B. bitt. A. sylest. A. B. nædran. 11. A. Eornostlice. A. yfele. A. synd. A. cunnon. A. mycele. A. eowre. 12. A. Eornostlice. A. wyllon. 13. A. in. B. nearuwe. A. foɪðam. A. get. A. -nysse. B. gelætt. A. synd. 14. A. nearu. B. ancsum. A. læt. A. synd. B. finden. 15. A. gegyrlum. B. reafiende. 16. A. hig. B. cwysþu. A. win-bergean. A. þyrcenum. 17. B. tryw (twice). 18. B. beoran. A. yfele (twice).

Various Readings.

9. sunu hyne; sylst þy. 10. fisces; næddran. 11. god sylen eowrum bearnum syllen; heofonum; syleð; þam. 12. Eornstlice; ǽ (for lage). 13. Gangeð inn; nearuwe; forþam þe; weg; swuðe; forspillednysse; synt; þone. 14. neara; ancsum; weyg; gelædt; fewe synt; þonne weyg finden. 15. Warniað; leasum witegum; sceapa gyrlum; byð innane. 16. undergeateð; cwyðst; gaderað; þornum; -æpplu. 17. elc; wæstmas; ælc yfel tryw bereð; wæstmas. 18. ne mæg; wæstmas.

第1章　アングロサクソン時代の言語　21

	☦	hua	is	from	iuh	monn	ðene	gif	he giuias	sunu	his	hlaf	cuiðestu
9		aut	quis	est	ex	uobis	homo	quem	si	petierit	filius	suus	panem	numquid

ðone stān	ræceð	☦ seles	him		☦	gif	ðone fisc	wilniað ☦ giuias		cuiðestu	ða nedrie	ræces
lapidem		porriget	ei	10	aut	si	piscem	petet		numquid	serpentem	porriget

him		gif	ðonne	iuh	mittŷ	ge aron	yflo	wutas ge	godo	gesealla	sunum	iurum
ei	11	si	ergo	uos	cum	sitis	mali	nostis	bona	dare	filiis	uestris

mara woen is	fader	iuer	seðe	in	heofnum	is	geselleð	godo	biddendum ☦ giuiendum	hine
quanto magis	pater	uester	qui	in	caelis	est	dabit	bona	petentibus	sé

	alle	ðonne ☦ forðon	sua huæt	gie welle	þ	hea gedoe	iuh	ða menn	J	gee	doeð ☦ wyrcas
12	*Omnia	ergo	quaecunque	uultis	ut	faciant	uobis	homines	et	uos	facite

him ðius	is	forðon	æ	J	witgas ☦ witgo		inngeonges	ðerh	nearuo	port ☦ dure ☦ gæt forðon
eis haec	est	enim	lex	et	prophetæ	13	*INtrate	per	angustam	portam quia

ðiu wide	geat	J	rumwelle	weg	ðiu	lædas	to	lose ☦ losing	J	monigo* sint	ða ðe	inngeongas	ðerh
	lata	porta	et	spatiosa	uia	quæ	ducit	ad	perditionem	et	multi sunt	qui	intrant	per

ða ilco		suiðe	naruu	port ☦ gæt	J	bogehte	woeg	ðiu	lædes	to	life	J	huon	aron ða ðe
eam	14	quam	angusta	porta	et	arta	uia	quæ	ducit	ad	uitam	et	pauci sunt	qui

onfindes	ða ilco		behaldas ge from	leasum	witgum	ða ðe	cymes	to	Iuh	in	wedum
inueniunt	eam	15	*Attendite á	falsis	prophetis	qui	ueniunt	ad	uos	in	uestimentis

scipa		Inna-ueard	uutedlice	sint	uulfes	férende		from	uæstmum	hiora	ongeatas ge ☦ oncnauæs
ouium		intrinsecus	autem	sunt	lupi	rapaces	16	á	fructibus	eorum	cognoscetis

hia ☦ ðailco cuiðestu ☦ hueðer		somnigas	of hryum ☦ of ðornum scearpum		☦ of haga-ðornum fic-beamas
eos		*Numquid	colligunt	de spinis	uuas aut de	tribolis	ficos

	suæ	eghwelc	treo☦	god	wæstmas		goda	doeð [☦] gewyrces	ðe yfle	uutedlice	treo	wæstmas
17	*Sic	omnis	arbor	bona	fructus (sic)		bonos	facit		mala	autem	arbor	fructus

yfle	doas		ne	mæg	treuo	god	wæstmas	yfle	gewyrca	ne	tre	yfle	wæstma
malos	facit	18	non	potest	arbor	bona	fructus	malos	facere	neque	arbor	mala	fructus

godo	gewyrce
bonos	facere

---

9. oþþa hwælc is eower monn þe hine bidde sunu his hlaf ah he stan ræceþ þæm (sic)　10. oþþe gif he fiscæs biddeth (sic) ah he nedra ræceþ him　11. nunu þonne ge þe ge sindun yfle cunneþ gód sellan beaearnum cowrum hu miccle mae fæder ewer seþe in heofunum is selleþ gód þæm þe biddaþ hine　12. all forþon swa hwęt swa ge willað þæt dóa cow menn gód swa J ge doþ heom þis is wiotudlice áe J witgu　13. gaþ inn þurh naarwe geate forþon wíd geatt J rúm weg þe lædeþ to for-wyrde ☦ forlore J monige sindun þa þe in-gan þurh þære ☦ þæne　14. hu naru ☦ wiðerdune geate J eorfeþe is se wég þe lædeþ to life J feawe sindun þa þe gemoetaþ þane ☦ cymeð in þara　15. behaldeþ eow wið lyge ☦ lease witgu þa þe cumaþ to eow in gewedum scépa in innan þonne sindun wulfas risænde ☦ woedende　16. from wæstmuum eora ge ongetaþ heo ah he somnigaþ of þornum winbegęr (sic) oþþe of gorstum ficos ☦ nyte　17. swa ægwilc treow gód godne węstmas bereþ ☦ wyrceþ yfel þonne treow yfle wæstmas ☦ blęd bereþ　18. ne mæg treow þæt góde yfle westmas beoran ☦ wyrcende ne þ treow yfle góde wæstmas ☦ blęd beoran

19 Ælc treow þe ne byrð godne wæstm sy hyt forcorfen ꝛ on fyr aworpen;
20 Witodlice be hyra wæstmum ge hig oncnawað;
21 Ne gæð ælc þæra on heofena rice þe cwyþ to me drihten drihten. ac se þe wyrcð mines fæder willan þe on heofenum is. se gæð on heofena rice;
22 Manega cweþað on þam dæge to me drihten drihten. hú ne witegode wé on þinum naman. ꝛ on þinum naman we út-awurpon deoflu. ꝛ on þinum naman we worhton mycle mihta.
23 þonne cweðe ic to him ꝥ ic eow næfre ne cuðe; Gewitað fram me ge þe worhton unrihtwysnesse;
24 Eornustlice ælc þæra þe ðas mine word gehyrð ꝛ þa wyrcð byþ gelic þam wisan were se hys hus ofer stán getimbrode.
25 þa com þær ren ꝛ mycele flod ꝛ þær bleowun windas ꝛ ahruron on ꝥ hus ꝛ hyt na ne feoll; Soðlice hit wæs ofer stan getimbrod.
26 ꝛ ælc þæra þe gehyrþ ðas mine word. ꝛ þá ne wyrcð se byþ gelic þam dysigan men þe getimbrode hys hus ofer sand-ceosel
27 þa rínde hit ꝛ þær cómun flod ꝛ bleowun windas ꝛ ahruron on ꝥ hus. ꝛ ꝥ hus feoll ꝛ hys hryre wæs mycel;

19 Ælch treow þe ne bered godne wæstme. syo hit for-corfen. ꝛ on fer aworpen.
20 Witodlice be heora wæstman ge hyo on-cnawað.
21 Ne gæð ælch þara on heofene riche þe cwyð to me drihten drihten. ac se þe wyrcð mines fæder willen þe on heofene ys. se gæð on heofene riche.
22 Manege cweðeð on þam daige to me drihten drihten. hu ne witegeden we on þinen namen. ꝛ on þinan namen we ut-awurpen deofel of mannen. ꝛ on þinen name we worhte mychele wundre ꝛ mihte.
23 Þanne cweðe ich to heom. þæt ich eow næfre ne cuðe. Ge-wítoð fram me. ge þe worhten un-rihtwisnysse.
24 Eornestlice ælch þare þe þas mine word ge-hereð ꝛ þa werceð beoð gelic þam wisen were se his hus ofer stan ge-tymbrede.
25 þa com þær ren ꝛ michel flod. ꝛ þær bleowan windas ꝛ ahruron on þæt hus. ꝛ hit naht ne feoll. Soðlice hit wæs ofer stan ge-tymbred.
26 ꝛ ælch þare þe ge-hyrð þas mine word ꝛ þa ne werceð. se beoð ge-lich þan desien men. þe getymbrede hys hus ofer sand-chisel.
27 þa rinde hyt. ꝛ þær com flod. ꝛ bleowen windes. ꝛ aruren on ꝥ hus. ꝛ ꝥ hus feol. ꝛ his ryre wæs mychel.

Various Readings.

19. A. sig. 20. A. heora. 21. A. hefena; B. heofona (*for 2nd* heofena). 22. A. witegodon. A. ut awurpan. A. mycele. 23. A. unryhtwysnysse. 24. A. Eornostlice. 25. A. mycel; B. micle. A. þar. A. bleowon. 26. A. dysegan. A. stan-ceosel. 27. A. com. A. bleowon.

Various Readings.

19. Elc; berð; wæstm; fyr. 20. wæstmum. 21. ælc; heofona rice; willan; heofenum (*twice*); rice. 22. drihten (*thrice*); witogede; þinum (*twice*); deofleo; manna; þinum; mycela wundra. 23. þonne; ic; eom; ic; gewiteð. 24. ælc; wyrcð byð; wisam; getimbrode. 25. micel; na (*for* naht). 26. ælc þara; wyrcð; byð gelic þam dysygum; -ciosel. 27. comen; bleowan windas; ahruren; feoll; mycel.

	eghuelc	tre	ðy ⊹ ðiu	ne	doeð	wæstm	god	gecorfen bið ⊹ gecearfas	ꝺ	in	fyr
19	omnis	arbor	quae	non	facit	fructum	bonum	exciditur	et	in	ignem

bið gesended⊹gesendes		ðonne	from	wæstmum	hiora	ongeatas ge ⊹ oncnaues	ða ⊹ hia		ne
mittitur	20	igitur	ex	fructibus	eorum	cognoscetis	eos	21 *	Non

eghuelc	seðe	cueðæs	to me	drihten	drihten	inngaas	in	ric	heofna	ah	seðe	doeð	willo
omnis	qui	dicit	mihi	domine	domine	intrabit	in	regnum	caelorum	sed	qui	facit	uoluntatem

faderes	mines	seðe	in heofnum	is	ðe	ingeonges	in	ric	heofna		monig wælle g[e]cneada
patris	mei	qui	in caelis	est	ipse	intrabit	in	regnum	caelorum	22 *	Multi dicent

to me	in	ðæm	dæg	drihten	drihten	ah ne	in	noma	ðinne ⊹ ðinum	we gewitgedon	ꝺ	in
mihi	in	illa	die	domine	domine	nonne	in	nomine	tuo	prophetauimus	et	in

noma	ðinne ⊹ ðinum	dioblæs	we fordrifon ⊹ forworpon	ꝺ	in	noma	ðinum	mæhto	monigo	we dydon
nomine	tuo	dæmonia	eiecimus		et	in nomine	tuo	uirtutes	multas	fecimus

	ꝺ	ða ⊹ ðonne	ic ondeto	him ⊹ ðæm	forðon	næfra	ic cuðe ⊹ oncneawu	iuih	afirres	from	me
23	et	tunc	confitebor	illis	quia	numquam	noui	uos	discedite	á	me

ða ðe	ge worhton	unrehtuisnisse		eghuelc	ðonne	se ðe	geheres	uorda	mina	ðas	ꝺ	does ða ilco
qui	operamini	iniquitatem	24 *	Omnis	ergo	qui	audit	uerba	mea	haec	et	facit ea

geefned	bið ⊹ geliced bið ⊹ geteled bið	wer	snotre	seðe	getimbres	hus	his	ofer ⊹ on	carr ⊹ stan
assimilabitur	uiro	sapienti	qui	ædificauit	domum	suam	supra	petram

	ꝺ	of-dune astag ⊹ gefeall	regn	ꝺ	cuomon	ea ⊹ streamas	ꝺ	ge-blewun	windas	ꝺ	in-ræsdon	in
25	et	descendit	pluuia	et	uenerunt	flumina	et	flauerunt	uenti	et	inruerunt	in

hus	ðæm	ꝺ	ne	gefeall	gewrynded * ⊹ geseted	forðon	wæs	ofer	stane		ꝺ	eghuelc
domum	illam	et	non	cecidit	fundata		enim	erat	supra petram	26 .	et	omnis

seðe	geheres	worda	mina	ðas	ꝺ	ne	doeð	ða ilco	gelic	bið	were	dysge	se ðe	getimberde
qui	audit	uerba	mea	haec	et	non	facit	ea	similis	erit	uiro	stulto	qui	ædificauit

hus	his	ofer ⊹ on	sonde		ꝺ	of-dune astag	regn	ꝺ	cuomon	streamas	ꝺ
domum	suam	supra	harenam	27	et	descendit	pluuia	et	uenerunt	flumina	et

gebleuun	windas	ꝺ	in-ræsdon	in	huse	ða ilco	ꝺ	gefeall	ꝺ	wæs	fæll	his	micel
flauerunt	uenti	et	inruerunt	in	domum	illam	et	cecidit	et	fuit	ruina	eius	magna

---

19. æghwilc þara treow þe ne bereþ westęm gódne bið acorfen ꝺ in fyre sended   20. forþon ⊹ cuþlice of wæstmum eora ge ongetaþ heo ⊹ hię   21. ne ⊹ nallæs æghwilc þara þe cweþ to me dryhten drihten gæþ in rice heofuna ah seþe wyrceþ wille fæder mines þæs þe in heofunum is se ⊹ he gǽeþ in heofuna rice   22. monige cweþaþ to me on ðæm dæge dryhten dryhten ah ne in þinum noma witgadun we ꝺ in þinum noma deoful ut wyrpon ꝺ in þinum noman mægen monige worhton   23. ꝺ ic þonne ondetu heom þæt ic næfræ cuþe eow gewitaþ from me ge þe wyrcaþ unrihtnisse   24. æghwilc þara þe ge-héreþ word min þas ꝺ fremmaþ hie he bið lic were þæm snottra þe ge-timbrade hus is on stane   25. ꝺ astág niþer rægn ꝺ cuomun eáé ꝺ blewun windas ꝺ fellun on hus þæt ꝺ hit no gefeoll gestaþulad soþlice hit wæs on stáne   26. ꝺ æghwilc þe ge-héreþ word min þas ꝺ ne fremmaþ þa gelic bið were dysig ⊹ dolum þæm þe timbrade hus his on sónde   27. ꝺ astag rægn niþer ꝺ cuomon eae ꝺ bleowen windas ꝺ feollun in hus þæt ꝺ hit gefeoll ꝺ wæs hryre his micel

28 Þa wæs geworden þa se hælend þas word ge-endode þa wundrode ꝥ folc his lare

29 soþlice he lærde swylce he anweald hæfde. ⁊ na swa swa hyra boceras ⁊ sundorhalgan;

28 Ða wæs ge-worðen þa se hælend þas word lærde ⁊ ge-endode. þa wundrede þæt folc. hys lare.

29 Soðlice he lærde swilce he anweald hæfde. ⁊ na swa swa heore bokeras ⁊ sunderhalgan.

第1章　アングロサクソン時代の言語　25

              ꝫ geworden is ɫ uæs mið ðy   ge-endade   ðe hælend worda ðas ge-uundrade weron ða ðreatas
28 *Et   factum   est   cum consummasset   *iesus*   uerba haec ammirabantur   turbae

ofer   lār   his   wæs forðon lærde hia suæ   mæht   hæfde ne suæ ɫ nalles suæ ɫ suelce
super doctrinam eius   29 erat enim docens eos sicut potestatem habens   non sicut

uðuta   hiora   ꝫ
scribae eorum et pharisaei

CHAPTER XIII.

1 On þam dæge þam hælende ût-gangendum of húse he sæt. wiþ ða sæ.
2 ꝛ mycle mænigeo wæron gesamnode to hym. swa ꝥ he eode on scyp ꝛ þær sæt. and eall seo mænigeo stod on þam waroþe.
3 ꝛ he spræc to hym fela on big-spellum cweþende; Soþlice ut-eode se sædere hys sæd to sawenne
4 ꝛ þa þa he seow. sume hig feollon wiþ weg. ꝛ fuglas comun ꝛ æton þá;
5 Soþlice sume feollon on stænihte þær hyt næfde mycle eorþan. ꝛ hrædlice upsprungon for-þam þe hig næfdon þære eorþan dypan;
6 Soþlice upsprungenre sunnan hig adruwudon ꝛ forscruncon. for þam þe hig næfdon wyrtrum;
7 Soþlice sume feollon on þornas. ꝛ þa þornas weoxon ꝛ for-þrysmudon þa.

CHAPTER XIII.

1 On þam dayge þam hælende ut-gangenden of huse he sæt wið þa sæ.
2 ꝛ michele menigeo wæren ge-samnode to hym. swa þæt he eode on scyp ꝛ þær sæt. ꝛ eall syo menigeo. stod on þam waruðe.
3 ꝛ he spæc to heom fele on bispellen cweðende. Soðlice ut-eode se sæwere hys sæd to sawenne.
4 ꝛ þa þa he seow. sume hye feollen wið weig. ꝛ fugeles comen ꝛ æten þa.
5 Soðlice sume feollon on stænette þær hyt næfde mychele eorðan. ꝛ rædlice upsprungen for-þan þe hyo næfdon þare eorðan deopan.
6 Soðlice up-sprungenre sunne hyo adruwedon ꝛ for-scrunken. for-þam þe hyo næfdon wyrtrum.
7 Soðlice sume feollon on þornen. ꝛ þa þornes weoxan ꝛ for-þrysmedon þa.

Various Readings.

48. A. moder. A. hylce. A. synd. 49. B. aþenude. 50. A. heofenum. A. broðer. A. swuster. A. myn moder; B. modur. Cap. xiii. 1. B. hælynde. 2. A. mycele. A. mænio (*twice*). A. gesomnode. 3. A. fæla. A. sawere. 4. B. feollun. A. fugelas. A. comon. 5. B. feollun. A. mycele. 6. A. adruwedon; B. adruwodun. A. wyrtruman. 7. B. feollun. A. forþrysmodon; B. forðrysmodun.

Various Readings.

48. seggendum; is min moder; swylce synt; gebroðra. 49. -cnihtas. 50. wylc; wyrcð; fæder; heofonum; is min broðor ꝛ min swustor ꝛ modor. Cap. xiii. 1. dæge; -gangendum. 2. micele mænigeo wæron; him; set; seo mænigeo. 3. bigspellum; sædere. 4. hyo; æton. 5. hit; mycelan; ræddlice. 6. sunnan; adruwodun ꝛ forscruncon. 7. feollun on þornum; þrornas (*sic*) weoxon ꝛ forþrysmodon.

CAP. XIII.

1 *In in ðæm dæge ge-eade ðe hælend of hus he gesætt ł wæs sittende æt ł neh sæ
  illo die exiens iesus de domo sedebat secus mare

2 ꓶ gesomnad weron ł sint to him menigo ł ðreatas monigo suæ ꝥ in scipp ł lyttel scipp
  et congregatae sunt ad eum turbae multæ ita ut in nauiculam

  astag ł wæs stigende gesætt ꓶ all ðreat gestód on* wearðe ꓶ spreccende wæs him
  ascendens sederet et omnis turba stabat in litore 3 et locutus est eis

  feolo ł monigo in bissenum cuoeð ł cuoeðende heonu ge-eade seðe sawes séde ł gesawe ł sedege
  multa in parabolis dicens ecce exiit qui seminat seminare

4 ꓶ mið ðy ł ða huile saues ðorlease ł sum oðer gefeollon neh ł æt strǽt ł woeg ꓶ
  et dum seminat quaedam ceciderunt secus uiam et

  cuomun ða flegendo* ꓶ gebrecon ł éton ł fréton ða ilco oðra uutedlice gefeallon
  uenenerunt (sic) uolucres et comederunt ea 5 alia autem ceciderunt

  in stæner ðer ne hæfde ł næbbend wæs eorðo micil ł monig ł foele* ꓶ mižðy sóna arisen weron
  in petrosa ubi non habebat (sic) terram multam et continuo exorta sunt

  forðon ne hæfdon ł næbbende weron heanisse eorðes sunna uutedlice mið ðy arrǽs
  quia non habebant altitudinem terrae 6 sole autem orto

  weron forberned ł besenced ꓶ forðon ne hæfdon ł næbbend wyrtrumme gescriungon ł weron gescrencde
  aestuauerunt et quia non habebant radicem aruerunt

  oðro uutedlice gefeollon in ðornum ł in hrygum ꓶ woxon ða ðornas ł hrygas ꓶ under-
7 alia autem ceciderunt in spinas et creuerunt spinae et suffoca-

  dulfon ða
  uerunt ea

---

48. he sylfe ondwyrde to þæm soeccende ꓶ cwæþ hwelc is moder min ꓶ broþer mine hwilce syndun
49. ꓶ aþenende hond in leornerum his cwæþ henu moder min ꓶ broþer min 50. swa hwa swa wyrceþ
willan fæder mines þe in heofunum is se min ge broþer ꓶ swuster ꓶ moder is
Cap. XIII. 1. on þæm dæge gangende se hælend of huse gesæt bi sǽé 2. ꓶ gesomnadun to him
mengu swa ꝥ he on scipe astigende gesett ꓶ all seo mengu stod on waraþe 3. ꓶ he sprec to heom
feola in gelicnissum cweþende henu ut code se sawend to sawenne 4. ꓶ þa he ˈseow sume gefeollun bi
wæge ꓶ cuomun fuglas heofun ꓶ frætun 5. þæt oþere þonne gefeollon on stanig lond þær ne hęfde eorðe
miccle ꓶ hræþe cuomun upp forþon þe hie næfdon heanisse eorðe 6. sunne þa upp cuom hatedun ꓶ forþon
þe hie nęfdun wy[r]tryme for-wisnadun 7. sume þonne gefetun in þornas ꓶ wexon þa þornas ꓶ smoradun hiæ

o 2

8 sume soþlice feollon on gode eorþan ⁊ sealdon weastm. sum hund-fealdne. sum sixtig-fealdne. sum þrittig-fealdne;
9 Se þe hæbbe earan to gehyrenne gehyre.
10 ⁊ þa genealæhton his leorning-cnihtas ⁊ cwædon to hym. for hwig spycst þu to hym mid big-spellum;
11 Ða andswarode he hym forþam þe eow is geseald to witanne heofena rices gerynu. ⁊ him nys na geseald;
12 Soþlice þam þe hæfþ. him byþ geseald ⁊ he hæfð. Soþlice se þe næfð ⁊ þ þe he hæfð him bið ætbroden.
13 forðam ic spece to him mid big-spellum. forþam þe lociende hig ne ge-seoþ. ⁊ gehyrende hig ne gehyraþ. ne ne ongytaþ.
14 þ on him si gefylled esaias witegung; Of gehyrnysse ge gehyraþ ⁊ ge ne ongytaþ ⁊ lociende ge ge-seoþ ⁊ [ge] ne ge-seoð;
15 Soþlice þises folces heorte is ahyrd. ⁊ hig hefelice mid earum gehyrdon. ⁊ hyra eagan beclysdon. þe læs hig æfre mid eagum geseon ⁊ mid earum gehyron. ⁊ mid heortan ongyton. ⁊ sin gecyrrede ⁊ ic hig gehæle.
16 Soþlice eadige synt eowre eagan forþam þe hig geseoþ. ⁊ eowre earan forþam þe hig gehyraþ;

8 sume soðlice* feollen on gode eorðan. ⁊ sealden wæstme. sume hundred-fealde. sum syxtig-fealde. sum þrittig-fealde.
9 Se þe hæbbe earan to ge-herenne gehere.
10 ⁊ þa genehlahten his leorning-cnihtes ⁊ cwæðen to hym. For-hwi spæcst þu to heom mid byspellum.
11 Ða answerede he heom. for-þan þe eow ys ge-seald to witene heofene riches geryne. ⁊ heom nys na ge-seald.
12 Soðlice þam þe hafð him beoð geseald. ⁊ he hæfð. soðlice se þe næfð. ⁊ þæt he hæfð him beoð æt-broden.
13 For-þam ic spece to heom mid byspellen. for-þam þe lokiende hyo ne geseoð. ⁊ ge-herende hyo ne ge-hereð. ne ne ongeteð
14 þæt on heom sy ge-felled ysaias gewitegung. Of ge-hernysse ge geheorað. ⁊ ge ne ongyteð*. ⁊ lokiende ge ge-seoð. ⁊ ge ne ge-seoð.
15 Soðlice þises folkes heorte. is aherd. ⁊ hyo hefylice mid earen ge-hyrden. ⁊ heora eagen be-clysdon. þe læs hye afre mid eagen ge-seagen. ⁊ mid earan ge-hyrdon. ⁊ mid heortan on-getan. ⁊ syon ge-cherde. ⁊ ic hyo ge-hæle.
16 Soðlice eadygen synd eowrum eagen for-þam þe hyo ge-seoð. ⁊ eowre earan forþam þe hyo ge-herað.

Various Readings.

8. B. feollun. A. godre. A. B. wæstm. A. þrytig-.
9. A. gehyranne. 10. A. sprycst. 12. A. seald.
13. A. sprece. A. lociende. 14. A. syg; B. sy. B. -nesse. A. B. lociende. A. B. *supply* 4th ge, which Cp. *omits*. 15. A. heflice. A. þylæs. A. oððe [*for 3rd* ⁊]. 16. A. synd.

Various Readings.

8. feollon; sealdom wæstm sum hund-faldne; -fealdne; þritig-fealdne. 9. gehearenne gehyre. 10. geneahlæcton; -cnihtas; hwy specst; big-spellum. 11. geseld; wytene; heofone rices; nis. 12. beað; Soðlyce; bið atbroden. 13. specce to eom mid bigspellen; -þan; locyennde; gehyrende; gehyoræð; ongyteð. 14. gefylled; eisaias; gehyrnysse; gehyoræð; ongyteð; lokyende; geseð ⁊ ne geseoð. 15. folces; hefelice; earum gehyrdon; hyora eagan; hyo æfre; eagum; earum gehyrdan; ongyton; syn gecyrrde. 16. eadigen sint; eowrun eagan; gehyrað.

第1章　アングロサクソンス時代の言語

	oðero	ec ł soðlice	gefeollon	in	eorðo	gód	ꝺ	sáldon ł gesald weron		wæstm	oðer
8	alia	uero	ceciderunt	in	terram	bonam	et	dabant		fructum	aliut

hundraŏ ł húnduelle	oðer	sexdeih (sic)	oðer	ðrittig		seðe	hæfeſ	earo	to herranne
centesimum	aliud	sexagesimum	aliud	trigesimum	9	qui	habet	aures	audiendi

geheraŏ	ꝺ	geneolecadon	ðegnas	cuedon	him	forhuon	bisenum	spreces ðu		seðe
audiat	10	et accedentes	discipuli	dixerunt	ei	quare	in parabolis	loqueris	11	qui

onduearde	cuoeð	to him	forðon	iuh	gesáld	is ł wæs	ꝥ ge witte ł to uutanne	clæno hryno ł gesægd-
respondens	ait	illis	quia	uobis	datum	est	nosse	mys-

nise ł diopnise	ríces	heofna	ðæm soðlice	ne	is	gesáld		seðe	forðon	hæfeð	gesald bið
teria	regni	caelorum	illis	autem	non	est	datum	12	*Qui	enim	habet	dabitur

him	ꝺ	monigfald bið	seðe	uutedlice	næfis ł ne hæfeð	ꝺ	ꝥ	hæfis	genummen bið	from	him
ei	et	abundabit	qui	autem	non habet	et	quod	habet	auferetur	ab	eo

	forðon ł foreðy	in	bissenum	ic spreco	him	forðon	gesegende ł seende ł ꝥ geseas ł gesegon		ne
13	*Ideo	in	parabolis	loquor	eis	quia	uidentes		non

seað ł ne sciolon gesea	ꝺ	ða geherdon	ne heras hia ł ne sciolon gehera	ne	oncnauas hia		ꝥ
uident	et	audientes	non audient	neque	intelligunt	14	ut

to sie gefylled	him	witgiung	essaies	cuoeð	from hernise	gie geheras	ꝺ	ne oncnæuge ł ne cuðon ge
adimpleatur	eis	prophetia	esaiae	dicens	"auditu	audietis	et	non intelligitis

ꝺ gesegende	ge sciolon gesea ł ge geseas	ꝺ	ne	geseað ł ne sciolon gesea	ðicce ł hefig	is
et uidentes	uidebitis	et	non	uidebitis	15 incrassatum	est

forðon	hearta	folces	ðisses	ꝺ	mið earum	píslice ł hefiglice	geherdon	ꝺ	ego	hiora	getyndon
enim	cór	populi	huius	et	auribus		grauiter	audierunt	et	oculos	suos	cluserunt

ðy	læs	*egum	hia geseað	ꝺ	*earum	heraŏ	ꝺ	mið heartæ	hia oncnaues	ꝺ	hwærfa hia ł se
ne	quando	oculis	uideant	et	auribus	audiant	et	corde	intelligant	et	conuer-

gehuerfde ł gecerre hia	ꝺ	ic hælo	hia ł ða		iuere	uutedlice	eadgo ł biðon	ego	forðon
tantur	et	sanem	eos"	16	*Uestri	autem	beati	oculi	quia

hia geseað	ꝺ	earo	iuere	forðon	héras hia	
uident	et	aures	uestrae	quia	audiunt	

---

8. Sume þonne gefetun on eorðe gode ꝺ saldun wæstem sume hund-teontig sume sextig sume þritig 9. seþe hæbbe earu gehernesse gehere 10. ꝺ gangende to him þa leorneras his cwædun forhwon in gelicnissum spreces þu heom 11. he þa onsuarade cweþ to heom forþon þe eow sald is gecunnan geryne rice heofuna heom þonne ne is sald 12. seþe þonne hæfþ sald bið him ꝺ ge-nyht-sumaþ seþe þonne ne hæfð ge þæt he [h]æfð afirred bið him 13. forþon in gelicnissum ic sprece heom þe hie gescende ne geseoþ ꝺ geherende ne gehoeraþ ne ongeotað 14. ꝥ sie gefylled heom witigdom esaias cweþende mid gehernisse ge geherað ꝺ ne ongetaþ ꝺ geseende geseaþ ꝺ ne geseoþ 15. gefætted is forþon heorte folkes þisses ꝺ earum heora hefiglice geherdun ꝺ egu heora fortyndon* þyles hie hwanne geseo egum ꝺ earan geheran ꝺ heorte on-geton ꝺ ge-cerrede ꝺ Ic hælo hiæ 16. eower þonne eadige ege þe hiæ geseoð ꝺ earan eowre þe hiæ geherað

17 Soþlice on eornust ic eow secge ꝥ manega witegan ⁊ rihtwise gewilnudon þa þing to ge-seonne þe ge geseoþ ⁊ hig ne ge-sawon; ⁊ gehyran þa þing þe ge gehyraðˑ ⁊ hig ne gehyrdon;
18 Ge-hyre ge soþlice þæs sawendan bigspell;
19 Ælc þæra þe godes wurd gehyrð ⁊ ne ongyt. þonne cymþ deoful ⁊ bereafað ꝥ on hys heortan asáwen is. ꝥ is se þe wiþ ðone weg asawen is;
20 Soþlice se þe ofer þone stan asawen is. ꝥ is seþe ꝥ godes wurd gehyrð. ⁊ hrædlice ꝥ mid blisse onfehþ.
21 Soþlice hyt næfþ þone wyrtrum on him. ac is hwilwendlic; Gewordenre gedrefednesse ⁊ ehtnesse for þam wurde hrædlice hig beoð geúntreowsode.
22 Soþlice ꝥ þe asáwen is on þornum. ꝥ is se þe ꝥ wurd gehyrþ ⁊ þonne eornfullness þisse worulde ⁊ leasung þissa woruldwelena forþrysmiaþ ꝥ wurd ⁊ hit is butan weastme geworden;
23 Soþlice ꝥ þe asawen wæs on ꝥ gode land ꝥ is se þe ꝥ wurd gehyrþ ⁊ ongyt ⁊ þone weastm bringð ⁊ þonne deþ sum hund-fealdne sum sixti-fealdne sum þrittifealdne;
24 He rehte him þa oþer bigspel ⁊ þus cwæð. heofona rice is geworden þam men gelic þe seow god sæd on his æcyre;

17 Soðlice on eornestlice ic eow segge þæt manega witegan ⁊ rihtwise ge-wilneden þa þing to ge-seonne þe ge ge-seoð. ⁊ hyo ne ge-seagen. ⁊ ge-hyran þa þing þe ge gehyrað. ⁊ hyo ne ge-hyrdon.
18 Ge-hyre ge soðlice þa sawenden byspellen.
19 Ælc þare þe godes word gehyrð ⁊ ne ongyt þanne cymð deofel ⁊ bereafað þæt on hys heortan asæwen is. þæt is se þe on þanne weig á-sawen is.
20 Soðlice se þe ofer stan asawen is. þæt is se þe þæt godes word ge-hyrð ⁊ hrædlice þæt mid blisse onfegð.
21 Soðlice hit næfð þanne wertrum on him ac is hwilwendlic. Geworðenre gedrefendnysse ⁊ ehtnysse for þam worde rædlice hyo beoð ge-untreowsede.
22 Soðlice þæt þe asawen is on þornen. þæt ys se þe þæt word ge-hyrð. ⁊ þanne geornfulnisse þisse worlde. ⁊ leasunge þissere worlde welen forþresmiað. þæt word. ⁊ hit is buten wæstme ge-worðen.
23 Soðlice þæt þe asawen wæs on þæt gode land þæt is se þe þæt word ge-herð. ⁊ on-gyt. ⁊ þane wæstme bringð ⁊ þonne deð sum hund-fealdne. sum sixtig-fealdne. sum þrittig-fealdne.
24 He rehte heom þa þa oðerne byspel ⁊ þus cwæð. heofene riche is geworðen þam men gelic þe seow god sæd on his akere.

Various Readings.

17. A. eornost. A. gewylnedon; B. gewilnodun. B. gesawun. A. ⁊ to gehyranne. 19. A. B. word. A. ongitt. A. deofol. A. *om. last nine words.* 20. A. B. word. 21. A. wyrtruman. A. gedrefednysse ⁊ ehtnysse. A. B. worde. B. hi. 22. A. B. word. A. eornfulnys; B. geornfullnes. A. weorulde. B. -welona. A. B. word. B. buton. A. B. wæstme. 23. A. *om.* þe *after* 1st ꝥ. A. B. word. A. on-gitt. A. B. wæstm. A. syxtig-. A. þryttig-; B. þriti-. 24. A. heofena. A. B. æcere.

Various Readings.

17. eornustlice; secge; gewilnodun; seoð; gesawan; hyrað. 18. þæs sawendum bigspell. 19. þæra; þonne; deoful; wið þone weg. 20. ofer þonne stan; onfehð. 21. þonne wurtrum; gewordenre gedrefednysse; hrædlice. 22. þonne; gornfulnysse; worulde; leasung þissa weorld-welena forþrysmiað; geworden. 23. gehyrð; ongit; þone wæstm; þonne; sixti-. 24. þa (*for* þa þa); oðer; heofone rice; geworden; gelice; accere.

	soðlic	forðon	ic cueðo	iuh	forðon	monigo	witgo	ᛝ	soðfæsto	gewillnadon	gesea
17	amen	quippe	dico	uobis	quia	multi	prophetæ	et	iusti	cupierunt	uidere

	ða ilco	ge seas	ᛝ	ne	gesegon	ᛝ	gehera	ða ilco	ge heres*	ᛝ	ne	herdon		gie
	quae	uidetis	et	non	uiderunt	et	audire	quae	auditis	et	non	audierunt	18	+Uos

	forðoñ	geheras + lysnas	bisena	ðæs sauende + sedere		eghuelc	seðe heres	word	rices
	ergo	audite	parabolam	seminantis	19	omnis	qui audit	uerbum	regni

	ᛝ	ne on-cneawu + ne ongæt	cuom	ðe ðiowl + ðɔ yfle	ᛝ	genom + gelahte	ꝥ	gesawen	wæs in
	et	non intellegit	uenit	malus	et	rapit	quod	seminatum	est in

	hearta	is	ðes	is + wæs	seðe	neh	strete + woeg	sawende	wæs		seðe	soðlice	ofer + on
	corde	eius	hic	est	qui	secus	uiam	seminatus	est	20	qui	autem	supra

	staener	sawende	wæs ðis is + wæs	seðe	word	geherde	ᛝ	sona + hræðe	mið	glædnisse	onfeng
	petrosa	seminatus	*est* hic	est	qui	uerbum	audit	et	continuo	cum	gaudio	accipit

	ðætt		ne hæfde	uut*edlice*	in him	wyrttrumma	ah wæs	lytle huile	awærð + geworden + gewærð
	illud	21	non habet	autem	in se	radicem	sed est	temporalis	facta

	soðlice	costung	ᛝ	oehtnisse	fore	word	mið ðon + sona	geondspurnad was		seðe
	autem	tribulatione	et	persecutione	propter	uerbum	continuo	scandalizat*ur*	22	qui

	uut*edlice*	wæs	sawænde	in	ðornum	ðes + ðis	is	seðe	word	heres	ᛝ	gemnisse + gælso
	autem	est	seminatus	in	spinis	hic	est	qui	uerbum	audit	et	sollicitudo

	woruldes	ðisses	ᛝ	esuica + gebrægdas + leasunga +	ðæra wlenca + walana	under-delfes	ꝥ	word	ᛝ	buta
	saeculi	istius	et	fallacia	diuitiarum	suffocat	uerbum	et	sine

	wæstm	gefunden bið		seðe	uut*edlice*	in	eorðo	godo*	sawende	wæs ðis	is + wæs	seðe
	fructu	efficitur	23	qui	uero	in	terra	bona	seminatus	est	hic	est	qui

	heres	word	ᛝ	oncnæw + ongæt	ᛝ	wæstm	gebrohte + gebrenges	ᛝ	doas + wyrcas	oðer	soðlice + ec
	audit	uerbu*m*	et	intellegit	et	fructum	affert	et	facit	aliud	quidem

	hundræð	oðer	soðlice	sexdig + sextih	ec + soð	oðer	ðritih		oðero	biseno
	centum	aliud	autem	sexaginta	porro	aliud	triginta	24	*Aliam	parabolam

	foresætt + foresægde	him + ðæm	cueð	gelic	geworden	wæs	ric	heofna	ðæm menn	seðe
	proposuit	illis	dicens	simile	factum	est	regnum	caelorum	homini	qui

	geseawu	god	sed	in	lond	his
	seminauit	bonum	semen	in	agro	suo

---

17. soþ ic sæcge eow forþon monige witgu ᛝ soþfeste wilnadun ꝥ geseon þa þe ge-seoþ ᛝ ne gesegon ᛝ gehera þa þe ge hoe[res] ᛝ ne geho[rdon]* 18. ge forþon geheraþ gelicnisse þæs sawendes 19. æghwilc þara þe geherað word ricces ᛝ ne on-getaþ cymþ se wærgad ᛝ geriseð ꝥte sawen wæs in heorte his ꝥ is seþe sawen wæs bi wæge 20. seþe þonne on þa stanige lond gesauwen wæs ꝥ is seþe gehereþ word ᛝ hraðe mid gefea onfoehþ þæm 21. ne hæfeþ þon*ne* in him wyrttryma ah is wilen geworden þonne swincnisse ᛝ oehtnisse for þæ*m* wordum hraðe *and*spurnisse þrowað 22. seþe þonne in ðornum gesauwen wæs þæt is seþe word gehereþ ᛝ be-hygdnis weorulde þisse ᛝ lygnisse weolan asmoraþ þæt word ᛝ butan [+] westemleas geworðræd 23. seþe þonne in eorðe godne gesauwen wæs ꝥ is seþe gehereð word ᛝ ongeteð ᛝ westem forð bereþ ᛝ wyrceþ sume þonne + eowic hund-teontig sume sextig sume þritig 24. oþer gelicnisse gesette + gesægde heom cwæþende gelic is rice heofunas menn ðæm þe seow god sed on lond his

25 Soþlice þa þa men slepon þa com his feonda sum ꝉ ofer-seow hit mid coccele on middan þam hwæte ꝉ ferde þanon ;

26 Soþlice þa seo wyrt weox ꝉ þone weastm brohte þa æt-eowde se coccel hine.

27 þa eodon þæs hlafordes þeowas ꝉ cwædon. hlaford hū ne seow þu god sæd on þinum æcere. hwanon hæfde he coccel

28 þa cwæþ he ꝥ dyde unhold mann þa cwædon þa þeowas wylt þu we gað ꝉ gadriað hig.

29 þa cwæð he nese þe læs ge þone hwæte awurtwalion. þonne ge þone coccel gadriaþ ;

30 Lætað ægþer weaxan oð rip-timan. ꝉ on þam riptiman ic secge þam riperum gadriaþ ærest þone coccel ꝉ bindaþ sceaf-mælum to for-bærnenne. ꝉ gadriaþ ðone hwæte into minum berne.

31 He rehte him þa gyt oþer big-spel þus cweþende. heofena rice is ge-worden gelic senepes corne ꝥ seow se man on hys æcre

32 ꝥ is ealra sæda læst; Soþlice þonne hit wyxþ hit is ealra wyrta mæst ꝉ hit wyrþ treow swa ꝥ heofnan fuhlas cumaþ ꝉ eardiaþ on his bogum ;

33 He spræc to him oþer big-spel ꝉ þus cwæð. heofena rice is gelic þam beorman þone ꝥ wif onfeng ꝉ behydde on þrim gemetum melwes oð he wæs eall ahafen ;

25 Soðlice þa þa men slepen. þa com hy. feonda sum ꝉ ofer-seow hit mid coccle oꞃ middam (sic) þam hwæte ꝉ ferden (sic) þanen.

26 Soðlice þa syo wert weox ꝉ þanne wæstm brohte þa atewede se coccel hine.

27 þa eoden þas hlaferdes þeowas. ꝉ cwæ-ðen. Hlaford hu ne seowe þu god sæd on þinen akere. hwanen hafde he coccel.

28 þa cwæðen he. þæt dyde unhold man. þa cwæðen þa þeowas. wilt þu we gað ꝉ gaderieð* hyo.

29 þa cwæð he ne se þe læs ge þanne hwate awertwalien. þanne ge þanne coccel gaderiað.

30 Læteð ayþer wexan oððe riptiman. ꝉ on þam riptiman ic segge þan riperen gaderiað ærest þanne coccel ꝉ bindeð* sceaf-mælen to for-bærnenne. ꝉ gaderiað* þane hwæte in-to mine berne.

31 He rette heom þa get oðer bispell þus cweðende. heofena rice is ge-worðen gelich senepes corn. þæt seow se man on hys akere.

32 þæt ys alre sæde læst. Soðlice þanne hyt wexað hyt ys alre wyrte mæst. ꝉ hyt wurð treow. swa þæt heofene fugeles cumað ꝉ eardigeð* þær on his bogen.

33 He spræc to heom oðer byspell ꝉ þus cwæð. heofene riche is ge-lic þam beorman þonne þæt wif onfeng ꝉ be-hydde on þrem gemitten melewes oð þæt hyt wæs eall ahafan.

Various Readings.

26. A. B. wæstm. A. ætywde. B. cocel. 27. A. seowe. 28. A. B. man. A. gaderiað. 29. A. þylæs. A. awyrt-walion. A. gaderiað. 30. A. wexan. A. gaderiað. A. B. forbærnanne. A. gaderiað. A. minon. 31. A. bigspell. A. æcere. 32. A. wyxt. A. heofen-fugelas. 33. A. bigspell. B. heofona. A. melewes.

Various Readings.

25. his; coccele; middum; hwate; ferdon þanon. 26. wyrt; þonne. 27. eodon; cwæðon; þinum acere. 28. mann; goð; gaderiað. 29. þonne hwæte awyrtwalien þonne; þonne; gæderiað. 30. ægþer weaxan oð; þam riperum; arest þonne; sceafmælum; þonne. 31. rehte eom þa geat; byspel; heofona; geworden gelic; his æcre. 32. ealra; þonne hit weoxð hit; ealra wyrta; hit; heofonan fuhlas cumeð ꝉ eardiað; bogum. 33. him; bigspel; heofona rice; þrim gemittum melewes; hit.

	mið ðy	uutedlice	geslepdon ⁊ geslepæ	waldon	ða menn	cuom	fiond	his	⁊	ofer-geseawu
25	cum	autem	dormirent		homines	uenit	inimicus	eius	et	super-

⁊ geseawde	wynnung ⁊ sifðe	In	middum	hwæte	⁊	gē-eade		mið ðy	uutedlice	gewóx
seminauit	zizania	in	medio	tritici	et	abiit	26	cum	autem	creuisset

brórd ⁊ niwe gers	⁊	wæstm	worhte ⁊ gedyde	ða	æd-eawadon	⁊	wynnunga		to-geneolecdon
herba	et	fructum	fecisset	tunc	apparuerunt	et	zizania	27	accedentes

soðlice	ðeas ⁊ ðegnas	faderes	hiorodæs ⁊ higna	cuoedon	him	drihten	ahne	god	sēd
autem	serui	patris	familias	dixerunt	ei	domine	nonne	bonum	semen

ðu geseawu	in	lónd	ðinum	huona	forðon	hafes	un-wæstm ⁊ átih ⁊ wynnung ⁊ wilde foter		⁊
seminasti	in	agro	tuo	unde	ergo	habet	zizania	28	et

cuoeð	ðæm	ðe fiond	monn	ðis	dyde	ðeas ⁊ ðegnas	uutedlice	cuoedon	him	we sohton	⁊
ait	illis	inimicus	homo	hoc	fecit	serui	autem	dixerunt	ei	uisimus*	et

we somnadon ⁊ we geadredon	ða		⁊	cueð	nese	ðylæs ⁊ eaða maeg ⁊ inwoenonga	gegeadredon
	colligimus	ea	29	et	ait	non	ne forte	colli-

⁊ gie geadrias	þ	un-wæstm	unwyrtrumias ⁊ unclænsias	ædgeadre ⁊ gelíc	⁊	ðone huæte	mið	him
gentes	zizania	eradicetis	simul	et	triticum	cum	eis

	forletas	egðer ⁊ boege	gewæxe	wið	to	hrípe .i. to domes dæg	⁊	in	tíd	hrípes
30	sinite	utraque	crescere	usque	ad	messem		et	in	tempore	messis

ic willo cuoeða	ðæm hrippe-monnum	geadriges ⁊ somniges	ærist	ða unwæstm ⁊ wilde ata*	⁊	bindas
dicam	messoribus	colligite	primum	zizania	et	alligate

ða	bunda ⁊ byrðenno ⁊ sceafa	to	bernenne*	ðone huætte	soð	somnias ⁊ geadrias	in
ea	[in]	fasciculos	ad	comburendum	triticum	autem	congregate	in

	ber-érn	mín		oðer	bisen+	fore-sætte ⁊ foresægde	him	cuoeð ⁊ cuoeðende	gelíc
	horreum	meum	31	*Aliam	parabolam	proposuit	eis	dicens	simile

is	ríc	heofna	córn	senepes	þ	onfeing ⁊ genóm	monn	geseawu	in	lónd	his
est	regnum	cælorum	grano	sinapis	quod	accipiens	homo	seminauit	in	agro	suo

þ	leasest	soðlice	is	from allum	sedum	mið ðy	soðlice	gewóx ⁊ gewæxe	mara	is
32	quod	minimum	quidem	est	omnibus	seminibus	cum	autem	creuerit	maius	est

allum	wyrtum	gelíc	tré	suoæ	þ	flegendo	heofnes	cymes	⁊	byes ⁊ eardegas	in	tyggum	his
omnibus	holeribus	effit (sic)	arbor	ita	ut	uolucres·	caeli	ueniant	et	habitant (sic)	in	ramis	eius

	oðer	bisen	sprecend wæs	him	gelíc	is	ríc	heofna	to dærste	þ	onfeng ⁊ genom
33	*Aliam	parabolam	locutus est	eis	simile	est	regnum	caelorum	fermento	quod	acceptum

wif	gehydde ⁊ degelde	in	mealo*	genoh	ðrím	wið ⁊ ða huile	gedærsted ⁊ gecnoeden	is	all
mulier	abscondit	in	farinae	satis	tribus	donec	fermentatum	est	totum

---

25. þa hie soþlice sleptun þa menn cuom feond his ⁊ ofer-seow weód in midle þæs hwætes ⁊ him aweg eode
26. þa soþlice weox se brord ⁊ westem dyde þa æt-eawde ek þa weod 27. ⁊ cumende þa esnas to fæder þas heoredes cwedun to him drihten no þu god sed geseowe on lond þin hwonan þonne hæfð hit þæt weod 28. ⁊ cweþ to heom unhold monn þæt gedyde cwedun þa him esnas wiltu we gæn ⁊ gesomnige hiæ 29. cweþ to heom nic þyles gesomnende þa weod alucæ somed mið ðæm ⁊ ek þone hwete 30. ah leteþ begen wexan oþþe to ripe ⁊ in tíd ripes ic cweðe to riftrum minum gesomnigæþ arest þa weod ⁊ gebindeþ hiæ sceafum to beornane hwete þonne gesomnigaþ in berern mine 31. oþer gelicnisse sægde heom cweþende gelic is rice heofunas corne sinapis* þæt genimende mon seow on londe his 32. þæt læsest þonne is alra seda ⁊ hit þonne wexeþ mara is wyrtum ⁊ gewyrð treow swa þæt fluglas (sic) heofun cumaþ ⁊ eardigað in telgrum his 33. oþer gelicnisse sprec to heom cweþende gelic is rice heofunas beorma þonne genimende wif ge-hydde in melwæs mittum ðrim oþþæt gebeormad wæs all

34 Ealle þas þing se hælend spræc mid big-spellum to þam weredum. ꝫ nan þing ne spræc he butan big-spellum
35 ꝥ wære gefylled. þæs witegan cwyde ic atyne minne muþ mid big-spellum. ic bodige digelnesse fram middaneardes gesetednesse;
36 He for-let þa ða mænegeo ꝫ com to his inne ꝫ þa genealæhton to him his leorning-cnihtas ꝫ cwædon arece us ꝥ big-spell þæs hwætes and þæs cocceles.
37 þa and-swarude he him seþe seow ꝥ gode sæd se is mannes sunu.
38 Soþlice se æcyr is þes middangeard ꝥ gode sæd ꝥ synt þæs heofonlican rices bearn. Se coccel synt soþlice þa manfullan bearn.
39 Se unholda man seþe þone coccel seow ꝥ is deoful; Soðlice ꝥ rip is worulde endung þa riperas synt englas.
40 eornustlice swa swa se coccel byþ gegaderud ꝫ mid fyre forbærned swa byð on worulde endunge.
41 mannes sunu sent his englas ꝫ hi gadriað of his rice ealle gedrefednesse ꝫ þa þe unrihtwisnesse wyrceað
42 ꝫ asendað hig on fyres ofen þær byþ wóp ꝫ toþa gristbitung.
43 þonne scinað ða rihtwisan swa swa sunne on hyra fæder rice;

34 Ealle þas þing se hælend spæc mid byspellen to þam weredum. ꝫ nan þing ne spæc he buton byspellen.
35 þæt wære ge-fylled þas witegan cwide. Ic untyne minne muð mid bispellen. ich bodige digelnysse fram midden-eardes gesetnysse.
36 He for-let þa þa menigeo. ꝫ com to his inne. ꝫ þa ge-neahlahten to hym his leorning-cnihtes ꝫ cwæðon. Areche us þæt bispell þas hwætes ꝫ þas coccles
37 þa andswerede he heom. se þe seow ꝥ gode sæd se is mannes sune.
38 Soðlice se aker is þis midden-eard. þæt gode sæd þæt synden þas heofenlican rices bearn. Se coccel synde soðlice þa manfulle bearn.
39 Se unhole man se þe þane coccel seow ꝥ is deofel. Soðlice ꝥ rip ys weorlde endunge. þa riperas sende englas.
40 Eornostlice swa swa se coccel byð ge-gadered ꝫ mid fere for-berned* swa beoð on werolde ændunge.
41 mannes sune sent his ængles ꝫ hyo gaderiað of hys riche ealle gedrefednysse ꝫ þa þe unriht-wisnesse wercheð*
42 ꝫ asendeð hyo on fyres ofen þær byð wop ꝫ toðe gritbitung (sic)
43 þanne scineð* þa rithwisa swa swa sunne on heora fæder riche.

Various Readings.

35. A. on-tyne. A. digolnyssa. A. gesetednysse. 36. A. mænio; B. menegeo. 37. A. ꝫswarode. 38. A. B. æcer. A. synd (*twice*). A. heofenlican. 39. B. sew. A. ryp is þysre (*for* rip is). A. synd. 40. A. Eornostlice. A. gegaderod. A. ge-endunge. 41. A. hig gaderiað. A. gedrefednysse. A. unryhtwysnysse. 42. A. þar. 43. A. heora. At the end of the verse A. adds ge-hyre seðe earan to ge-hyranne hæfð.

Various Readings.

34. big-spellum; werodum; spræc; bigspellum. 35. ware; þæs; bigspellum. ic; middan-eardes. 36. geneahlæhton; -cnihtas; cwæðon. Arece; bispel; þæs (*twice*); cocceles. 37. sunu. 38. acer is þes middan-eard; synt þæs; sinde; manfullan. 39. þonne; deoful; is weorulde; sind. 40. Eornustlice; gegoderod; fyre forbærned; byð; weorulde endunge. 41. engles; hio; his rice; unrihtwysnysse wirceð. 42. bið; toða. 43. þonne scyneð; rihtwisa; sunna; hyora; rice.

34 *Haec omnia sprecende wæs hælend in bisenum to ðæm menigum ⁊ buta bisenum
    Haec omnia locutus est iesus in parabolis ad   turbas et sine parabolis non

sprecende wæs him   ꝥ to-gefylled wære   ꝥ gecuedon wæs ðerh ðone witgo cuoeðen
loquebatur   eis   35 ut adimpleretur quod dictum erat per prophetam dicentem

ic ædeawe* ⁊ ic ontyno in bisenum muð mín ic loccete ⁊ ic ge-yppe ⁊ deiglo from   setnesse
   "aperiam   in parabolis ós meum   eructabo   abscondita á constitutione

middangeardes   ða ⁊ mið ðy forletnum ðreatum† cuom in hus ⁊ geneolecdon to him
   mundi"   36 *Tunc   dimissis   turbis uenit in domum et accesserunt ad eum

ðegnas his cuoedon to-scead us   bisen *wun-wæstma londes   seðe onduearde cueð
discipuli eius dicentes dissere nobis parabolam zizaniorum agri 37 qui respondens ait

seðe sawæs gód sed is   sunu   monnes   lond uutedlice is middangeard gód
qui seminat bonum semen est filius hominis 38 ager autem   est mundus   bonum

soðlice   ða sindon suno ríces ða winnunga ⁊ áta ⁊ sifða ⁊ unwæstın soðlice suno* sindon
uero   semen hí sunt filii regni   zizania   autem filii sunt

yfelwyrcende [⁊] wohful*   ðe fiond wutedlice seðe sawes ⁊ seawu ða is diowl hrípet ⁊ hrípnis
nequam   39 inimicus autem qui seminauit ea est diabolus   messis

uutedlice   endung   woruldes is ða hripemenn soðlice engles sindon   suæ forðon
  uero   consummatio saeculi est ða messores autem angeli sunt   40 sicut ergo

gesomnad biðon ða un-wæstma ⁊ mið fyr forberned biðon suæ bið in énde   woruldes
colliguntur zizania et   igni comburuntur sic erit in consummatione saeculi

       sendes sunu monnes engles his ⁊ geadriges hia of ríc   his alle ondspyrnisse ⁊
41 mittet filius hominis angelos suos et colligent de regno eius omnia scandala   et

ðailco ða ðe wyrcas unrehtuisnisse   ⁊ sendas hia ⁊ ða in   ofn fyres ðer bið wóp
 eos qui faciunt iniquitatem   42 et mittent eos in caminum ignis ibi erit fletus

 ⁊ gristbittung* toða   ða soðfæsto† scines ⁊ lixeð suæ sunna in ríc   fadores
et   stridor   dentium   43 tunc   iusti   fulgebunt   sicut sol   in regno patris

his seðe hæfes hearo gehere ðe
sui qui habet aures audiat

---

34. þas all sprec hælend to mængum in gelicnissum ⁊ butan gelicnissum ne sprec he to heom   35. þæt
gefylled węre þætte gecweden wæs þurh esaias þone witgu cweþende ic on-tyno in gelicnissum muð minne roket-to
forð ⁊ bilket-to forð þa þe ahyded werun from setnisse middangeardes   36. þa forletende þa mengu cuom in
huse ⁊ eodun to him leorneras his cwæþende arecce us þa gelicnisse hwæte ⁊ weode londes 37. he þa ondswarede ⁊ cwæþ seþe sauweþ god séd sunu monnes ꝥ is   38. ꝥ lond þonne is middangeard ꝥ gode wiotudlice
scæd sindun bearn rices þa weod þonne bearn syndon þa nænegu   39. se fiond þonne seþe seow hiæ is deoful
þa rip þonne endunge weorulde is þa riftra þonne endung englas sy[n]dun   40. swa beoþ gesomnad þa weod ⁊ fyre
forberned swa bið in endunge weorulde   41. sendeþ sunu monnes englas his ⁊ hiæ asomnigaþ of rice his
all geswicu ⁊ þa fremmende unreht   42. ⁊ sendeþ þa in ofne fyres beornende þær bið wop ⁊ gristbitung toþa
43. þanne þa soþfeste scinaþ* swa swa sunne in rice fader heora seþe hæbbe earan gehernisse gehoēre

44 Heofona rice is gelic gehyddum goldhorde on þam æcere þone behyt se man þe hyne fint ꝉ for his blysse gæð ꝉ sylþ eall ꝥ he ah ꝉ gebigþ þone æcer;

45 Eft is heofena rice gelic þam mangere þe sohte ꝥ gode mere-grot

46 þa he funde ꝥ án deorwyrðe meregrot þa eode he ꝉ sealde eall ꝥ he ahte ꝉ bohte ꝥ meregrot;

47 Eft is heofena rice gelic. asendum nette on þa sǽ ꝉ of ælcum fisc-cynne gadrigendum.

48 þa hi þa ꝥ nett úpp-atúgon ꝉ sǽton be þam strande. þa gecuron hig þa godan on hyra fatu. þa yflan hig awurpon út;

49 Swa byþ on þisse worulde endunge þa englas farað ꝉ asyndriað þa yfelan of þæra godra midlene.

50 ꝉ aworpað hig on þæs fyres ófen. þær byð wóp ꝉ tóða grist-bitung.

51 ongyte ge ealle þas þing. þa cwædon hig witodlice we hit ongytað

52 þa sæde he him. forþam is ælc gelæred bocere on heofenan rice gelic þam hiredes ealdre þe forð-bringð of his goldhorde níwe þing ꝉ ealde;

53 And hit wæs geworden þa se hǽlend geendode þas big-spel þa ferde he þanone

54 ꝉ þa he com to his earde he lærde hig on hyra gesamnungum swa ꝥ hig wundredon ꝉ cwædon hwanon ys þysum þes wisdom. ꝉ þis mægen.

44 Heofene rice is ge-lic gehydden goldhorden. on þam akere þanne be-bit (sic) se man þe hine fint ꝉ for hys blisse gæð. ꝉ silð æll þæt he hæfð ꝉ ge-beið þanne Aker.

45 Eft is heofene riche gelic þam mangere þe sohte ꝥ gode meregrot

46 þa he funde ꝥ an derwurðe meregrot þa eode he ꝉ sealde all þæt he ahte ꝉ bohte þæt meregrot.

47 Eft ys heofene rice ge-lic. asende nytte on þa sæ. ꝉ of ælche fyskenne gaderiende.

48 þa hyo þa þæt nyt up-atugen ꝉ sæten be þam strande. þa ge-curen hyo þa goden on heora fate. þa yfele hy atorfedon ut.

49 Swa beoð on þissere worulde endunge. þa ængles fareð*. ꝉ asyndrieð ða yfele of þare godere midlene.

50 ꝉ a-wurpeð hyo on þas feres ofen. þær byð wop ꝉ toke (sic) gristbyting.

51 ongete ge ealle þas þing. þa cwæðen hyo. witodlice we hyt on-getað.

52 þa sægde he heom. for-þan is ælc læred bokere on heofene riche ge-lic þam heordes ealdre þe forð-bringð of hys goldhorde nywe þing ꝉ ealde.

53 Ænd hyt wæs worðen þa se hælend ge-endode þas byspell. þa ferde he þanon.

54 ꝉ þa he com to hys earde he lærde hyo on heora samnungen swa þæt hyo wundredon ꝉ cwæðen. hwanen ys þisum. þes wisdom ꝉ þis maigen.

Various Readings.

44. A. Heofena. 45. B. heofna. 47. B. heofona. A. gaderiendum. 48. A. hig. A. heora. A. B. yfelan. 49. B. worolde. 50. B. awurpað. A. þar. 51. A. hig (for hit). 52. A. om. he. A. om. is. A. heofena; B. heofonan. A. rice byð gelyc. 54. A. gesomnungum. A. þyssum.

Various Readings.

44. Heofone; gehiddum goldhordum; acere þone; sillð eal; gebyg þonne æcer. 45. hefone rice. 46. derewurðe; eall. 47. heofone; ælce fyscynne gaderiendum. 48. hy; hyora; yfel hyo awurpon ut. 49. byð þysse weorulde eandunge: engles; asyndrieð; yfelen; þara godra. 50. þæs fyres; toþa gristbytung. 51. ongeate; cwæðen; hit ongeoteð. 52. for-þam; lærd (alt. to læred) bocere; heofone; hyrdes; forðbrincð; niwe. 53. End hit; geworden; ge-ændede; bygspel. 54. his; hyora; wundreden; cwæðon hwanon hys; þes mægen.

第 1 章　アングロサクソン時代の言語　37

```
            ōngelīc    is      rīc    heofna    strion   to-gedeglede   in   lōnd   ðone    seðe    infand ᛫ onfindes
         44 *Simile   est   regnum  caelorum  thesauro   abscondito    in   agro   quem    qui             inuenit

         monn   gehydde    ꝫ    fore   glædnisse    ðæs    geongeð ᛫ gæð     ꝫ     bebyges    alle     ða  ðe    hæfes   ꝫ
         homo  abscondit   et   prae    gaudio    illius      uadit        et    uendit    uniuersa  quæ   habet   et

         byges  lōnd  ðone ᛫ þ              eft sona  ongelīc   is      rīc    heofna    menn    ðæm cepe   soecende
         emit   agrum   illum           45  iterum   simile   est   regnum  caelorum   homini  negotiatori  quaerenti

         godo   mere-groto              begetna ᛫ begeten was    uut edlice     an    *᛫ wyrðe ᛫ diorwyrðe   meregreota
         bonas  margaretas          46              inuenta     autem         una              pretiosa      margarita

         ge-eade    ꝫ   bobohte    alle   ða  ðe   ahte      ꝫ   bohte    ða                eft    ongelīc   is     rīc
           abiit   et  uendidit  omnia   quae   habuit    et   emit    eam             47 iterum  simile   est  regnum

         heofna    segne    sende    in    sae    of    all ᛫ eghwelc   cynn      fisca     somnende ᛫ geadrigende
         caelorum saginae  missae   in   mare    ex       omni      genere   piscium            congreganti

              ðiu ᛫ þ  mið ðy  gefylled   was   of-gelædon ᛫ gebrohton    ꝫ   neh  warðe  geseton   gecuron     godo
         48  quam    cum    impleta   esset         educentes          et  secus  litus  sedentes elegerunt   bonos

         in   fetelsum ᛫ in fatum ᛫ in sciopum       ða yflo   soðlice    ūt    gesendon               suæ     bið    in
         in              uasa                        malos   autem     foras  miserunt            49  sic     erit    in

         endung       worldes  *gæs   englas    ꝫ   tosceadas ᛫  ða yfle  of  middum   soðfestra                    ꝫ
         consummatione saeculi exibunt angeli   et  separabunt  malos    de  medio   iustorum              50 et

         sendes  hia ᛫ ða   in     ofn     fyres   ðer   bið   wōp    ꝫ   gristbiotung   toðana                    oncneaw
         mittent* eos      in   caminum   ignis   ibi   erit  fletus  et    stridor    dentium        51         in-

         gie ᛫ ongete ge  ðas    alle   cwoedon ᛫ sægdon him                cueð  him  forðon  eghwelc  wuðuta
         tellexistis     haec   omnia     dicunt         ei    etiam   52  ait  illis   ideo    omnis   scriba

         gelæred in   rīc   heofna  gelīc   is   *menn   feder iorodes   seðe  ahefes   of  striona    his    niwea
         doctus  in  regno caelorum similis est homini  patri-familias  qui  profert  de thesauro·  suo    noua

           ꝫ    alda        ꝫ   geworden  wæs  mið ðy   ge-endade     ðe hælend    biseno   ðas    gefoerde
          et  uetera       53  et  factum  est  cum  consummasset    iesus    parabolas  istas   transiit

         ðona              ꝫ    cuom    in oeðel ᛫ in eard   his   gelærde  hia   in  somnungum   hiora   suæ   þ
         inde          54  *Et Ueniens    in patriam        suam  docebat  eos   in  synagogis   eorum   ita   ut

         hia gewundradon   ꝫ   gecuedon huona  ðissum   snytry   ðius    ꝫ    mægn
            mirarentur    et   dicerent  unde  huic   sapientia haec    et   uirtus
```

---

44. gelic is rice heofunas gold-horde gehyded in eorðe þæm seþe findeþ þe monn ahydeþ ꝫ for gefea his gæþ ꝫ bebygið ᛫ sellaþ all þ he hæfeþ ꝫ bygiþ lond þæt　45. eft gelic is rice heofunas menn ceape sohte gode ercnan-stanas　46. ꝫ gemoetend þa ænne ercna-stan diorwyrðe code ꝫ salde eall þæt he hæfde ꝫ gebohte þanne　47. ꝫ eft gelic is rice heofunas nett asendun in sæe ꝫ of æghwilce cynne fisca þ somnendum　48. þa hit gefylled wæs upp-teonde ꝫ bi waraðe gesittende gecuron þa gode in fatu þa yfle þonne sendun ūt　49. swa bið in endunge weoruldes ꝫ þonne gæþ englas ꝫ ascedeþ yfle of midle soðfestra　50. ꝫ sendaþ hiæ in ofn fyres þer bið wop ꝫ gristbitung toþa　51. ongetaþ ge þas call cwedun hie la drihten　52. cweþ to heom forþon æghwilc bokere gelæred in rice heofunas is gelic menn fæder hina þæm þe forð-bereð of gold-hord his þa neowe ꝫ þa ealde.　53. ꝫ gelamp þa ge-endade se hælend gelicnisse þas foerde þonan　54. ꝫ cuom in oeþel hia gelærde hiæ in gesomnungum heora swa þæt hiæ wundradun ꝫ cweden hwonan þissum þas snottre ꝫ mægn

55 witodlice þes ys smiþes sunu hú ne hatte hys modor maria. ⁊ hys broþru iacob ⁊ ioseph. ⁊ simon ⁊ iudas.

56 ⁊ hu ne synt ealle hys swustra mid us hwanon synt þisum ealle þas þing

57 ⁊ hig wæron ge-úntrywsode on him; Ða soþlice sæde se hælend him nys nan witega butan wurþ-scype buton on hys earde ⁊ on hys huse.

58 ⁊ he ne worhte þær manega mægena for hyra ungeleafulnysse.

55 Witodlice þes is smiðes sune. ⁊ hu ne hatte his moder MARie ⁊ hys broðra iacob ⁊ ioseph. ⁊ symon ⁊ iudas.

56 ⁊ hu ne synd ealle hys swustre mid us. hwanen synðon þisen ealle þas þing.

57 ⁊ hyo wæren untreowsede* on him. Ða soðlice saigde se hælend heom. nis nan witege buton wurðscipe bute on hys earde. ⁊ on his huse.

58 ⁊ he ne worhte þær manega mænege* buto for heora ungeleaffulnysse.

| | ah ne | ðis | is | smiðes ┼ wyrihta | sunu | | ah ne | moder | his | acweden | maria | ꝫ | broðer |
| 55 | nonne | hic | est | fabri | filius | | nonne | mater | eius | dicitur | maria | et | fratres |

| is | | | | | | | | | ꝫ | suoester | his | ah ne | alle | mið | us * |
| eius | iacobus | et | ioseph | et | simon | et | iuda | | 56 et | sorores | eius | nonne | omnes | apud | nos |

| sint | hwona | forðon | ðissum | alle | ðas | | ꝫ | ge-ondspurnedon ┼ ge-ondspurnedo | woeron | in him |
| sunt | unde | ergo | huic | omnia | ista | 57 et | scandalizabantur | | | | in eo |

| hælend | uutedlice | cueð | him | ne | is | witge | buta | are | nymðe | in eard ┼ in oeðel | his | ꝫ | in |
| *Iesus | autem | dixit | eis | non | est | propheta | sine | honore | nisi | in patria | sua | et | in |

| hus | his | | ꝫ | ne | dyde | ðer | mæhto ┼ mægno | monigo | fore | ungeleaffulnisse ┼ ungelefenise |
| domo | sua | 58 et | non | fecit | ibi | uirtutes | multas | propter | incredulitatem |

hiora ┼ ðæra
illorum

CHAPTER XX.

1 Soþlice heofona rice ys gelic þam hiredes ealdre. þe on ærne mergen ut-eode á-hyrian wyrhtan on hys wíngeard;
2 Gewordenre gecwydrædene þam wyrhtum he sealde ælcon ænne penig wiþ hys dæges worce. he asende hig on hys wíngeard;
3 ꝉ þa he út-eode embe undern-tide. he ge-seah oþre on stræte idele standan;
4 Ða cwæð he. gá gé on minne wíngeard. ꝉ ic sylle eow ꝥ riht byþ. ꝉ hig þa ferdon;
5 Eft he út-eode embe þa sixtan ꝉ nigoþan tide. ꝉ dyde þam swá gelíce;
6 Þa embe þa endlyftan tide he út-eode. ꝉ funde oþre standende. ꝉ þa sæde he; Hwi stande ge her eallne dæg idele.
7 þa cwædon hig forþam þe ús nan mann ne hyrode; Ða cwæð he. ꝉ gá gé on minne win-geard;

CHAPTER XX.

1 Soðlice heofene rice ys ge-lic þam hyrdes ealdre. þe on ernemorgen ut-eode áhyrian wyrhten on hys wingeard.
2 Ge-wordenre ge-cwydredene þam werhtan he sealde ælchen ænne pænig wið hys dæges weorke. he sente hyo on hys wingeard.
3 ꝉ þa he ut-eode ymbe under-tide. he ge-seah oðre on stræte ydele standen.
4 Þa cwæð he. ga ge on minne wingeard. ꝉ ic gyfe eow ꝥ riht beoð. ꝉ hy þa eoden.
5 Eft he ut-eode embe þa syxten ꝉ þa nigeþan tyde. ꝉ dyde þam swa ge-lice.
6 Ða ymbe þa endlyftan tide heo (sic) ut-geode. ꝉ funde oðre standende. ꝉ þa sægde he. Hwi stande ge her ealne dayg ydele.
7 Ða cwæðen hye. for-þan þe nan mann us ne herde. Ða cw̄. he gað on minne wingeard.

Various Readings.

29. A. moder. A. hund-fealdum. 30. A. ytemyste (*twice*).
Cap. xx. 1. A. heofena. A. wyn-eard. 2. A. gecwydrædenne. A. weorce. A. wyn-eard. 3. A. ymbe.
5. A. ymbe. A. ꝉ þa nygeðan. A. *om.* swá. 6. A. ymbe. A. hwig. A. B. ealne. 7. A. B. man. A. byrede.

Various Readings.

29. minum næmen; gebroðra; geswustra; modor; hundfeoldan; hæfð ecce. 30. bið ytemesta; fyrmeste. Cap. xx. 1. heofone; ærne-; wyrhtan. 2. wyrhton; ælcen; penig; his daiges wyrce; sende. 3. geseagh. 4. sylle (*for* gyfe); ryht byð; hyo; feorden (*for* eoden). 5. syxton; *om.* þa. 6. endleftan; he; -eode; Hwy; daig. 7. hyo; man; ge-hyrde; ꝉ ga ge (*for* gað); mine.

CAP. XX.

1 *Símile / gelic / est / is / enim / forðon / regnum / ríc / caelorum / heofna / homini / ðæm menn / patri-familias / fador† hiorodes / qui / seðe / exiit / foerde / primo / ærist ɫ ár

mane / in merne / conducere / efne-gelæda / operarios / ða woercmenn / in / in / uineam / win-geard / suam / his / 2 conuentione / gesomnung / autem / uutedlice / facta / gewearð

cum / mið / operariis / ðæm wyrcendum ɫ woerc-monnum / ex / of / denario / penning / diurno / dæghuæmlice / misit / sende / eos / hia / in / in / uineam / win-geard / 3 et / ꝫ

egressus / gefoerde / circa / ymb / horam / tíd / tertiam / ðy ðirdda / uidit / gesæh / alios / oðero / stantes / standende / in foro / in sprec ɫ in ðing-stow / otiosos / ídlo / 4 et / ꝫ

illis / ðæm / dixit / cueð / ite / gaað / et / ꝫ / uos / gie / in / in / uineam / win-geard / et / ꝫ / quod / ꝥ te / iustum / reht / fuerit / bið / dabo / ic selo / uobis / iuh / illi / ða / autem / uutedlice

abierunt / ge-eodon / 5 iterum / eftsona / autem / soðlice / exiit / ge-eode / circa / ymb / sextam / ða seista / et / ꝫ / nonam / non / horam / tíd / et / ꝫ / fecit / dyde / similiter / gelic

6 circa / ymb / undecimam / ða ællefta / uero / ec / exiit / ge-ende / et / ꝫ / inuenit / gemoette / alios / oðero / stantes / standende / et / ꝫ / dicit / cuoeð / illis / him / quid / hwæt / hic / her

statis / stondes ge / tota / allen / die / dæge / otiosi / idlo / 7 dicunt / cuoedun / ei / him / quia / forðon / nemo / ænig* menn / nos / usig / conduxit / efne-gelæde / dicit / cuoeð

illis / him / ite / gaað / et / ꝫ / uos / gie / in / in / uineam / win-geard

---

29. ꝫ æghwilc þonne ðe for-leteþ hus oþþe broþer oþþe swuster oþþe fæder oþþ moder oþþe wif oþþe bearn oþþe lond for noman minum hundteantig falde onfoþ her ꝫ lif æce gesitteþ   30. monige þonne beoþan þa ærestu næhstu ꝫ þa næhstu ærestu

Cap. XX. 1. gelice is rice heofunas monn fæder hina ðæm ðe eode on ærne morgen bycgæ wyrhta in win-geard his   2. ꝫ þa geþingadun wið þæm wyrhtum be dinere ꝫ deglicum sende hio in þone win-geard   3. ꝫ ut-eode æt þære ðridda tid ɫ hwile gesæh oþre standende on prot-bore unnytte   4. ꝫ cwæþ to heom gæþ ge ek in win-geard mine ꝫ þætte reht biþ ic selle cow hie þa eodun   5. eft uteode æt þæm sextan ꝫ þæm nigoþan tide ɫ hwile ꝫ dyde gelice   6. æt þære ællefta soþlice tide þa eode ut ꝫ gemette oþre standende   7. ꝫ cwæð to þæm hwæt stondeþ ge her unnytte ealne dæg cwædun hie forþon nænig usic mið leane gebohte cwæþ to heom gáþ ge ek swilce in win-geard mine

8 Soþlice þa hyt wæs æfen geworden. þa sæde se wín-geardes hlaford hys geréfan; Clypa þa wyrhtan. ꝉ agyf him heora mede. agynn fram þam ytemestan oþ þone fyrmestan;

9 Eornostlice þa ðæ ge-comon þe embe þa endlyftan tíde comon. þa onfengon hig ælc his pening;

10 ꝉ þa þe þær ærest comon wendon ꝥ hig sceoldon mare onfón. þa onfengon hig syndrige penegas;

11 Ða ongunnon hig murcnian. ongen þone híredes ealdor

12 ꝉ þus cwædon; Þas ytemestan worhton áne tide. ꝉ þu dydest hig gelice us þe bæron byrþena on þises dæges hætan;

13 Ða cwæð he andswarigende hyra anum; Eala þu freond. ne dó ic þe nænne teonan; Hú ne come þu to me to wyrceanne wið anum peninge.

14 nim ꝥ þin ys ꝉ ga; Ic wylle þysum ytemestan syllan eal swa mycel swa þe.

15 oþþe ne mot ic dón ꝥ ic wylle. hwæþer þe þin eage mánful ys. forþam þe ic gód eom;

16 Swa beoð þa fyrmestan ytemeste. ꝉ þa ytemestan fyrmeste; Soþlice manega synt geclypede ꝉ feawa gecorene;

17 ÐA ferde se hælend to hierusalem. ꝉ nam hys leorning-cnihtas on-sundron ꝉ þus cwæþ;

8 Soðlice þa hyt wæs æfen ge-worðen. þa sægde þas wingeardes hlaford hys gerefen. Clepe þa werhtan. ꝉ gyf heom heore mede. agyn fram þam ytemestan. oð þanne fyrmesten.

9 Eornestlice þa ða ge-comen þa ymbe þa ændlyften tide comen. þa onfengon hi ælch hys panig.

10 ꝉ þa þe þær ær comen wenden þæt hyo mare scolden on-fon. þa on-fengen hyo sindrie paneges.

11 Ða ongunnen hyo murcnian ongean þanne heorde alder.

12 ꝉ þus cwæðen; Ðas ytemestan worhtan ane tíde. ꝉ þu dydest hyo ge-liche us. þe bæren byrdene oððe þises dayges hæten.

13 þa cwæð he andsweriende hyora anen. Eale þu freond ne do ich þe nane teonen. hu ne come þu to me to wyrcenne for ænne panig.

14 nym þæt þe þin ys ꝉ gá. ic wille þisen ytemestan gyfan eal swa mycel swa þe.

15 Oððe ne mot ic don þæt ic wille. hwader þe þin eage manfull ys. forþam þe ich gód eom.

16 Swa beoð þa fyrmestan ytemeste. ꝉ þa ytemesta fyrmesta. Soðlice manega synde ge-clypede. ꝉ feawe ge-corena.

17 ÞA ferde se hælend to Ierusalem. ꝉ nam hys leorning-cnihtes on-sundren ꝉ þus cwæð to heom.

Various Readings.

8. A. hyra. A. agin; B. aginn. B. ðæne. 9. A. Eornestlice. A. *om.* ðæ ge-comen. A. ymbe. A. penig. 10. A. þar. 11. A. on-gean. 12. A. hi. 13. A. ꝉswariende heora. A. wyrcanne. A. penige. 14. A. þyssum ytemystum. 15. A. ege. B. mánful. 16. A. synd. A. B. ge-clypode.

Various Readings.

8. afen ge-worden; ge-reafan; clypa; wyrhtan ꝉ geaf com heora; agin; ytemestam; ðenne. 9. Eornostlice; embe; endlefte tyde; onfengon hyo ælc his pening. 10. wendon; sindrige panegas. 11. on-gunnan; þonne hyrde ealder. 12. worhten; tid; gelice; byrðene; on (*for* oððe). 13. hyra; Eala; ic; næn teonan; wið (*for* for); æne panige. 14. *om.* þe; wylle ðysen; syllan (*for* gyfan). 15. wylle. hwæðer; man-ful; ic. 16. byð; ytemeste fyrmeste; mæga (*for* manega) sint; feawa. 17. man (*for* nam); -cnihtas; onsundran; *om.* to heom.

```
         miðði    efern ł ic sædi  uutedlice  geworden  were    cuoeð   hlafard    ðære win-gearde   giroefæ
      8  cum           sero           autem    factum   esset    dicit  dominus       uineae        pro-curatori

         his    ceig    ða wercmenn  ꝫ    geld     him      meard      ongann     from    ðæm laetmestum    wið
         suo    uoca      operarios  et   redde    illis    mercedem   incipiens    a       nouissimis    usque

         ðæm forðmestum           mið ðy   gecuomun   uutedlice   ða ðe    ymb     ða ællefta    tid      gecuomon
           ad primos          9    cum     uenissent    ergo      qui     circa    undecimam    horam    uenerant

         onfengon   suindrigo   penningas          cymende     uutedlice  ꝫ   ða forðmesto  gedoemendo*  weron
         acceperunt  singulos   denarios      10   uenientes     autem    et    .primi       arbitrati   sunt

          ꝥ       forðor     weron    onfengendo    onfengon    uutedlice ł ec   ꝫ    ða ilco   syndrigo   penningas
         quod     plus      essent    accepturi    acceperunt     autem        et    ipsi      singulos   denarios

          ꝫ    mið ðy gefengon    hia huæstredon ł deglice yfle sprecon   wið      ðæm hiorodes          cuoeðendo
         11 et   accipientes        hia murmurabant                     aduersus   patrem familias    12  dicentes

         ðas   hlætmesto   an      tid ł huil    dydon ł worohton    ꝫ    ðu efnes ł gelic*     ða     ús      ðu dydest
          hi   nouissimi   una       hora          fecerunt         et      pares               illos  nobis    fecisti

         we ða ðe     beron      hefignise ł byrðen    ðæs dæges   ꝫ    hæto ł byrn             soð   he    onduearde
               qui    portauimus      pondus           diei       et     aestus           13    at    ille  respondens

         anum   hiora   cueð    la freond ł la meg   ne   dóm ic   ðe    laæðo ł baeligniso    ah ne     for     penning
          uni   eorum   dixit      amice             non   facio   tibi   iniuriam             nonne     ex     denario

         ðu cuome    mec mið                nim     ꝥte    ðin    is     ꝫ   gaa ł geong    ic willo   uutedlice   ꝫ    ðissum
         con-uenisti mecum           14   tolle    quod    tuum   est   et      uade         uolo       autem     et    huic

         hlætmesto   sealla    sua    ꝫ    ðe              ł      ne      is rehtlic    me      ꝥ      ic willo   doa    ł
         nouissimo   dare      sicut  et   tibi      15   aut    non      licet        mihi    quod     uolo      facere  án

         ego   ðin   wohgfull    is    forðon     ic   gód   amm                   suæ    biðon    ða hlætmesto    forðmest
         oculus tuus  nequam    est    quia      ego  bonus  sum           16      sic    erunt     nouissimi       primi

          ꝫ    ða forðmest   hlætmest    monigo   sint   forðon    geceigdo   lythwon   uutedlice   gecoren     ꝫ
         et      primi       nouissimi    multi   sunt    enim     uocati      pauci     autem      electi   17 *Et

         astág      ðe hælend                  genóm       tuoelfo    ða ðegnas   déglice    ꝫ    cueð    him
         ascendens    iesus       hierosolymis  assumsit   duodecim   discipulos  secreto    et   ait     illis
```

---

8. þa hit þa efen geworden wæs cwæþ he se hlaford þæs win-geardes to his geroefa cege þæm wyrhtum
ꝫ gef heom heora lean ingingende from þæm næhstum oþ þe ærestu   9. þa cumende þa þe æt þære
elleftan hwile ł tide comen ꝫ-fengon æghwilc anum dinere   10. cumende þa ek þa ærestu wendon þæt
hie mare sculdon onfoon onfengon ꝫ hie þonne swilce anum dinere   11. ꝫ þa onfengon grornadun wið
þæm fæder hina   12. cweþende þas næhstu ane tide worhtun ꝫ gelice þu hiæ us dydest seþe berou
mægen þisses dæges ꝫ hætu   13. ꝫ he ondswarede anum heora ꝫ cwæþ freond ne do ic ðe teane ah ðu
be dinere dægullicum* geþingdest wið me   14. genim þætte þin is ꝫ ga ic wille ek ꝫ ðissum næhsta
sellan swilce ꝫ þe   15. ah me is alæfed to sellan min þæt ic wille doan þa egan þin nawiht is forþon
þe god ic eam   16. swa beoþ þa næhstu æreste ꝫ þa erestu næhsta monige forþon sindun gecæged ꝫ
feawe soðlice gecoren   17. ꝫ astigende hælend hiervsolymis* genom þa twelf leorneras his degullice ꝫ
cwæþ to heom

18 Nú wḗ faraðto hierusalem. ꝫ mannes sunu byþ ge-seald þæra sacerda ealdrum ꝫ bocerum. ꝫ híg ge-nyþeriað hyne to deaþe.

19 þeodum to bysmrigenne ꝫ to swingenne ꝫ to ahónne ꝫ þam þryddan dæge hḗ arist;

20 Ða cṓm to him zebedeis bearna modor mid hyre bearnum hig ge-eadmedende. ꝫ sum þingc fram him biddende;

21 þa cwæð he hwæt wylt-tu; Ða cwæð heo. sege ꝥ þas míne twegen suna sittan án on þine swiþran healfe. ꝫ án on þine wynstran on þínum rice;

22 Ða ꝫswarode him se hælend; Gyt nyton hwæt gyt biddaþ. mage gyt drincan þone calic ðe ic to drincenne hæbbe þa cwædon hig. wyt magon;

23 Ða cwæð he. witodlice gyt minne calic drincaþ to sittanne on mine swiþran healfe oððe on wynstran nys me inc to syllanne. ac þam þe hyt fram minum fæder gegearwod ys;

24 ꝫ þa ða tyn leorning-cnihtas gebulgon wiþ ða twegen gebroðru;

25 þa clypode se hælend hig to him ꝫ cwæð; Wite ge ꝥ ealdor-menn wealdað hyra þeoda. ꝫ þa ðe synt yldran habbað anweald on him.

26 ne byþ swa betweox eow. ac swa hwylc swa wyle be-tweox eow beon yldra sy he eower þen.

18 Nu we fareð to ierusalem. ænd mannes sune beoð ge-seald þare sacerda eldren ꝫ bokeren. ꝫ hyo ge-niðeriað hine to deaðe.

19 þeoden to bisemerienne. ꝫ to swingenne. ꝫ to ahonne. ꝫ þam þridde daige he arist.

20 Ða com to hym zebedeis bearne moder mid hire bearnen. hyo ge-eadmedende ꝫ sum þing fram him byddende.

21 Ða cwæð he. hwæt wilt þu. Ða cwæð hye. sege þæt þas twege mine sunas sittan an on þinen swiðren healfe. ꝫ se oþer on þinen wenstron on þinen rice.

22 Ða andswerede heom se hælend. gyt nyston ge hwæt gyt bydde‍ð. mugen gyt drinken þanne calic ðe ic to drinken hæbbe. Ða cwæðen hye wit mugen.

23 Ða cwæð he. witodlice gyt minne calic drinkeð. to sittenne on mine swiðre healfe oððe on wenstren nis me inc to sellenne. ac þan þe hit fram minen fæder gegarewed ys.

24 ꝫ þa þa teon leorning-cnihtes gebolgen wið þa twegen broðren.

25 þa clypede se hælend hyo to hym ꝫ cwæð. Wite ge þæt ealdormen wealdeð heora þeode. ꝫ þa þe synd ealdran hæbbed anweald on heom.

26 ne beoð swa be-twex eow. ac swa hwile swa wile betweox eow byon eldra syo heo eowre þeing.

Various Readings.

18. A. deðe. 19. A. bysmrianne. A. swinganne. 20. A. *om.* to him. A. suna (*for* bearna). A. moder. A. ge-eaðmedende. A. þing. 21. A. ðu. B. sæge. A. sytton. 22. A. drincanne. 23. B. syllenne. A. ge-earwod. 25. B. hi. A. wytodlice (*for* wite ge ꝥ). A. -men. A. heora. A. synd. 26. A. betwyx. A. wylle. A. yldran sig.

Various Readings.

18. faræð; byð; eldrum ꝫ bocerum; deadum. 19. bysemirigenne. 20. bearna; biddende. 21. wylt; hyo sæge; *om.* mine; sitten; þinum swyðrum; an (*for* se oþer); þine winstron; þinum. 22. him; git biddaæ; drincan þonne; drincan habbe; cwaðen hyo. 23. drincað; sittanne; swyðran; winstrum; syllenne; þam; mynum. 24. -cnihtas ge-bulgon; broðra. 25. halend; ðyda (*for* þeode); sint; habbað; eom. 26. byð; be-twux; beon yldra; he eower þen.

```
         heonu  we stiges ⊦ we scilon stige                     ] sunu   monnes   gesåld bið  forwuostum ⊦
    18   ecce            ascendimus        hierosolymam  et  filius  hominis   tradetur          princi-

aldormonnum    ðæra sacerda  ] wuðuutum  ] geniðredon ⊦ geteldon  hine   to deaðe               ]  sellas
pibus             sacerdotum  et  scribis  et  condemnabunt      eum    morte       19  et  tradent

hine    hæðnum     to telenne ⊦ to besuicanne   ]   to suinganne    ]   to hoanne     ]  ðirdda   dæg
eum   gentibus      ad deludendum           et   flagellandum    et  cruci-figendum  et  tertia   die

eft arisæs              ða     cuom ⊦ geneolecde    to   him   moder   suno    zebedics   mið   sunum  hire
resurget            20  *Tunc     accessit        ad  eum   mater  filiorum  zebedaei   cum   filiis  suis

to-bæd ⊦ worðade     ]   giwude   huelc-huoegu   from  him              seðe   cueð   him   huæt   wilt ðu
adorans           et   petens        aliquid      ab   eo       21   qui    dixit    ei    quid    uis

cueð him ⊦ sægde him    cueð  ðæt   gesitta*   ðas  tuoeg  suno   minne   enne   to     suiðra    ðinum
     ait illi            dic   ut    sedeant    hi   duo   filii   mei    unus   ad   dexteram   tuam

 ]  enne  to   winstra   in   ric              geonduorde*   uutedlice   ðe hælend   cueð   ne uutuge
et  unus  ad  sinistram  in  regno  tuo    22  respondens     autem       iesus     dixit  nescitis

huæt    ge giwas ⊦ bidas    magage    drinca    calic    ðone     ic     drincende beom ⊦ drinca willo    cuedon
quid       petitis        potestis   bibere   calicem  quem    ego           bibiturus  sum                 dicunt

him    we magon           cueð    him    ðe calic    ec soð   mín    gie drinces    sitta    uutedlice   to
ei     posumus       23   ait    illis   calicem    quidem  meum    bibetis       sedere     autem      ad

suiðra     minra   ]   winstra     ne   Is    min    sella    iuh   ah    ðæm    gegearwad    is   from
dexteram   meam   et  sinistram   non  est   meum   dare   uobis   sed  quibus   paratum    est    a

feder   min              ]    geherdon    teno     wuraðe    weron   of   ðæm twæm    broðrum
patre   meo        24   *Et  audientes   decem   indignati   sunt    de   duobus     fratribus

   ðe hælend    uutedlice   geceigde   hia   to    him    ]   cueð    gie wuton    forðon     aldormenn    hæðna
25  iesus        autem      uocauit    eos   ad    se    et   ait    scitis       quia      principes    gentium

ricsað       hiora     ]    ða ðe   heist ⊦ maast   sint    mæht ⊦ onweald    geðencas    in him ⊦ in ða ilco
dominantur   eorum    et    qui     maiores       sunt    potestatem        exercent        in eos

    ne    swæ   bið ⊦ sie   betuih   iuh   ah    ða ðe ⊦ suachuelc    welle     betuih   iuh    maast ⊦ heest
26  non   ita     erit     inter    uos   sed     quicumque       uoluerit    inter    uos    maior

wosa   sie   iuer    embehtmonn
fieri  sit  uester   minister
```

---

18. henu we astigað...] sunu monnes bið sald aldor sacerd] bokerum   19.] gedoemeþ hine to deade] sellaþ hine ðeodum to bismerene] to swinganne] to hóanne] ðrydda dæg eft ariseþ   20. þa eode to him moder sunu zebedes mid sunu hire to gebiddanne] hine boensendu hwæt-hwugu from him   21. cwæþ he to hire hwæt wiltu cwæþ hio cwæþ þæt sittæ þas twægen mine sunæ an on þa swiðran healfe þine] oþer on þa winstran healfe þin in rice þinum   22. ondswarade þa heom se hælend] cwæþ ge nytan hwæt ge bidaþ magon git ðene kælic drincan þe ic drincande beom cwædun hiæ wit magun   23. cwæþ he to heom se hælend kælic git minne drincan sitte git þonne on þa swiðran halfe min] þa winstran min nis me to sellanne inc ah ðæm ðe Iarward (sic) is from fæder minum   24.] geherendo þa tene abolgenne werun be þæm twæm broþrum   25. hælend þa ceigde þæm to him] cwæþ ge cunun þæt ðeoda aldormenn agun gewald þara ⊦ heora] þa þe mare sindun mæhte begæþ ofer heo   26.] ne bið swa betwihc eow ah swa hwa swa wille betwix eow mare geweorðan beo he eower ðægn

27 ꝺ seþe wyle betweox eow beon fyrmest sy he eower þeow;
28 Swa mannes sunu ne com þ him man þenode. ac þ he þenode. ꝺ sealde his sawle lif to alysednesse for manegum;

Ge wilniað to geþeonne on ge-hwædum þinge. ꝺ beon gewanod on þam mæstan þinge; Witodlice þonne gē to gereorde ge-laþode beoð ne sitte ge on þam fyrmestan setlum þe læs þe arwurðre wēr æfter þe cume ꝺ se husbonda hāte þe arisan ꝺ ryman þam oðron* ꝺ þu beo gescynd. gyf þu sitst on gereorde on þam ytemestan setle ꝺ æfter þe cymþ. oþer gebeor ꝺ se laþigenda cweþe to þe site innor leof þonne byþ ðe arwurðlicor þonne þe man uttor scufe;
29 And þa hig ferdon fram hiericho. him fyligde mycel menegu;
30 ꝺ þa sæton twegen blinde wiþ ðone weg ꝺ ge-hyrdon þ se hælend ferde. ꝺ þa clypodon hig to him ꝺ cwædon; Drihten gemiltsa unc dauides sunu;
31 Ða bead seo menegu him þ hig suwodon. þa clypodon hig þæs ðe má; drihten gemiltsa unc dauides sunu;
32 Þa stod se hælend ꝺ clypode hig to him ꝺ cwæð; Hwæt wylle gyt þ ic inc do;
33 Ða cwædon hig. drihten þ uncre eagan sin gē-openede.
34 Ða ge-miltsode he him. ꝺ hyra eagan æt-hran. ꝺ hig sona gesawon. ꝺ fyligdon him;

27 ꝺ se þe wile beo-tweox eow beon fyrmest syo he eower þeow.
28 Swa mannes sune ne com þæt hym man þenode. ac þæt he þenode ꝺ sealde hys sawle lyf to alesendnysse for manegen.

Ge wilniað to ge-þeonne on gehwaden þinge. ꝺ to beon ge-wunod on þam mæsten þingen. Witodlice þanne ge to reorde gelaðode beoð ne sytte ge on þam fermestan sætlen. þe lest þe arwurðoen wer æfter þe cume. ꝺ se husbunde hate þe arisan ꝺ ryman þam oðren ꝺ þu beo ge-scend. gyf þu sitst on ge-reorde on þam ytemestan setle. ꝺ æfter þe cymð oðer gebeorn. ꝺ se laðiende cweð to þe site innor leof. þanne byoð þe arwurdlicor. þanne þe man utter scufe.
29 ꝺ þa he ferde* fram ierico hym felgde mycel maniga.
30 ꝺ þa sæten twegen. blinde wið þanne weig. ꝺ hyo ge-herden þæt se hælend þær forð-ferde. ꝺ þa clypeden hyo to hym and cwæðen. drihten ge-miltse unc dauiðes sune.
31 Ða bed syo manige heom þæt hyo swugedon. þa clepedon hyo þæs þe mare. Drihten ge-miltse unc dauiðes sune.
32 Ða stod se hælend ꝺ clypede hyo to hym ꝺ cwæð. hwæt wille git þæt ic inc do.
33 Þa cwæðen hio. Drihten þæt uncor eagen seon ge-openede.
34 Ða ge-miltsede he heom. ꝺ heora eagen æt-ran. ꝺ hyo ge-seagen. ꝺ felgedon hym.

Various Readings.

27. A. wylle. A. sig. 28. A. -nysse. A. gereordum. A. þylæs. A. arwyrðra; B. arwurðra. A. husbunda. A. oðrum; B. oðron. A. laðienda. A. lyof. A. arweorðlycor. B. utor. 29. A. iericho. A. mænigeo. 30. A. clypedon. 31. A. mænio. A. swigedon. A. clypedon. 32. A. om. hig. A. heom. 33. A. ge-openode. 34. A. heora.

Various Readings.

27. be-twux. 28. lif; alysendnysse; manegum; wylniað; ge-hwadum; sitte; fyrmestan setlum; læs (for lest); husbonde; ruman; oðrum; be; gif; settle; laðigende; þonne byð; þonne; uttor. 29. hyo ferdon; Iericho him fylgde; manega. 30. sæton; þonne weg; geherdon; þære fyrde; clypedon; cwæðon. 31. bæd sy menega; clypedon; ma; ge-miltsa; dauides. 32. halend; cleopede; hinc. 33. hyo; uncre eagan syn. 34. eagan; sawen ꝺ fylgdon.

                    ꝛ   seðe   wælle   betuih   iuh   forðmest ł foruuost   wossa   sie ł bia   iuer .   ðea ł ðegn
               27   et qui   uoluerit inter   uos   primus   esse   erit   uester   seruus

                     sua   sunu   monnes   ne   cuom   him to heranne   ah   he to embehtane oðrum   ꝛ   sella
               28 *Sicut   filius   hominis   non   uenit   ministrari   sed   ministrare   et   dare

                    sawel   his   eft-lesing ł alesenis   fore   monigum   færendum   ðæm   from
                   animam   suam   redemtionem   pro   multis   29   *Et - egredientibus illis ab

                   hiericho   gefylged   wæs   hine   ðreatas monigo   ꝛ   heonu   tuoege   blindo*   sittende   æt
                   hiericho   secuta   est   eum   turba   multa   30   et   ecce   duo   caeci   sedentes   secus

                   weg   geherdon   forðon   ðe hælend   oferfoerde ł bi-eode ł wæs færende   ꝛ   ceigdon   cueðendo
                   uiam   audierunt   quia   iesus   transiret   et   clamauerunt   dicentes

                   drihten   milsa ús ł help usig   sunu   dauides   ðy ł ða menigo   uutedlice   geðreadade ł
                   domine   miserere nostri   fili   dauid   31   turba   autem   incre-

                  weron geðreatne hia   þte   hia suiꞇdon   soð   ða ilco   suiðor   weron ceigendo   ðus cuoeðendo   drihten
                  pabat   eos   ut   tacerent   at   illi   magis   clamabant   dicentes   domine

                   milsa   ús   sunu   dauides   ꝛ   stod   ðe hælend   ꝛ   ceigde   hia   ꝛ   cueð   huæt
                   miserere nostri   fili   dauid   32   et   stetit iesus   et   uocauit eos   et   ait   quid

                  wallað gie   þ   ic gedoa   iuh   cuedon   him   drihten   þte   untynde sie   ego   usra
                  uultis   ut   faciam   uobis   33   dicunt   illi   domine   ut   aperiantur   oculi nostri

                        milsande wæs   uutedlice   hiora   ðe hælend   gehran   ego   hiora   ꝛ   sona   gesegon   ꝛ
                  34   misertus   autem   eorum   iesus   tetigit oculos eorum   et   confestim   uiderunt   et

                  fylgende   weron   hine
                  secuti   sunt   eum

               ───

               27. ꝛ se þe wile se forma beon beo he eower esne   28. swa sunu monnes ne cwom þ him wære
               ðægnad ah he ðægnade ꝛ salde ferh his for mongum to alesnisse   29. ꝛ þa ut eodun hiæ from hiericho
               folgadun him micel mengu   30. ꝛ henu twægen blinde sittende bi ðæm wæge geherdun þ se hælend
               foerde ł liorde ꝛ cliopadun cwæþende dryhten miltsa unc sunu dauiðes   31. sio mengu þa ðreattan hiæ
               þ hi swigadun ꝛ hiæ swiðor cleopadun cweþende gemiltsa unc sunu dauiðes   32. ꝛ gestód se hælend
               ꝛ cliopade heom ꝛ cwæþ hwæt willaþ git þ ic do eow   33. ꝛ cwædun heo dryhten þ ontyned sie egna
               ure   34. miltsende þa heom se hælend ꝛ hrán egum heora ꝛ sona gesægun ꝛ folgadun him

6. Appendix

最後にマタイ伝第7章、第13章、第20章の最初の部分の逐語訳を参考までに添えておく。

Matthew VII. 24-27

Each of those who these my words hears, and those does, will be like the wise man, who his house on rock built. Then came there rain and great flood, and there blew winds, and fell into that house, and it not not fell: Truly it was on rock built.

And each of those who hears these my words, and those not does, he will be like the foolish man, who built his house on sand. Then rained it, and there came floods and blew winds, and fell into that house, and that house fell; its fall was great.

Matthew XIII. 24-30

Kingdom of heavens is the man like who sowed good seed in his field. Truly, when men slept, then came one of his enemy, and sowed (over) it with corn-cockle in the midst of the wheat, and went away. Truly, when the plant grew, and the fruit brought forth, then appeared the corn-cockle itself. Then went servants of this lord and said: ' Lord, how, sowed thou good seed in your field? Whence had it corn-cockle?' Then said he: ' That did hostile man.' Then said the servants: ' Wish thou, we go and gather them?' Then said he: ' No: lest you the wheat root up, when you the corn-cockle gather. Let each grow until harvest; and in the harvest I say to the reapers: " Gather first the corn-cockle, and bind in sheaves (in bundles) to burn; and gather the wheat into my barn." '

Matthew XX. 1-16

Kingdom of heavens is like the master of family who in early morning out went (to) hire workers in his vineyard. Made agreement to the workers (Agreement made to the workers (with the workers), he gave each one penny for / towards his day's work, and sent them into his vineyard. And when he out went about the third hour of the day (9:00 a.m.), he saw others in (on) street idle stand. Then said he : ' go you into my vineyard, and I give you that which (what) right will be.' And they then went. Again he out went about the sixth and ninth hour, and did to them as likewise (equally). Then about the eleventh hour he out went, and found others standing, and then said he : ' Why stand you here all day idle ? Then said they : ' Because us no man not hired.' Then said he : 'And go you into my vineyard.'

Truly when it had evening become, then said the lord of vineyard to his reeve : ' Call the workers, and give them their reward(s) ; begin from the last until (to) the first.' Indeed when those came who about the eleventh hour came, then received they each his penny. And those who there first came thought that they should more receive ; then received they separate pennies. Then began they (to) complain against the master of family, and thus said : These last worked one hour and you did them like us, who carried burdens in this day's heat.' Then said he answering to one of them : Oh ! thou friend, not do I thee no injury (insult) ; how, not came you to me to work for one penny ? Take that which thine is, and go ; I will to this last give just as much as to thou. Or not may I do that which I wish ? Your eye wicked is because I good am ? So will be the first last and the last first ; Truly many are called and few chosen.'

テキスト及び参考文献

1. テキスト
Skeat[a], W.W. (ed.): *The Gospel according to Saint Matthew and according to Saint Mark*. Darmstadt, 1970

2. 参考書

Crystal, D.: *The English Language*. Cambridge University Press, 1995
Fennell, B.A.: *A History of English*. Blackwell, 2001
Fisiak, J.: *An Outline History of English*. Kantor Wydawniczy Saww, 1993
Jones, Sir W.: *The Works of Sir William Jones*. I-IV. Robinson & Evans, 1799
Miller, T.: *The Old English Version of Bede's Ecclesiastical History of the English People*. EETS. OS. 95, 96, 110, 111, 1890–98 (1959)
Mynors, R.A.B.: *Bede's Ecclesiastical History of the English people*. Oxford (Clarendon), 1969
Robinson, O.W.: *Old English and Its Closest Relatives*. Stanford University Press, 1992
Rass, R.: *The Shape of English*. J.M. Dent & Sons Ltd, 1987
Skeat[b], W.W. (ed.): *The Gospel according to Saint Luke and according to Saint John*. Darmstadt, 1970

3. 聖書
The Holy Bible. Oxford University Press
『聖書　新共同訳　旧約聖書続編つき』日本聖書教会　1987

4. 辞書
Klein, E.: *A Comprehensive Etymological Dictionary of the English Language*. Elsevier Scientific Publishing Company, 1971
Murray, J.A.H. and others: *The Oxford English Dictionaries*. 13 vols., Oxford (Claredon), 1933. [*OED*]

第2章　言語と文化——
　　　　社会文化的なアプローチを中心に

はじめに

　言語文化という概念とその対象領域は広範囲に及ぶ。厳密に言えば、言語自体が文化の一部であり、言語は人間がそれを生み出して以来、有力な文化の伝達手段および創造手段となっている。例えば、私たちは、文学を通してある社会や民族の思想を表現し、象徴的な文化的価値観を文学という手法によって表現する。その結果、文学自体が文化の一部として残り、その手法も受け継がれていく。

　また、文学以外に、言語によってどのような人間の知識が伝えられているかを考えてみると、それは、私たちが携わっている広範で多様な学問領域によってその多くを代表することができる。例えば、物理学や生物学のような学問領域は広く共有されている知識である。また、民族（文化人類学、西洋思想史、東洋史）や言語圏（比較言語学、日本語学、比較文化論）という範疇で、知識の一般化を図ることもできる。このような分類は細分化の問題でもあるが、私たちの思考や行動様式を体系化した結果つくりだされたものである。より一般化すれば、社会の中で有形無形に存在する意義ある思考形体や行動様式などの総体が文化といえる。

　本章では、言語と文化の関係について社会における人間の言語活動とそのはたらきについて考察していく。そして、それが社会文化的価値観の形成と理解にどのように関わっているのかについて、言語とその使用者である人間とそれをとりまく社会との関係に焦点をあてていく。

　本章で使用する文献資料は、M.A.K. Halliday（1978）の論文'Language and social man'から抜粋した。これらをもとに、第1節では、言語という記号体

系が社会の中でどのように位置づけられているか略述した。第2節では、人間の社会化というプロセスと言語の果たす役割についてまとめた。最後に、第3節では、言語とその社会文化的な役割についてまとめた。そして補足説明としてHallidayの理論を理解するためのいくつかの概念を紹介した。また、各節を通して文化の継承者である人間と言語使用、その伝達の場を提供する社会的空間、そして文化との関連性についてより深い理解が得られるよう解説をほどこした。以下、英語資料を先に示し、日本語による解説および要点の説明を行っていくことにする。

1. テキスト1 — Language and the environment

If we ever come to look back on the ideology of the 1970s, as suggested by the writer of an imaginary ' retrospect from 1980 ' published in *The Observer* in the first issue of the decade, we are likely to see one theme clearly standing out, the theme of ' social man '. Not social man in opposition to individual man, but rather the individual in his social environment. What the writer was forecasting — and he seems likely to be proved accurate — was, in effect, that while we should continue to be preoccupied with man in relation to his surroundings, as we were in the 1960s, the 1970s would show a change of emphasis from the purely physical environment to the social environment. This is not a new concern, but it has tended up to now to take second place; we have been more involved over the past twenty years with town planning and urban renewal, with the flow of traffic around us and above our heads, and most recently with the pollution and destruction of our material resources. This inevitably has distracted us from thinking about the other part of our environment, that which consists of people — not people as mere quanta of humanity, so many to the square mile, but other individuals with whom we have dealings of a more or less personal kind.

The ' environment ' is social as well as physical, and a state of wellbeing, which depends on harmony with the environment, demands harmony of both kinds. The nature of this state of wellbeing is what environmental studies are about. Ten years ago we first came to hear of 'ergonomics', the study and control of the environment in which people work; many will remember London Transport's advertising slogan 'How big is a bus driver?', announcing the design of new buses 'on ergonomic principles'. This was characteristic of the conception of the environment at that time. Today we would find more emphasis laid on the social aspects of wellbeing. No one would assert that the shape of the bus driver's seat is unimportant; but it no longer seems to be the whole story. There are other aspects of environmental design which seem at least as significant, and which are considerably more difficult to adjust.

Consider for example the problem of pollution, the defensive aspect of environmental design. The rubbish creep, the contamination of air and water, even the most lethal processes of physical pollution appear to be more tractable than the pollution in the social environment that is caused by prejudice and animosity of race, culture and class. These cannot be engineered away. One of the more dangerous of the terms that have been coined in this area is 'social engineering'; dangerous not so much because it suggests manipulating people for evil ends — most people are alert to that danger — but because it implies that the social environment can be fashioned like the physical one, by methods of demolition and construction, if only the plans and the machines are big enough and complicated enough. Some of the unfortunate effects of this kind of thinking have been seen from time to time in the field of language and education. But social wellbeing is not definable, or attainable, in these terms.

'Education' may sound less exciting than social engineering, but it is an older concept and one that is more relevant to our needs. If the engineers and the town planners can mould the physical environment, it is the teachers who exert the most influence on the social environment. They do so not by manipulating the social structure (which would be the engineering approach) but by playing a major part in the process whereby a human being becomes social man. The school is the main line of defence against pollution in the human environment; and we should not perhaps dismiss the notion of ' defence ' too lightly, because defensive action is often precisely what is needed. Preventive medicine, after all, is defensive medicine; and what the school has failed to prevent is left to society to cure.

In the development of the child as a social being, language has the central role. Language is the main channel through which the patterns of living are transmitted to him, through which he learns to act as a member of a ' society ' — in and through the various social groups, the family, the neighbourhood, and so on — and to adopt its ' culture ', its modes of thought and action, its beliefs and its values. This does not happen by instruction, at least not in the pre-school years; nobody teaches him the principles on which social groups are organized, or their systems of beliefs, nor would he understand it if they tried. It happens indirectly, through the accumulated experience of numerous small events, insignificant in themselves, in which his behaviour is guided and controlled, and in the course of which he contracts and develops personal relationships of all kinds. All this takes place through the medium of language. And it is not from the language of the classroom, still less that of courts of law, of moral tracts or of textbooks of sociology, that the child learns about the culture he was born into. The striking fact is that it is the most ordinary everyday uses of language, with parents, brothers and sisters, neighbourhood children, in the home, in the street and the park, in the shops and the trains and the buses, that serve to transmit, to the child, the essential qualities of society and the nature of social being.

This, in brief, is what this chapter is about. It is a general discussion of the relation of language to social man, and in particular language as it impinges on the role of the teacher as a creator of social man — or at least as a midwife in the creation process. That this does not mean simply language in school is already clear. It means, rather, language in the total context of the interaction between an individual and his human environment:

between one individual and others, in fact. But the point of view to be adopted will be an educational one, emphasizing those aspects of language and social man that are most relevant to the teacher in the classroom.

It might seem that one could hardly begin to consider language at all without taking account of social man, since language is the means whereby people interact. How else can one look at language *except* in a social context? In the last resort, it is true that the existence of language implies the existence of social man; but this does not by itself determine the point of vantage from which language is being approached. Let us think for a moment of an individual human being, considered as a single organism. Being human, it is also articulate: it can speak and understand language, and perhaps read and write as well. Now the ability to speak and understand arises, and makes sense, only because there are other such organisms around, and it is natural to think of it as an inter-organism phenomenon to be studied from an inter-organism point of view. But it is also possible to investigate language from the standpoint of the internal make-up of that organism: the brain structure, and the cerebral processes that are involved in its speaking and understanding, and also in its learning to speak and to understand. So there is an intra-organism perspective on language as well as an inter-organism one. The two standpoints are complementary; but there tend to be shifts of emphasis between them, trends and fashions in scholarship which lead to concentration on one, for a time, at the expense of the other. In the 1960s the major emphasis was on what we are calling intra-organism studies, on the investigation of language as knowledge, of 'what the speaker knows', running parallel to, and probably occasioned by, the relative neglect of man's social environment. There has now been a move back towards a greater concern with the social aspects of language, a restoring of the balance in linguistic studies, with account once more being taken of the inter-organism factor-that of language as social behaviour, or language in relation to social man.

A diagrammatic representation of the nature of linguistic studies and their relation to other fields of scholarship will serve as a point of reference for the subsequent discussion (figure 1). The diagram shows the domain of language study — of linguistics, to give it its subject title — by a broken line; everything within that line is an aspect or a branch of linguistic studies.

In the centre is a triangle, shown by a solid line, which marks off what is the central area of language study, that of language as a system. One way of saying what is meant by 'central' here is that if a student is taking linguistics as a university subject he will have to cover this area as a compulsory part of his course, whatever other aspects he may choose to take up. There are then certain projections from the triangle, representing special sub-disciplines within this central area: phonetics, historical linguistics and dialectology — the last of these best thought of in broader terms, as the study of language varieties. These sometimes get excluded from the central region, but probably most linguists would agree in placing them within it; if one could give a three-dimensional representation they would not look like excrescences.

Then, outside this triangle, are the principal perspectives on language that take us beyond a consideration solely of language as a system, and, in so doing, impinge on other disciplines. Any study of language involves some attention to other disciplines; one cannot draw a boundary round the subject and insulate it from others. The question is whether the aims go beyond the elucidation of language itself; and once one goes outside the central area, one is inquiring not only into language but into language in relation to something else. The diagram summarizes these wider fields under the three headings, 'language as knowledge', 'language as behaviour', 'language as art'.

The last of these takes us into the realm of literature, which is all too often treated as if it was something insulated from and even opposed to language: 'we concentrate mainly on literature here — we don't do much on language', as if 'concentrating on literature' made it possible to ignore the fact that literature is made of language. Similarly the undergraduate is invited to 'choose between lang. and lit.'. In fact the distinction that is being implied

第 2 章　言語と文化——社会文化的なアプローチを中心に　57

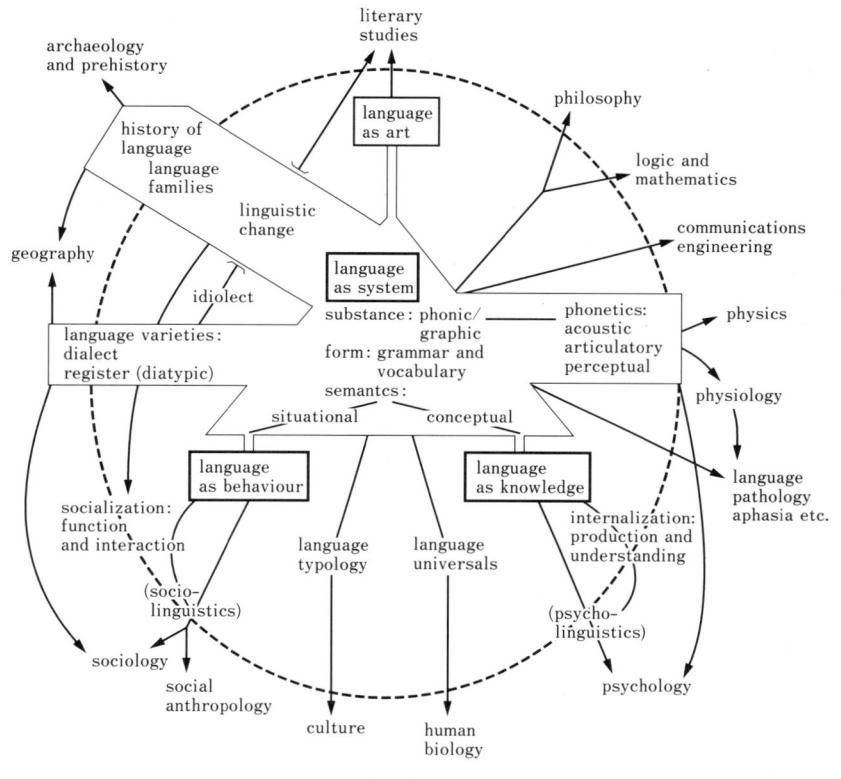

Fig. 1

is a perfectly meaningful one between two different emphases or orientations, one in which the centre of attention is the linguistic system and the other having a focus elsewhere; but it is wrongly named, and therefore, perhaps, liable to be misinterpreted. One can hardly take literature seriously without taking language seriously; but language here is being looked at from a special point of view.

The other two headings derive from the distinction we have just been drawing between the intra-organism perspective, language as knowledge, and the inter-organism perspective, language as behaviour. These both lead us outward from language as a system, the former into the region of psychological studies, the latter into sociology and related fields. So in putting language into the context of 'language and social man', we are taking up one of the options that are open for the relating of language study to other fields of inquiry. This, broadly, is the sociolinguistic option; and the new subject of sociolinguistics that has come into prominence lately is a recognition of the fact that language and society — or, as we prefer to think of it, language and social man — is a unified conception, and needs to be understood and investigated as a whole. Neither of these exists without the other: there can be no social man without language, and no language without social man. To recognize this is no mere academic exercise; the whole theory and practice of education depends on it, and it is no exaggeration to suggest that much of our failure in recent years — the failure of the schools to come to grips with social pollution — can be traced to a lack of insight into the nature of the relationships between language and society: specifically of the processes, which are very largely linguistic processes, whereby a human organism turns into a social being.

2. 記号体系としての言語とそのはたらき

(1) 言語と人間と社会

　押し並べて言えば、人間の世界は、おおよそ物理的なものと精神的なものに大別することができる。そして、人間はその成長過程で、さまざまな社会経験をしながら、自己の経験世界を広げていく。ある文化を継承した社会集団の中で生まれた子供達は、その中で思考・行動様式を学んでいくが、この学習過程で重要な知識の伝達手段を果たすものが言語である。

　言語活動による知識の伝達や行為の遂行はさまざまな社会環境の中で行なわれる。例えば、私たちは生後、伝達手段としての言語を習得し、社会経験を知識として記憶する。この点、言語と言語を使用する人間をとりまく環境との関係は非常に密接なものと考えられる。例えば、生後間もない日本人であっても、

英語圏で生活し英語を通して教育を受ければ、英語を話し欧米などの文化を理解できる人間として育つことになる。とりわけ、教育現場では、言語を介した情報や文化的価値観の伝達が重要となってくる。この社会化のプロセスは、人間の言語能力の発達と言語の持つ社会的機能の両面から捉えることができる。前者は、環境によって、使用言語と思考・行動様式が決定され、特定言語の能力と思考行動パターンモデルが学習される。後者は、社会における言語自体の存在が人間形成と社会化のプロセスに欠かせないものであるという見方である。どちらに重点をおいて言語活動をみていくかという方向性の違いはあるにせよ、情報や経験を受容する人間、その伝達手段としての言語体系、そして人間をとりまく環境との間には、人間の進化の過程で有機的な結びつきが生まれたと考えられる。本節では、伝達手段としての言語について基本的な理解を深めるために、記号体系としての言語についてまとめていく。

(2) 言語研究のパラダイム

言語体系を捉える場合、いくつかの側面が考えられるが、テキスト1のFig.1では、言語を、①体系としての言語（language as system）、②知識としての言語（language as knowledge）、③行為としての言語（language as behaviour）、④芸術としての言語（language as art）の4つの側面から捉えている。言い換えれば、①は言語体系自体を記述するための理論構築を目的とする言語研究であり、記号体系と意味の具現化に関することが研究の中心となる。例えば、語彙論・文法論・意味論など言語体系の分析に必要な理論や言語の歴史的な発達理論などがその主要分野となる。②は言語を使用する人間の持つ言語知識と運用能力に関する研究で、言語習得理論などがその中心となっている。③は社会における言語使用と役割などとの関連から、方言学・社会言語学などが主要分野となる。④は言語の表現様式の持つ芸術性に関するもので、文学・文学理論などがこの分野に入る。以下、これら4つの側面から私達と言語の関わり合いについて説明する。

(3) 体系としての言語（language as system）

記号体系としての言語は、手話・信号機の信号・モールス信号など他のさま

ざまな記号体系と同様に、人間にとって何らかの意味を伝達する記号体系のひとつである。ここでの関心は、記号体系としての言語がどのように人間にとって意味あることを表現するのかということである。そして、記号と意味との関係や理論的記述方式の体系化が従来の言語学の中心テーマである。

言語のしくみとはたらきを体系的に分析するといくつかの分析レベルに分けられる。まず、われわれはことばを使うときに物理的な意味でその表現媒体——言語素材（phonic / graphoric substance）——を持つ。そして、その表現手段として音声手段と書記手段を基本的に使用する。例えば、私達は、話し言葉では相手の発する言語音を耳で捉え、書き言葉では文字を読んで、意味を理解することができる。言語学では、前者に関しては、音韻論（phonology）や音声学（phonetics）、後者の文字体系や用法については、形態論（morphology）や正書法（orthography）という研究分野が発達し、それぞれの言語にどのような言語素材があるか体系化している。例えば、書記言語においては、日本語のひらがな・カタカナ・漢字などが、また、英語ではアルファベットが、それぞれ意味ある言語単位を形成する言語素材である。

また、このような言語素材がつくりだす小さな意味ある言語単位が語彙（lexis——その代表が単語）と呼ばれるものである。そして、それぞれの言語の中で、言語単位の形成に携わっている素材を形式（form）と呼ぶ。例えば、単語は、文を形成するための形式ということになる。そして、単語レベルの言語形式がどのように結びつき文を形成するかをまとめ、その規則を体系化する分野を統語論（syntax）と呼ぶ。文法（grammar）という用語がこれを代用する場合も多い。例えば、英語で「僕は野球が好きだ」という場合、「I like baseball.」となるわけだが、統語的には動詞と目的語が両言語では逆の位置になっている。

また、形式によって表現される意味（meaning）を扱う分野は意味論（semantics）と呼ばれ、言語形式と意味との関係を中心に扱っていく。そして、この形式と意味を備えた言語メッセージがある言語環境の中でどのように使用されて、我々の意図を伝達しているのかを研究する分野が語用論（pragmatics）と呼ばれる分野である。すなわち、話し手や聞き手はコミュニケーションの中で発生する意図によって、さまざまな表現様式をある伝達内容に対して選択する。例えば、映画館で上映の合間に流される他の映画の予告編を見ながら、Oh, I don't like it. や Oh, I am glad I can miss this. のように隣りの友達に言ったとする。両者ともその映画に興味がないという共通したメッセージを持つが、前者は直接嫌いだということを表現し、後者は予告編を見るだけで十分でありこの映画の本編を今後見ないですむというニュアンスが含まれる。このように私達は状況に応じた表現様式を選択し、その中に言語使用者としての意図を組み込みながら、あるメッセージを形成している。

　このように、言語はそれ自体が独立した記号体系の1つであり、人間にとって意味あるものを表現するために体系化されたものである。

(4) 内在化された知識としての言語（language as knowledge）

　私達は1つの記号体系である言語を駆使してあるまとまった意味ある言語メッセージをつくりあげる。この言語能力の発達に大きく関わっているものは、私達の認知活動とそれを体系化し内在化する脳の存在である。何を認知し記憶するかは、一言で言えば、人間のあらゆる経験とそれを可能な限り表現したり想像したりするための言語運用の仕方である。したがって、私達は文字や言語音を知識として認知し理解しているだけではなく、それによって具現化される意味を理解し発信するための言語知識を内在化し使用している。

(5) 社会的行為としての言語（language as behaviour）

　また、言語は行為として捉えることができる。私たちは言語体系を駆使しながら知識や経験を伝達する能力を備えているが、それはとりもなおさず社会生活を営むための手段のひとつとなっている。Halliday（1978）では、このような私たちの存在をある種の社会機能を備えた人間（social man）として捉えている。このように考えると、私たちは何らかの社会的な行為を象徴したり促進したりするために言語を使用していると言うことができる。また、言語活動は、多くの場合人間の思考や行動様式を、社会的な場面に適合させ具現させるために不可欠なものである。例えば、憲法は、条文化と法的な手続きを経て初めてその効力を発揮する。その際、言語の果たす役割はこの社会的な制定プロセスに不可欠なものとなる。そして、条文によって示される内容は、社会的・法的にも国家や国民のあり方を具現化したものとなる。

また、さまざまな日常的な場面でも言語活動が大きな役割を果たしている。例えば、言語活動は考え方を共有し、人間関係を築くための意志疎通には欠かせないものである。また、社会的な背景を共有するための要素として、方言の共有化なども大きな要素のひとつとなっている。同時にまた、社会集団特有の価値観の共有も言語によって伝達される部分が大きい。

このように、人間の社会化（socialization）を推進する重要な要素として言語の存在を挙げることができる。

(6) 芸術としての言語（language as art）

言語の表現様式の持つ芸術性に視点をおいて言語を捉えることもできる。言語は伝達手段としての記号体系であると同時に、無限に広がる人間の創造性と思考形体をさまざまな様式で表現する多様性と芸術性を持ち合わせている。その結果、文学・詩学などに代表される優れた表現の手法がつくりだされている。

このように言語とその関連領域との関わり合いを概観することで、人間の活動領域と言語の関係がどれほど重要かつ密接なものであるかその一端を窺うことができる。ここでは特に、人間と言語の結びつきについていくつかの視点から解説した。

3. テキスト 2 — Inter-organism and intra-organism perspectives

The diagram[注1] in section 1 suggests a context for language study, placing it in the environment of other fields of investigation. It also suggests where 'language and social man' fits into the total picture of language study. The discussion of the diagram will perhaps have made it clear (and this harks back to what was said at the beginning) that when we talk of ' social man ' the contrast we are making is not that of social versus individual. The contrast is rather that of social versus psychophysiological, the distinction which we have attempted to draw in terms of inter-organism and intra-organism perspectives.

When we refer to social man, we mean the individual considered as a single entity, rather than as an assemblage of parts. The distinction we are drawing here is that between the behaviour of that individual, his actions and interactions with his environment (especially that part of his environment which consists of other individuals), on the one hand, and on the other hand his biological nature, and in particular the internal structure of his brain. In the first of these perspectives we are regarding the individual as an integral whole, and looking at him from the outside; in the second we are focusing our attention on the parts, and looking on the inside, into the works. Language can be considered from either of these points of view; the first is what we called on the diagram ' language as behaviour ', the second ' language as knowledge '. ' Language and social man ' means language as a function of the whole man; hence language man to man (inter-organism), or language as human behaviour.

These are two complementary orientations. The distinction between them is not a difficult one to make; in itself it is rather obvious and simple. But it has become complicated by the fact that it is possible to embed one perspective inside the other: to treat language behaviour as if it were an aspect of our knowledge of language (and hence to see it in terms of the capacity of the human brain), and also, though in a rather different sense, to treat the individual's knowledge of language as a form of behaviour. In other words we can look at social facts from a biological point of view, or at biological facts from a social point of view.

The study of language as knowledge is an attempt to find out what goes on inside the individual's head. The questions being asked are, what are the mechanisms of the brain that are involved in speaking and understanding, and what must the structure of the brain be like in order for the individual to be able to speak and understand language, and to be able to learn to do so?

Now one important fact about speaking and understanding language is that it always takes place in a context. We do not simply ' know[9] our mother tongue as an abstract system of vocal signals, or as if it was some sort of a grammar book with a dictionary attached. We know it in the sense of knowing how to use it; we know how to communicate with other people, how to choose forms of language that are appropriate to the type of situation we find ourselves in, and so on. All this can be expressed as a form of knowledge: we know how to behave linguistically.

Therefore it is possible, and is in fact quite usual in what is nowadays called 'sociolinguistics', to look at language behaviour as a type of knowledge; so that although one's attention is focused on the social aspects of language — on language as communication between organisms — one is still asking what is essentially an intra-organism kind of question: how does the individual know how to behave in this way? We might refer to this as psychosociolinguistics: it is the external behaviour of the organism looked at from the point of view of the internal mechanisms which control it.

We said above that the two perspectives were complementary, and it would be reasonable to conclude that they are really inseparable one from the other. But if so the inseparability holds in both directions. It is true that the individual's potential for linguistic interaction with others implies certain things about the internal make-up of the individual himself. But the converse is also true. The fact that the brain has the capacity to store language and use it for effective communication implies that communication takes place: that the individual has a 'behaviour potential' which characterizes his interaction with other individuals of his species.

Since no doubt the human brain evolved in its present form through the process of human beings communicating with one another, the latter perspective is likely to be highly significant from an evolutionary point of view. But that is not our main point of departure here. There is a more immediate sense in which the individual, considered as one who can speak and understand and read and write, who has a 'mother tongue', needs to be seen in a social perspective. This concerns the part that language has played in his own development as an individual. Let us start with the notion of the individual human organism, the human being as a biological specimen. Like the individual in many other species, he is destined to become one of a group; but unlike those of all other species, he achieves this — not wholly, but critically — through language. It is by means of language that the 'human being' becomes one of a group of 'people'. But 'people', in turn, consist of 'persons'; by virtue of his participation in a group the individual is no longer simply a biological specimen of humanity — he is a person. Again language is the essential element in the process, since it is largely the linguistic interchange with the group that determines the status of the individuals and shapes them as persons. The picture is as in figure 2

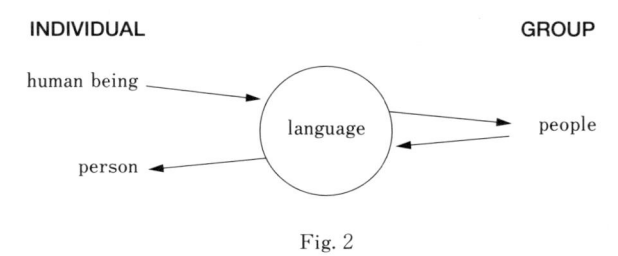

```
   INDIVIDUAL                          GROUP
   human being ──────→
                       ( language ) ──────→ people
   person      ←──────
```

Fig. 2

In other words, instead of looking at the group as a derivation from and extension of the biologically endowed mental power of the individual, we explain the nature of the individual as a derivation from and extension of his participation in the group. Instead of starting inside the organism and looking outwards, we can adopt a Durkheimian perspective and start from outside the organism in order to look inwards.

But when we do adopt this perspective it becomes apparent that we can take the dialectic one stage further, and that when we do so language will still remain the crucial factor. The individual as a 'person' is now a potential 'member': he has the capacity to function within society, and once more it is through language that he achieves this status. How does a society differ from a group, as we conceive it here? A group is a simple structure, a set of participants among whom there are no special relations, only the simple coexistence that is implied by participation in the group. A society, on the other hand, does not consist of participants but of relations, and these relations define social roles. Being a member of society means occupying a social role; and it is again by means of language that a ' person ' becomes potentially the occupant of a social role.

Social roles are combinable, and the individual, as a member of a society, occupies not just one role but many at a time, always through the medium of language. Language is again a necessary condition for this final element in the process of the development of the individual, from human being to person to what we may call ' personality ', a personality being interpreted as a role complex. Here the individual is seen as the configuration of a number of roles defined by the social relationships in which he enters; from these roles he synthesizes a personality. Our model now looks like figure 3:

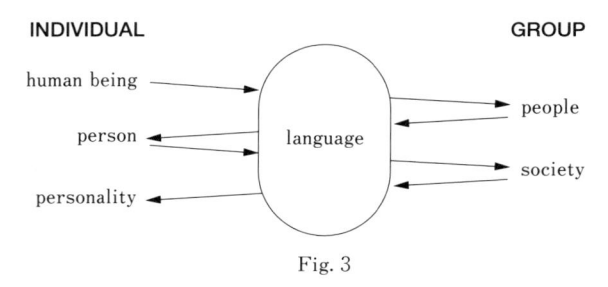

INDIVIDUAL   **GROUP**

human being → language ← people
person ← language → society
personality ←

Fig. 3

Let us now interpret this in terms of a perspective on language. We have gone some way round in order to reach this particular angle of vision, certainly oversimplifying the picture and perhaps seeming to exaggerate the importance of language in the total process. The justification for this is that we have been trying to achieve a perspective that will be most relevant in an educational context. From this point of view, language is the medium through which a human being becomes a personality, in consequence of his membership of society and his occupancy of social roles. The concept of language as behaviour, as a form of interaction between man and man, is turned around, as it were, so that it throws light on the individual: the formation of the personality is itself a social process, or a complex of social processes, and language — by virtue of its social functions — plays the key part in it. Hence just as the view of language as knowledge, which is essentially an individual orientation, can be used to direct attention outwards, through such concepts as the speech act, towards language in society, so the essentially social interpretation of language as behaviour can be used to direct attention onto the individual, placing him in the human environment, as we expressed it earlier, and explaining his linguistic potential, as speaker-hearer and writer-reader, in these terms. This does not presuppose, or preclude, any particular theory about the nature of the mental processes that are involved in his mastery of language, either in how he speaks and understands or in how he learnt to do so in the first place. There are conflicting psychological theories on these questions, as we shall see in the next section; but our present perspective is neutral in this respect.

The ability to speak and understand, and the development of this ability in the child, are essential ingredients in the life of social man. To approach these from the outside, as inter-organism phenomena, is to take a functional view of language. The social aspect of language becomes the reference point for the biological aspect, rather than the other way round. In the next two sections we shall consider briefly what this means.

注1) 本章57ページのFig.1を指す。

4. 人間の社会化へのプロセス

　人間がことばを使って社会生活を送る過程で明らかに指摘できる点は、人間が唯一無二の個性を育んでいくということである。ことばによる影響がすべて

の個性の形成に関わっているというわけではないが、ひとつの重要な要因となっていることは言うまでもない。前節でも、言語活動を区別した際に、知識としての言語 (language as knowledge) と社会的行為としての言語 (language as behaviour) について略述したが、その根底には生物学的—社会的人間の存在という考え方が根ざしている。本節では、テキスト2を基にして、この2つの側面の繋がりをまとめていく。また、人間の社会化 (socialization) という視点から言語がどのように関係しながら個性を形成し、人間としてある社会文化的集団の価値観を反映した思考と行動様式を身につけていくのか (how to behave linguistically) について、テキスト中の考え方を略述する。

社会化のプロセスにおける言語の役割 (social perspectives)

Halliday (1978) は、人間の社会化と言語活動についていくつかの要因を挙げ、下記の図のようにまとめている (テキスト2のFig. 3より)。

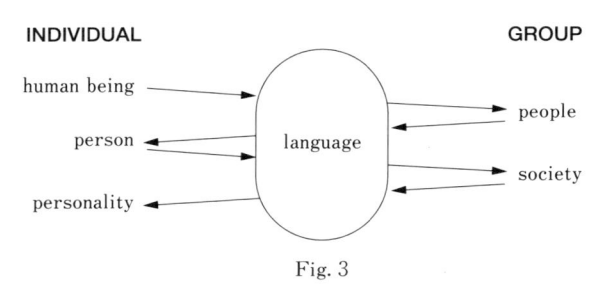

```
INDIVIDUAL                        GROUP
human being  ──→            ──→ people
person       ←──  language
                            ──→ society
personality  ←──
```

Fig. 3

(1) 個人 (individual) と集団 (group)

まず、生物学的特性の1つである人間の言語能力は、人間の成長発達に大きな役割を果たしている。人間 (human being) は生後、膨大な量の情報にさらされながら成長していくが、人間が処理しなければならない知識や情報の質と量も大きく変化する。例えば、人間が成長するにつれ、より一般的で抽象度の高い情報が加わってくる。また、種種雑多な知識や情報はある有機的なまとまりを持つ個々の集まりであり、人間の思考や社会の様々な部分を象徴している。そして、知識や情報を形成し発信する相手は環境によって異なる。例えば、家族や遊び友達による情報伝達が中心となる幼児期を過ぎ学校に通うようになる

と急速に広範囲な情報や知識を受容するようになる。同時にまた、言語を通して様々な知識を吸収する力もついてくる。また、この過程において、私達は人間そして個人（individual）としてより多くの人々（people）と接するようになり、社会経験を積んでいくことになる。

(2) 社会 (society) と社会的役割 (social roles)

さらに Halliday (1978) は、単なる人々の集まりとしての人間集団（people）とその中の個人が何らかの社会的関係で繋がって形成されている社会集団（society）とを区別する。そして、個人は社会集団の構成員となる可能性を持っており、その構成員となる過程で言語の果たす役割は重要なものであるという立場をとっている。

また、このような社会的な関係が成立する際には、構成員であるための社会的役割（social role）が発生すると考える。そして、個人は複数の社会的役割を持ち合わせ、ある社会体系網（social network）の中で位置づけられた人間関係を保ちながら社会的機能を果たしている。例えば、親子関係においては、親・子供・兄・妹などがこの役割に当たる。また、学校では、先生と生徒、アルバイト先での店長とアルバイトの店員、職場での上下関係や職業による社会的役割の分類などが可能となる。社会の構成員は、このような役割を一人何役もこなしながら社会生活を営んでいることになる。そして、このような社会的な関係を認識したり築きあげる際に、言語が大きく貢献する。例えば、法廷で法律用語を駆使しながら裁判を進める裁判官も、その一方では、友達とゴルフに行けばリラックスした気分で話しながら余暇を楽しむことができる。そして、そこではそれぞれの社会的な場面に適した内容と言語様式が使われる。前者（＝法廷での社会活動）は特に、言語活動なしではまったく成立しない社会活動でもある。そして、社会化のプロセスの結果、人間は唯一無二の個性を発達させ、ある人格を持つ個人（personality）となる。

このように見ると、言語習得能力という人間の能力（intra-organism phenomena / language as knowledge）と人間の社会的な存在に大きく影響している社会活動（inter-organism phenomena / language as behaviour）との間には深い関わり合いが存在していることになる。

5. テキスト 3 — Language and social structure

Here we are adopting a sociolinguistic perspective on language — or rather a perspective which in terms of the earlier discussion would be inter-organism. Language is being regarded as the encoding of a ' behaviour potential ' into a ' meaning potential '; that is, as a means of expressing what the human organism ' can do ', in interaction with other human organisms, by turning it into what he ' can mean '. What he can mean (the semantic system) is, in turn, encoded into what he ' can say ' (the lexicogrammatical system, or grammar and vocabulary); to use our own folk-linguistic terminology, meanings are expressed in wordings. Wordings are, finally, receded into sounds (it would be nice if we could say ' soundings ') or spellings (the phonological and orthographic systems). Terms like *meaning*, *wording* and *spelling* are so familiar in everyday speech that we are hardly aware of them as ways of talking about language. But every time we say, to a pupil, or to a committee chairman perhaps, ' I think you'll have to alter the wording ', we are making systematic assumptions about language, bringing into play what Peter Doughty calls ' a " folk linguistic ", a " common sense " about the language we live by ' (Doughty *et al.* 1972, 8).

This perspective is valuable to the linguist because it affords an insight into *why* language is as it is. There is no *a priori* reason why human language should have taken just the evolutionary path that it has taken and no other; our brains could have produced a symbolic system of quite a different kind. But if we consider what language is required to do for us, there are certain functions which it must fulfil in all human cultures, regardless of differences in the physical and material environment. These are functions of a very general kind.

1. Language has to interpret the whole of our experience, reducing the

indefinitely varied phenomena of the world around us, and also of the world inside us, the processes of our own consciousness, to a manageable number of classes of phenomena : types of processes, events and actions, classes of objects, people and institutions, and the like.

2. Language has to express certain elementary logical relations, like ' and ' and ' or ' and ' if ', as well as those created by language itself such as ' namely ', ' says ' and ' means '.

3. Language has to express our participation, as speakers, in the speech situation ; the roles we take on ourselves and impose on others ; our wishes, feelings, attitudes and judgements.

4. Language has to do all these things simultaneously, in a way which relates what is being said to the context in which it is being said, both to what has been said before and to the ' context of situation '; in other words, it has to be capable of being organized as relevant discourse, not just as words and sentences in a grammar-book or dictionary.

It is the demands posed by the service of these functions which have moulded the shape of language and fixed the course of its evolution. These functions are built into the semantic system of language, and they form the basis of the grammatical organization, since the task of grammar is to encode the meanings deriving from these various functions into articulated structures. Not only are these functions served by all languages, at least in their adult form ; they have also determined the way human language has evolved.

So when we study the language development of young children, we are really investigating two questions at once. The first concerns the language they invent for themselves, on the basis of the set of elementary uses or functions of language which reflect the developmental needs, potentialities and achievements of the infant — instrumental, regulatory and so on. The second concerns their transition to the adult language, a language which is still functional in its origins but where the concept of 'function' has undergone a significant change : it is no longer simply synonymous with ' use ', but has become much more abstract, a kind of 'metafunction' through which all the innumerable concrete uses of language in which the adult engages are given symbolic expression in a systematic and finite form. To what extent the individual child traces the evolutionary path in moving from one to the other is immaterial; it appears that at a certain point he abandons it, and takes a leap directly into the adult system. Be that as it may, he has to make the transition, and in doing so he carves out for himself a route that reflects the particular circumstances of his own individual history and experience. Geoffrey Thornton expresses this very well when he says that the language which each child learns

> is a unique inheritance. It is an inheritance because he is endowed, as a human being, with the capacity to learn language merely by growing up in an environment in which language is being used around him. It is unique, because ... no two people occupy identical places in an environment where language learning is taking place, and this must mean that the language learnt is unique to the individual. (Doughty *et al.* 1972, 48).

This takes us back to the perspective outlined in section 2. Biologically we are all alike, in so far as the language-learning capacity is concerned; we have this ability, as a species, just as we have the ability to stand upright and walk, and it is quite independent of the usual measures of 'intelligence' in whatever form. Ecologically, on the other hand, each one of us is unique, since the environmental pattern is never exactly repeated, and one individual's experience is never the same as another's.

However, the uniqueness of the individual, in terms of his personal experience, must be qualified by reference to the culture. Our environment is shaped by the culture, and the conditions under which we learn language are largely culturally determined. This point is significant at two levels, one of which is very obvious, the other less so. It is obviously true in the sense that a child learns the language he hears around him; if he is growing up in an English-speaking society, he learns English. This is a matter of the linguistic environment, which is itself part of the culture, but in a special sense. Moreover he learns that dialectal variety of English which belongs to his particular socioregional subculture: working-class London, urban middle-class Northern, rural Dorset and so on. (He may of course learn more than one dialect, or more than one language, if the culture is one in which such linguistic diversity is the norm.) It is equally true, but much less obvious, in another sense: namely that the culture shapes our behaviour patterns, and a great deal of our behaviour is mediated through language. The child learns his mother tongue in the context of behavioural settings where the norms of the culture are acted out and enunciated for him, settings of parental control, instruction, personal interaction and the like; and, reciprocally, he is 'socialized' into the value systems and behaviour patterns of the culture through the use of language at the same time as he is learning it.

We can now see the relevance of this to linguistic theories of educational failure, which were referred to briefly in the last section. There has been much discussion of educability lately, and various theories have been put forward. One school of thought has concentrated on the effect of the child's *linguistic* environment — namely, the particular form of language he has grown up to speak. In practice, since educational failure is usually associated with the urban lower working class, this means the particular socioregional dialect; and we find two versions of the ' language failure ' theory here, sometimes known as the ' deficit theory ' and the ' difference theory '. According to the deficit theory, the whole dialect is simply defective; it lacks some essential elements — it is deficient, perhaps, in sounds, or words, or structures. Now this is not merely nonsense; it is dangerous nonsense. Unfortunately it has rarely been explicitly denied; probably because, as the American educator Joan Baratz put it, ' linguists ... consider such a view of language so absurd as to make them feel that nobody could possibly believe it and therefore to refute it would be a great waste of time ' (Williams 1970a, 13). There is no such thing as a deficient social dialect. But, on the other hand, if a teacher believes that there is, and that some or all of his pupils speak one, then, as Frederick Williams has very convincingly shown in his investigations in American schools, he thereby predisposes the children to linguistic failure. This is known as the 'stereotype hypothesis': children, no less than adults, will come to behave like the stereotype to which they are consigned (Williams 1970a, ch. 18).

This then leads us into the 'difference' version of the theory, according to which the problem is not that the child's speech is deficient but that it is different — different, in implication, from some received standard or norm. This would obviously be important if it meant that the child did not understand the language in which he was being taught (as happens with many immigrant children). But for the native English-speaking child, this is not the problem. Wherever he comes from, and whatever section of society he comes from, the speech differences are relatively slight and superficial, and in any case he has heard the teacher's language frequently on television and elsewhere, so that he never has more than very temporary difficulty in understanding it, and in fact is usually rather competent at imitating it — an activity, however, which he tends to consider more appropriate to the playground than to the classroom. So the difference theory resolves itself into a question of prejudice: if the child fails as a result of differences between his language and that of the school, it is not because there are difficulties of understanding but because the child's variety of English carries a social stigma: it is regarded by society as inferior. If 'society' here includes the teacher, the child is, effectively, condemned to failure from the start.

To that extent, then, the difference theory, unlike the deficit theory, is at least partially true: there *are* prejudices against certain varieties of English, and *they are* shared by some teachers. But they are by no means shared by all teachers; and it is difficult to believe that this factor by itself could be sufficient explanation of the full extent of educational failure, especially since children have a great capacity for adaptation — if one form of behaviour does not pay off they will usually switch to another, and they are quite capable of doing so where language is concerned. Moreover the prejudices are getting less, whereas the general view is that educational failure is increasing.

We return to this discussion in chapter 5 below, with reference to the work of Basil Bernstein. Educational failure is really a social problem, not a linguistic one; but it has a linguistic aspect, which we can begin to understand if we consider the cultural environment in the second of the two senses mentioned above. It is not the linguistic environment, in the sense of which language or dialect the child learns to speak, that matters so much as the cultural or subcultural environment as this is embodied in and transmitted through the language. In other words, the 'language difference' may be significant, but if so it is a difference of function rather than of form.

It is this fundamental insight which lies behind Professor Bernstein's theoretical and empirical work in the field of language and society; together with a further insight, namely that what determines the actual cultural-linguistic configuration is, essentially, the social structure, the system of social relations, in the family and other key social groups, which is characteristic of the particular subculture. Bernstein (1971, 122) writes:

> A number of fashions of speaking, frames of consistency, are possible in any given language and ... these fashions of speaking, linguistic forms or codes, are themselves a function of the form social relations take. According to this view, the form of the social relation or, more generally, the social structure generates distinct linguistic forms or codes and *these codes essentially transmit the culture and so constrain behaviour.* [His italics.]

If we accept that, as the American sociological linguist William Stewart expressed it, " so much of human behaviour is socially conditioned rather than genetically determined ', it is not difficult to suppose an intimate connection between language on the one hand and modes of thought and behaviour on the other.

This view is associated first and foremost with the work of the great American linguist Benjamin Lee Whorf, who wrote 'An accepted pattern of using words is often prior to certain lines of thinking and modes of behaviour / Whorf emphasized that it is not so much in ' special uses of language '' (technical terms, political discourse etc.) as " in its constant ways of arranging data and its most ordinary everyday analysis of phenomena that we need to recognize the influence [language] has on other activities, cultural and personal ' (1956, 134-5). Bernstein (1971, 123) points out that, in Whorf's thinking, ' the link between language, culture and habitual thought is *not* mediated through the social structure ', whereas his own theory

> places the emphasis on changes in the social structure as major factors in shaping or changing a given culture through their effect on the consequences of fashions of speaking. It shares with Whorf the controlling influence on experience ascribed to '' frames of consistency ' involved in fashions of speaking. It differs [from] Whorf by asserting that, in the context of a common language in the sense of a general code, there will arise distinct linguistic forms, fashions of speaking, which induce in their speakers *different* ways of relating to objects and persons.

Bernstein has investigated *how* this connection is made, and suggests that it is through linguistic codes, or fashions of speaking, which arise as a consequence of the social structure and the types of social relation associated with it. As Mary Douglas put it, ' The control [of thought] is not in the speech forms but in the set of human relations which generate thought and speech ' (1972, 312).

What are these linguistic codes, or fashions of speaking? They relate, essentially, to a functional interpretation of language. It is not the words and the sentence structures — still less the pronunciation or ' accent '— which make the difference between one type of code and another; it is the relative emphasis placed on the different functions of language, or, to put it more accurately, the kinds of meaning that are typically associated with them. The ' fashions of speaking ' are sociosemantic in nature; they are patterns of meaning that emerge more or less strongly, in particular contexts, especially those relating to the socialization of the child in the family. Hence, although each child's language-learning environment is unique, he also shares certain common features with other children of a similar social background; not merely in the superficial sense that the material environments may well be alike — in fact they may not — but in the deeper sense that the forms of social relation and the role systems surrounding him have their effect on the kind of choices in meaning which will be highlighted and given prominence in different types of situation. Peter Doughty comments : ' the terms elaborated and restricted refer to characteristic ways of using language to interact with other human beings; they do not suggest that there are two kinds of " meaning potential " ' (Doughty et al. 1972, 104-5).

This dependence on social structure is not merely unavoidable, it is essential to the child's development; he can develop only as social man, and therefore his experience must be shaped in ways which make him a member of society and his particular section of it. It becomes restrictive only where the social structure orients the child's thinking away from the modes of experience that the school requires. To quote Bernstein again, ' the different focusing of experience ... creates a major problem of educability only where the school produces discontinuity between its symbolic orders and those of the child ' (1971, 183-4). In other words, the processes of becoming educated require that the child's meaning potential should have developed along certain lines in certain types of context, especially in relation to the exploration of the environment and of his own part in it. To what extent this requirement is inherent in the very concept of education, and to what extent it is merely a feature of education as it is at present organized in Britain and other highly urbanized societies, we do not know; but as things are, certain ways of organizing experience through language, and of participating and interacting with people and things, are necessary to success in school. The child who is not predisposed to this type of verbal exploration in this type of experiential and interpersonal context ' is not at home in the educational world ', as Bernstein puts it. Whether a child is so predisposed or not turns out not to be any innate property of the child as an individual, an inherent limitation on his mental powers, as used to be generally assumed; it is merely the result of a mismatch between his own symbolic orders of meaning and those of the school, a mismatch that results from the different patterns of socialization that characterize different sections of society, or subcultures, and which are in turn a function of the underlying social relations in the family and elsewhere. Mary Douglas says of Bernstein that he asks ' what structuring in society itself calls for its own appropriate structures of speech ' (1972, 5); and she goes on to add 'A common speech form transmits much more than words; it transmits a hidden baggage of shared assumptions ', a ' collective consciousness that constitutes the social bond '.

It is all too easy to be aware of subcultural differences in speech forms, because we are all sensitive to differences of dialect and accent. Unfortunately this is precisely where we go wrong, because differences of dialect and accent are in themselves irrelevant; in Bernstein's words, There is nothing, but nothing, in the dialect as such, which prevents a child from internalizing and learning to use universalistic meanings' (1971, 199), and dialect is a problem only if it is *made* a problem artificially by the prejudice and ignorance of others. It is much harder to become aware of *insignificant* differences, which are masked by dialectal variation (and which by no means always correspond to dialect distinctions), and which do not appear in the obvious form of differences in vocabulary or grammatical structure. We are still far from being able to give a comprehensive or systematic account of the linguistic realizations of Bernstein's codes or of the ways in which language operates in the transmission of culture. But the perspective is that of language and social man, and the functional investigation of language and language development provides the basis for understanding.

In essence, what seems to happen is this. The child first constructs a language in the form of a range of meanings that relate directly to certain of his basic needs. As time goes on, the meanings become more complex, and he replaces this by a symbolic system — a semantic system with structural realizations — based on the language he hears around him; this is what we call this ' mother tongue ''. Since this is learnt, and has in fact evolved, in the service of the same basic functions, it is, essentially, a functional system; but its functionality is now built in at a very abstract level. This is what was referred to at the beginning of this section, when I said that the adult linguistic system has, in effect, the four generalized functional components, or ' metafunctions ', experiential, logical, interpersonal and textual. These form the basis for the organization of meaning when the child moves from his original protolanguage into language proper.

But he does not abandon the original concrete functional elements of the system as he invented it. These still define the purposes for which language is used; and out of them evolve the social contexts and situation types that make up the patterns of use of language in daily life — including those contexts that Bernstein has shown to be critical in the socialization process. Herein lies the basis of the significant subcultural variation that we have been looking at. In *which* particular contexts of use will the child bring to bear *which* portions of the functional resources of the system? Seen from a linguistic point of view, the different ' codes ', as Bernstein calls them, are different strategies of language use. All human beings put language to certain types of use, and all of them learn a linguistic system which has evolved in that context; but what aspects of the system are typically deployed and emphasized in one type of use or another is to a significant extent determined by the culture — by the systems of social relations in which the child grows up, including the roles he himself learns to recognize and to adopt. All children have access to the meaning potential of the system; but they may differ, because social groups differ, in their interpretation of what the situation demands.

6. 言語とその社会文化的な役割

　本節では、社会文化的な観点から、文化の継承者である人間と言語使用について見ていく。まずは、社会における言語の役割と言語分析へのアプローチについて Halliday の提唱する言語理論を中心に説明し、次に言語と文化のコンテクストとのつながりについて考察していく。

社会的―記号的視点に立った言語へのアプローチ
　Halliday (1978) は、文化の形成と継承に重要な役割を果たしている言語の役割を社会言語学的な視点から解説している。以下、テキスト3で述べられている理論的な立場を中心に、Halliday の提唱する言語理論の一部を紹介し、その枠組みの骨子を説明していく。

(1) M.A.K. Halliday の機能的な言語分析
　Halliday の提唱している言語理論は、現在では選択体系機能言語学（Systemic Functional Linguistics――以下 SFL）と呼ばれ、社会的―記号的視点（social-semiotic perspective）から言語を捉えている。ここでいう記号的（semiotic）とは以下の引用にもあるように、言語を独立した記号体系として狭義的に捉えるのではなく、記号体系とそれによって生み出される意味体系との研究を視野に入れたアプローチを意味する。

> The sign has tended to be seen as an isolate, as a thing in itself, which exists first of all in and of itself before it comes to be related to other signs. Even in the work of Saussure, despite his very strong conception

of language as a set of relationships, you will still find this rather atomistic conception of the linguistic sign. For that reason, therefore, I would wish to modify this definition of semiotics and say that, rather than considering it as the study of signs, I would like to consider it as the study of sign systems — in other words, as the study of meaning in its most general sense. [Halliday and Hasan 1985:3-4]

また、記号体系と意味体系との関係は、例えば、映像・絵画・服装のモードなど言語以外のさまざまな表現様式にも認められると考えられる。そして、Hallidayは様々な記号体系によって具現化される意味体系の存在を視野に入れながら、その中の記号体系の1つである言語体系と意味体系の関係を分析する立場をとっている。そして、その意味体系は言語以外の意味体系と体系的にネットワーク化されており、その意味体系の総和が、ある文化に存在する意味の総和であるとHallidayは考える。Hallidayはそのような意味体系を「体系（system）」（Halliday and Hasan 1985:4）と呼ぶ。

また、社会的（social）という概念には、「社会的体系（文化）全体」と「言語と社会構造との関係」の2つの意味合いが含まれている（Halliday and Hasan 1985:4）。当然のことながら、言語によって生み出される意味の認識と解釈、そのような認知活動が行なわれる脳のはたらきなど、言語と意味をどのように研究していくかについてはさまざまな視点が考えられるが、人間が社会の中で言語を使って社会生活を営んでいることを考えれば、人間がどのようにして意味体系を消費しながら社会活動を行っているかという社会的観点から言語を理解していくことは欠かせないことである。

このような視点から人間の言語使用をみると、言語は人間の社会行動を遂行する手段のひとつと考えることができる。Halliday（1978）は、このような側面を次のように捉えている。

Language is being regarded as the encoding of a 'behaviour potential' into a 'meaning potential'; that is, as a means of expressing what the human organism 'can do', in interaction with other human organisms, by turning it into what he ' can mean '. What he can mean (the semantic system) is, in turn, encoded into what he ' can say ' (Halliday 1978：21ページ)

言い換えれば、言語は記号の持つ意味を単に伝達する記号体系ではなく、言語使用者の思考や行動様式を反映した意味や行動の象徴をカプセル化するはたらきをしていることになる。

また、Halliday (1978) は、このような言語と社会行動とのつながりを前提とし、記号体系がどのような機能を発達させながら様々な意味具現に貢献しているか考察し、言語に備わっていると考えられる4つの機能を提唱している。

1. 経験的意味機能：実際の世界の出来事や現象を表現する機能
2. 論理的意味機能：実際の出来事や現象といった内容を論理的に組み立てるための言語的手段としての機能
3. 対人関係的意味機能：社会の中で言語を使用するときに発生する対人関係を反映し表現する意味機能
4. テクスト形成的意味機能：上記の3つの機能を状況に合わせて具現化させる機能で構造的、意味的に一貫性のあるメッセージを構成する手段としての機能

また、最初の2つの機能は観念構成的意味機能としてまとめられている。これらの機能は言語のメタ機能 (metafunctions) と呼ばれ、言語の機能的な意味を束ねる役割を果たしている。Halliday (1978) に従えば、これらの機能は人間の言語使用において広く用いられている機能であると考えられている。

なお、言語体系——特に、文法体系——がどのように上記の機能を果たすのかについては、Halliday and Hasan (1985) を参照のこと。

(2) 状況のコンテクスト

また、Halliday (Halliday et al. 1964, Halliday 1978, Halliday and Hasan 1985) は Malinowski (1923, 1935) と Firth (1935, 1950) の流れを汲みながら、状況のコンテクスト (context of situation) という概念を体系化し、言語体系との体系的な関係を探っている。これらは「談話のフィールド (field of discourse)」、「談話のテナー（tenor of discourse)」、「談話のモード（mode of discourse)」と呼ばれる概念で、言語メッセージがつくられる状況コンテクストを解釈するときに役立つものである。

　Halliday and Hasan（1985：12）の説明を要約すれば、まず「談話のフィールド（field of discourse)」とは言語活動領域のことで、実際に起きている社会的活動の本質的なものを指す。言い換えれば、どのような事柄に言語使用者が関っているのか、またその中で言語がどの程度重要な役割を果たしているのかということを記述するための概念である。「談話のテナー（tenor of discourse)」とは役割関係のことで、誰が関与しているのか、関与者達の特徴、社会的地位や役割、そして関与者達の間にどのような（一時的・永続的）役割関係が生じているのかなどを示す概念である。また、この役割関係とは「ことばを使いながらどのような役割を果たしているか」ということと、「あらゆる社会的な有意義な関係」の両方を含んでいる。そして「談話のモード（mode of discourse)」とは言語の伝達様式のことで、言語がどのような役割を果たしているかということを指す。具体的には、どのような記号上の組織の中に組み込まれるテキストとして産出されるのか、テキストの地位、コンテクストにおけるテキストの機能（話されているものか、書かれているものか、またはその両者の組み合わせなのかというチャネル（channel）も含む）などを記述するものである。そして、もう1つ重要な要素として挙げられている点は、テキストの持つ修辞上の伝達様式（the rhetorical mode）としての役割である。つまり、説得的（persuasive)、説明的（expository)、教訓的（didactic）というような修辞的効果はテキストによって達成されるものであり、伝達様式の重要な役割と考えられている。

　SFLではまた、言語のメタ機能（metafunctions）と文法（lexicogrammar）という2つの理論的枠組が関係しながら、前者が後者を体系化する理論的基盤を与えていると考えられている。そして言語体系は社会的—記号的空間（social semiotic space）において意味を具現化し整理するための手段であると考えられている（Halliday 1994, Matthiessen 1995)。文法の記述体系も意味の機能的な側面を具現化するための記述体系として理論化されている。さらに、これらは上述した状況のコンテクストの3つの構成概念——談話のフィールド、テナー、

モード——と連動しながら、意味選択を体系的に行っていると解釈されている。要約すると、状況のコンテクストの3つの概念——談話のフィールド、テナー、モード——は機能的に構成された意味体系部門——経験的意味部門、対人関係的意味部門、テキスト形成的意味部門——とそれぞれ相互関係を持っているという仮説が立てられている（詳しくは Halliday and Hasan（1985：26）を参照）。

そして、SFL では、状況のコンテクスト、機能的な意味選択、そのような意味選択を可能にする機能的な言語の記号体系（文法）との間に有機的で体系的な関係が存在するという仮説に基づき理論の構築を進めている。

(3) 文化のコンテクスト

文化人類学者である Malinowski は、トロブリアンド諸島（the Trobriand Islands of the South Pacific）の住民の文化を研究する過程で、彼らの原語であるキリウィナ語のテクストを理解しそれを説明する際に、テクストの語義に加え「テクストが発話される状況（the situation in which the text was uttered）」（Halliday and Hasan 1985：6）が必要であると指摘し、その際「全体的な文化的な背景」もその解釈には必要であると述べている。

このように、あるテクストを理解するために必要な情報をコンテクストと呼ぶが、それは狭義的なものと広義的なものに大別することができる。狭義的な解釈に基づくコンテクストとは、我々が一般的に使用している文脈という意味が代表するように、語や文の意味を解釈するために必要な前後関係の情報を指しているが、それに対し、広義的な解釈に基づく場合、テキストがある環境で産出されるときに我々が経験的に獲得している状況的な情報（...it (= the context) serves to make a bridge between the text and the situation in which texts actually occur. [Halliday and Hasan 1985：5]）が含まれる。

Malinowski（1923, 1935）の2つの概念——状況のコンテクスト（context of situation）と文化のコンテクスト（context of culture）——は後者に含まれるが、両者は言語・非言語コミュニケーションの場面で言語を含む意味伝達を理解するのに欠かせないものである。これらの概念はまた Firth（1935、1950）や Halliday へと受け継がれ体系化されていった。

言語と文化のコンテクスト

　テキスト3では、文化というパラダイムによって唯一無二の個人の存在について言及されている。つまり、私たちが身を置く環境は文化によって特徴づくられ、言語を学ぶ状態もおおよそ文化的な影響を受け決定されるということである。そして、人間の言語活動と文化的な影響について2つの側面があると指摘されている。

　まずは、言語的な現象である。子どもは生後言語を習得するがその言語にはある文化的な特徴が付加されている。つまり、ある地域のある社会集団で生まれ育てば、そこの方言や人々の思考や行動様式を反映した言語知識と運用を身につけることになる。また、観察される言語使用に対して、所属する社会集団も社会階級やその他の社会的、文化的な特徴づけが可能となる。また、もう1つは、言語活動を通して、行動様式とその中に潜在する文化的な価値体系を身につけるという点である。これは人間の社会化というプロセスに言語活動がどう貢献するかという点を明らかにするために重要である。そして、複数の異なる言語と社会環境の中で育った人間が社会の中で共存して初めて、言語やその他の表現様式を通してその文化的な価値観の違いというものを認識することになる。また、文化や社会体系網の構造もこのプロセスに大きな影響を及ぼしている。テキスト3では、言語が関わる社会的な場面として教育に関する例を挙げているが、その他にさまざまな日常的な場面で、言語が重要な媒体として機能している。また、個々の人間が発信する言語メッセージと社会的、文化的価値観は表裏一体なものであり、言語から個人の社会的、文化的な価値体系を垣間見ることもできれば、その逆をたどることが可能なのである。

おわりに

　本章では、言語という視点から、人間・社会・文化を関連づけながら、言語と文化の関わり合いについて社会的な側面から解説してきた。ここで扱ったアプローチは、言語活動と社会文化的な要因がどのように関連しながら人間を社会的に意義のある存在としているのかということを探る1つの考え方を示すも

のであるが、言語と文化の結びつきについてさらに深く考えていくための糸口にしていただきたい。

〔参考文献〕

Baratz, Joan C. (1970) ' Teaching reading in an urban Negro school system '. In Williams 1970

Bernstein, Basil (1971) *Class, codes and control 1 : theoreical studies towards a sociology of language* (Primary Socialization, Language and Education) London : Routledge & Kegan Paul

Douglas, Mary (1972) ' Speech, class and Basil Bernstein ' London : The Listener 2241 (9 March)

Doughty, Peter S. *et al*. (1972) *Exploring language* (Explorations in Language Study) London : Edward

Firth, J.R. (1935) " The technique of semantics," *Translations of the Philological Society*. Reprinted in J.R. Firth, *Papers in Linguistics 1934–1951*, London, Oxford University Press, 1959

Firth, J.R. (1950) " Personality and language in society," *Sociological Review* 42, 37–52. Reprinted in J.R. Firth, Papers in Linguistics 1934–1951, London, Oxford University Press, 1959

Halliday, M.A.K. 1978 *Language as social semiotic : The social interpretation* of language and meaning London : Edward Arnold

Halliday, M.A.K. (1994) *An Introduction to Functional Grammar*, London, Edward Arnold

Halliday, M.A.K. and Hasan, R. 1985 *Language, context, and text : spects of language in a social-semiotic perspective* Deakin University Press

池上嘉彦 (1984) 『記号論への招待』 岩波新書

Malinowski, B. (1923) ' The problem of meaning in primitive languages," Supplement 1 in C.K. Ogden & I.A. Richards (eds.) *The Meaning of Meaning* (International Library of Philosophy, Psychology and Scientific Method), London, Kegan Paul

Malinowski, B. (1935) *Coral Gardens and their Magic*, Vol.2, Allen & Unwin, London. Reprinted as *The Language of Magic and Gardening* (Indiana University Studies in the History and Theory of Linguistics), Bloomington, Ind, Indiana University Press, 1967

Matthiessen, C. (1995) *Lexicogrammatical Cartography : English Systems.* Tokyo : International Language Science Publishers

Whorf, Benjamin Lee (1956) *Language, thought and reality:selected writings*, ed. John B. Carroll Cambridge, Mass : MIT Press

Williams, Frederick (ed.) (1970) *Language and poverty : perspectives on a theme.* Chicago : Markham

第3章 フィッツジェラルドの
『偉大なギャツビー』を読む

　この章では1920年代のアメリカの空気を見事に捉えたF.スコット・フィッツジェラルド（F. Scott Fitzgerald 1896-1940）の『偉大なギャツビー』(*The Great Gatsby* 1925) を取り上げ、作者と作品の時代背景、その意義などについて3回に分けて解説を行いたい。

1

　In my younger and more vulnerable years my father gave me some advice that I've been turning over in my mind ever since.

　'Whenever you feel like criticizing anyone,' he told me, 'just remember that all the people in this world haven't had the advantages that you've had.'

　He didn't say any more, but we've always been unusually communicative in a reserved way, and I understood that he meant a great deal more than that. In consequence, I'm inclined to reserve all judgements, a habit that has opened up many curious natures to me and also made me the victim of not a few veteran bores. The abnormal mind is quick to detect and attach itself to this quality when it appears in a normal person, and so it came about that in college I was unjustly accused of being a politician, because I was privy to the secret griefs of wild, unknown men. Most of the confidences were unsought — frequently I have feigned sleep, preoccupation, or a hostile levity when I realized by some unmistakable sign that an intimate revelation was quivering on the horizon; for the intimate revelations of young men, or at least the terms in which they express them, are usually plagiaristic and marred by obvious suppressions. Reserving judgements is a matter of infinite hope. I am still a little afraid of missing something if I forget that, as my father snobbishly suggested, and I snobbishly repeat, a sense of the fundamental decencies is parcelled out unequally at birth.

And, after boasting this way of my tolerance, I come to the admission that it has a limit. Conduct may be founded on the hard rock or the wet marshes, but after a certain point I don't care what it's founded on. When I came back from the East last autumn I felt that I wanted the world to be in uniform and at a sort of moral attention forever; I wanted no more riotous excursions with privileged glimpses into the human heart. Only Gatsby, the man who gives his name to this book, was exempt from my reaction — Gatsby, who represented everything for which I have an unaffected scorn. If personality is an unbroken series of successful gestures, then there was something gorgeous about him, some heightened sensitivity to the promises of life, as if he were related to one of those intricate machines that register earthquakes ten thousand miles away. This responsiveness had nothing to do with that flabby impressionability which is dignified under the name of the ' creative temperament '— it was an extraordinary gift for hope, a romantic readiness such as I have never found in any other person and which it is not likely I shall ever find again. No — Gatsby turned out all right at the end; it is what preyed on Gatsby, what foul dust floated in the wake of his dreams that temporarily closed out my interest in the abortive sorrows and shortwinded elations of men.

Already it was deep summer on roadhouse roofs and in front of wayside garages, where new red petrol-pumps sat out in pools of light, and when I reached my estate at West Egg I ran the car under its shed and sat for a while on an abandoned grass roller in the yard. The wind had blown off, leaving a loud, bright night, with wings beating in the trees and a persistent organ sound as the full bellows of the earth blew the frogs full of life. The silhouette of a moving cat wavered across the moonlight, and, turning my head to watch it, I saw that I was not alone — fifty feet away a figure had emerged from the shadow of my neighbour's mansion and was standing with his hands in his pockets regarding the silver pepper of the stars. Something in his leisurely movements and the secure position of his feet upon the lawn suggested that it was Mr Gatsby himself, come out to determine what share was his of our local heavens.

　I decided to call to him. Miss Baker had mentioned him at dinner, and that would do for an introduction. But I didn't call to him, for he gave a sudden intimation that he was content to be alone — he stretched out his arms toward the dark water in a curious way, and, far as I was from him, I could have sworn he was trembling. Involuntarily I glanced seaward and distinguished nothing except a single green light, minute and far away, that might have been the end of a dock. When I looked once more for Gatsby he had vanished, and I was alone again in the unquiet darkness.

　今回は作者フィッツジェラルドの生涯と作品について解説する。フランシス・スコット・キー・フィッツジェラルド（Francis Scott Key Fitzgerald）は1896年9月24日、ミネソタ州セント・ポールに生まれた。彼の名前は父方の親戚で、アメリカ国歌となる詩（The Star-Spangled Banner）を書いたFrancis Scott Key（1779–1843）から取られたもので、由緒ある名前である。父方の祖先は17世紀にアイルランドからメリーランド州に渡ってきていて、アメリカでも古い家柄であった。フィッツジェラルドの父は家具工場を経営していたが、1893年の不況で経営に失敗し、彼が生まれた頃はProctor & Gambleという家庭用品の会社の旅回りのセールスマンをしていた。母は19世紀の中頃やはりアイルランドから移住してきた移民の娘で、実家はセント・ポールで成功した食品会社を経営していた。フィッツジェラルドのなかに両親の双方からアイルランドの濃い血が流れ込んでいるのは注目に値する。
　彼の生家はセント・ポール市の中心の高級住宅街にあったが、家計は不安定で、彼らは必ずしも裕福な部類には入らなかった。一家には「家柄はいいがある種のみすぼらしさ」があったという。近所の裕福な家庭の子供たちと遊んだ

幼・少年時代に、後のフィッツジェラルドの上流社会への憧れが芽生えたと考えることができる。

　一家は父親の仕事の関係で、セント・ポールとニューヨーク州のシラキュース、バッファローの間で転々と住処を変えた。しかし、父親にはその道の才能がなかったらしく、1908年旅回りのセールスマンの仕事を成績不振のため解雇され、一家は再びセント・ポールへ戻ってくる。そして、主に母親の実家の経済的支援に頼って彼らは生きてゆくことになった。

　フィッツジェラルドの両親はセント・ポールの街の上流社会の人間とはあまり付き合わなかったが、息子の教育には金を惜しまず、1908年彼らは息子を上流階級の師弟の行くセント・ポール・アカデミーに入れた。父親はまた息子に文学への手ほどきをし、ポーやバイロンの作品を読んで聞かせたり、自分の祖先の功績を語って聞かせた。早熟なフィッツジェラルドは、面白い本を読んだり芝居を観たりすると、自分でも早速それをまねた物語や芝居を書くようになり、1909年にはアカデミーの雑誌に「レイモンド家証書の謎」という短編を発表するまでになる。

　フィッツジェラルドのセント・ポール・アカデミーでの学業は、議論と体育には優れていたが、その他の面ではあまりパッとしなかった。そこで1911年両親は息子を、東部のニュージャージー州にあるカトリック系の寄宿学校ニューマン・スクールへ送り、否応なく勉強せざるを得ない情況に彼を置いた。後にフィッツジェラルドは、このニューマン・スクールでの2年間を「浪費された2年間」といい、「得るところなく過ごした不幸の歳月」と記している。午前中は授業で、午後は運動、夜は監督つきの自習という、おおよそこのようなこの学校の日課が、両親に甘やかされて育ったフィッツジェラルドに楽しかったはずもない。空想の世界にひたる一人だけの寝室がなかっただけに、セント・ポール・アカデミー時代よりも一層つらかったらしい。

　しかし、集団生活をすることで、彼の自己中心的な性格に修正が加えられ、ここでの生活はフィッツジェラルドの人間としての成長に有益であったはずである。事実、彼はこのカトリックの学校のフェイ神父と親交を結ぶようになり、そして神父は彼の人生の師となり、彼に文学的才能をみがき発展させるよう励ますことになる。この学校時代にもフィッツジェラルドは、学校新聞に「つい

てないサンタ・クロース」とその他いくつかの短編を発表している。

　1913 年フィッツジェラルドは 2 度の入学試験の失敗の後、かろうじて東部の名門プリンストン大学に入学をはたす。彼にとってプリンストン大学は東部の富と権力、栄光を表わす象徴だった。彼の父は東部の名門の旧家の出で、事業の成功を求めて中西部のセント・ポールへやってきたがそれに失敗し、家の富と栄光は潰えてしまっていた。プリンストン大学への入学は、彼にとって、一家の失われた富と栄光を回復するための第一歩だったのである。

　大学に入るとまもなく、フィッツジェラルドはキャンパスのユーモア雑誌『プリンストン・タイガー』に短編を発表し始める。またニューマン・スクール時代から演劇に興味があった彼は、ミュージカル公演で有名な「トライアングル・クラブ」に加わり、ミュージカル・コメディの脚本を書き出す。それに加えて、1 年先輩のエドマンド・ウィルスン（Edmund Wilson　1895～1972）の編集する雑誌『ナッソー文学』に詩や小説を発表するようになる。ウィルスンは後年アメリカ有数の批評家となり、またフィッツジェラルドの生涯の友となって、彼の死後未完のまま残された『最後の大君』やエッセイを編集することになる。

　このようにフィッツジェラルドは大学キャンパス内の社交界では華々しい活躍をするが、学業の方はあまり振るわなかったらしい。大学 3 年の後半には大学当局から退学勧告を受け、3 年生をもう一度やり直すはめになる。しかし、やり直しの 3 年目が終わろうとする 1917 年 4 月、アメリカがドイツに宣戦を布告して第 1 次世界大戦に参戦することになり、フィッツジェラルドの人生に大きな転機が訪れる。

　彼は自発的に陸軍の少尉任官試験を受け、合格したのを機にプリンストン大学を退学し、1917 年 11 月正式に陸軍に任官した。この軍隊志願の動機がはっきりしない。文学や演劇を愛する若者は、戦争の熱狂とは無縁のはずである。親類の者にあてた手紙の中で「アメリカのために死ぬかも知れないが、ぼくは自分自身のために死ぬつもりです」と語っているから、国への愛国的忠誠心からというわけでもなさそうである。大学の友人たちも戦争へ行き、その上プリンストン大学卒業の見込みもたたず、プリンストンに託した成功の夢も潰え、その傷をいやすために死というロマンティックな幻想に慰めを見いだしたのかもしれない。

第3章　フィッツジェラルドの『偉大なギャツビー』を読む　93

　それはどうあれ、フィッツジェラルドは1918年6月中尉に昇進し、陸軍第67連隊への配属が決まった。そして10月には派遣命令が出され、ニュージャージー州の港からフランス戦線へ送られようとする矢先の11月11日、休戦条約が結ばれるのである。彼は結局戦争へは行かず、1919年2月に正式に除隊となる。

　この軍隊時代に、彼はその後の人生を決める運命の女性と出会っている。それは、1918年アラバマ州モンゴメリーに駐屯している時にパーティで出会った、当時18歳になるゼルダ・セイヤー（Zelda Sayre　1899〜1948）だった。彼女は州最高裁判所判事の末娘で、フィッツジェラルドの言葉によれば「アラバマとジョージアに並ぶもののいない美女」であった。才気活発で、生気にあふれ、しかも華やかな雰囲気をもつゼルダは、フィッツジェラルドの憧れていた上流社会の女性であった。彼は一目で恋に落ち、彼女に結婚を申し込むが、しかし陸軍の一将校の力では上流階級の娘の望む生活をかなえられるはずもなく、即座に断られていた。

　除隊となったフィッツジェラルドは、ニューヨークの広告会社に勤めながら、雑誌の出版社にそれまで書き貯めておいた短編を送るが、ほとんど断られる。そこで、前に一度送って断られていた長編『ロマンティックなエゴイスト』を大幅に書き改め、タイトルも『楽園のこちら側』(*This Side of Paradise*)と改題し、前と同じスクリブナーズ社に送った。すると今度はそれは受諾され、1920年3月出版された。

　『楽園のこちら側』はフィッツジェラルドの自伝的物語である。親に甘やかされて育った主人公エイモリー・ブレインがプリンストン大学で文学に打ち込み、大学社交界で上流階級の美しい若者たちと交わり、いくつか恋愛も経験する。戦争でフランス戦線に送られるが、帰国すると母の死に遭遇し、経済的困難を経験する、というものである。この小説には飲酒やペッティング、フラッパーの流行など、第1次大戦後の青春の開放感が描かれていて、読者に好評のうちに迎えられ、たちまちベストセラーになった。

　いまや「売れっ子」になったフィッツジェラルドの結婚の申し出に、ゼルダも今度は同意し、1921年4月2人は結ばれる。それは彼にとって、まさにおとぎ話が現実のものとなったようなものだった。あっと言う間の財政的成功と、

夢だった上流社会の女性を、同時に手にしたのだった。彼はまたたく間にアメリカ文学界の「寵児」となり、後にアメリカ史上〈狂乱の 20 年代〉と呼ばれる新時代を象徴する若き天才と見なされるようになる。

『楽園のこちら側』の大成功の後、出版社はフィッツジェラルドの短編を高額の料金で引き取るようになり、最初の短編集『フラッパーと哲学者』(*Flappers and Philosophers*) が 1920 年 8 月に出版される。結婚後のフィッツジェラルドとゼルダはマンハッタンの高級アパートに住み、連日連夜パーティと観劇、ナイトクラブ、演奏会めぐりを繰り返し、ニューヨーク社交界の花形になった。彼ら夫婦のどちらにも金銭感覚というものがなく、フッツジェラルドが稼いだ大金を、文字通り湯水のごとく使い尽くしたという。そういう生活を維持するために、彼は猛烈な勢いで短編を書きまくり、それらは 1922 年 9 月、『ジャズ・エイジの物語』(*Tales of the Jazz Age*) としてまとめられ出版された。

同じ年の 3 月、雑誌に連載されていた『美しく呪われた人々』(*The Beautiful and Damned*) がやはり出版されている。この物語もまたインテリ青年の堕落の物語である。ニューヨークの大富豪の孫アンソニー・パッチがハーヴァード大学を出て、イタリア遊学から帰った後も定職につかず、ニューヨークの高級アパートで気ままな生活を送っている。南部出身の女性と結婚するが、夫婦の放蕩三昧の生活は改まらず、激怒した祖父は遺産相続人のリストからアンソニーの名前をはずし、死亡する。アンソニーは異議申し立ての訴訟を起こすが、勝訴の見込みも立たず、酒におぼれ破滅の道をたどる。最後は突然、勝訴の連絡が届き、パッチ夫妻がヨーロッパへ旅立つところで終わる。この小説は、少なくとも財政的成功をフィッツジェラルドにもたらした。

フィッツジェラルド夫婦は頻繁にヨーロッパとの間を行き来したが、最初のヨーロッパ訪問は 1921 年 5 月のことで、フランス、イタリア、イギリスを回り、7 月に帰国している。そして 10 月に長女 "スコティ" (Frances Scott) が生まれる。1922 年 10 月夫婦はマンハッタンの南に位置する、映画俳優や金持ちの多く集まるロング・アイランドのグレート・ネックに引っ越し、連日騒々しいパーティを繰り広げた。その間もフィッツジェラルドは生活費を稼ぐために短編を書き続けたが、またブロードウェイのヒットを狙って戯曲『植物』(*The Vegetable*) を書き上げた。しかし、これは完全な失敗作で、1923 年 11 月にア

トランティック・シティで一晩上演されただけで中止となった。

　1924年4月フィッツジェラルド一家は2度目のヨーロッパ旅行に出発し、南フランスのサン・ラファエルに落ち着く。ここで彼はこれまでにないほど芸術性を意識して、彼の代表作となる『偉大なギャツビー』に全力を投入した。というのは、それまでフィッツジェラルドの書いていたのは、出版社の求める大衆の嗜好に合った短編小説で、その方が収入もよく、彼の「名声」も高まった。しかし、それでは文学界からは一人前の芸術家としては扱われないというジレンマに陥っていた。そこで彼は、大衆性と芸術性を兼ね備えた本格的な作品を目指したのだった。

　『偉大なギャツビー』は1925年4月スクリブナーズ社から出版され、フィッツジェラルドは大成功を予感した。文学界からの反応は好評だった。詩人のT・S・エリオット（T.S. Eliot　1888～1965）はこの小説を「ヘンリー・ジェイムズ以来アメリカ小説が初めて一歩前進した作品」と手紙の中でほめた。小説家のイーディス・ウォートン（Edith Wharton　1862～1937）やガートルード・スタイン（Gertrude Stein　1874～1946）などもこの小説を称賛し、彼は一人前の芸術家として認められた。しかし、フィッツジェラルドの予想に反して、大衆の反応はいまひとつで、この本の売れ行きは『美しく呪われた人々』の半分にとどまった。その後彼は、1934年まで長編小説は発表していない。

　フランス滞在中、フィッツジェラルドはパリでアーネスト・ヘミングウェイ（Ernest Hemingway　1899～1961）と出会っている。後世2人は〈失われた世代〉の作家と目されることになるが、この当時フィッツジェラルドは『われらの時代に』（*In Our Time*　1925）を発表したばかりのヘミングウェイの才能を認め、彼を出版社に紹介している。しかし、2人の間にかなりのライヴァル意識はあったようである。

　1926年12月アメリカに帰国したフィッツジェラルドに、ハリウッドの映画製作会社ユナイテッド・アーティスツから映画の脚本の依頼が届く。翌年1月ハリウッドを訪れるが、脚本のでき具合が悪くて拒否され、3月にはそこを去っている。

　1928年4月一家は3度目のフランス旅行へ出るが、今回は妻ゼルダのバレーのレッスンのためであった。ゼルダは突然バレーに凝り始め、プロのバレリー

ナを目指して本格的に練習していた。9月に一家は一旦帰国するが、翌年の3月再びパリへ戻る。パリ滞在の1930年4月、ゼルダが極度の不安状態のため入院し、5月にスイスの病院で精神分裂病と診断される。

　2人の結婚生活は初めから緊張をはらんでいた。酒びたりの生活とパーティの連続は、彼らの健康と神経を蝕んでいた。社交界におけるスキャンダラスなゴシップ、絶えざる借金の恐怖、創作行為からくるストレスなどのために、強い個性を持った2人の間に、いさかいが止むことはなかった。ゼルダの発病の裏にはこのような要因があったと考えられる。

　ゼルダの症状は一時好転し、1931年9月に退院して帰国する。10月フィッツジェラルドはハリウッドのMGMと契約し、映画のシナリオを書くが、今回もうまく行かなかった。1932年1月父親の死の衝撃からゼルダの病気が悪化し、再び入院する。そんな中の1934年4月、フィッツジェラルドは9年ぶりに長編小説『夜はやさし』（*Tender Is the Night*）を出版した。

　『夜はやさし』は1920年代のフランスのリヴィエラを舞台に、現地のアメリカ人社交界と、理想に燃える若き精神科医ディック・ダイヴァーの破滅へ向かういきさつが語られる。ディックは留学先のチューリッヒの精神病院で、分裂病に苦しむ同国人の美しい患者、ニコル・ウォレンと恋に落ち結婚する。しかし、不倫や近親相姦、ニコルのために医者と夫を買う、というような考え方をする上流社会の道徳的腐敗のなかで生きてゆくうち、ディック自身もそうした汚れに染まり、酒におぼれ、崩壊の道を転げ落ちてゆく。最後は、彼がアメリカの片田舎でひっそりと開業医として暮らしているところで終わる。

　この小説はスクリブナーズ社から1万3,000部印刷されたが、フィッツジェラルドが期待したほど売れなかった。好意的に評価する批評家も少なくなかった。しかし、時代は「大恐慌」の後の30年代不況の真っ直中にあり、生活の糧にも困る一般大衆に、20年代の売れっ子作家による上流社会の物語を読む余裕などなかった。時はマイケル・ゴールド（Michael Gold 1893〜1967）の『金無しユダヤ人』（*Jews Without Money* 1930）やジャック・コンロイ（Jack Conroy 1898〜1990）の『文無しラリー』（*The Disinherited* 1933）など左翼プロレタリア小説全盛の時代だったのである。

　その後もフィッツジェラルドは、ゼルダの入院費を稼ぐため、アルコールと

借金返済のプレッシャーと闘いながら、長編小説や短編小説、エッセイなどを書き続けた。1937年7月、再びMGMと契約し、ハリウッドで映画の脚本の仕事をする。何本かの脚本を仕上げたが、1938年12月MGM側はフィッツジェラルドとの契約を更新しなかった。しかしその後も彼はハリウッドにとどまり、パラマウントやユニヴァーサル、コロンビアといった映画会社と次々と契約を結び、1940年12月21日心臓発作で亡くなるまで、ハリウッドで仕事を続けた。

彼の最後を看取ったのは、シーラ・グレアム（Sheilah Graham）というイギリス人女性記者だった。フィッツジェラルドは1937年7月、当時28歳の彼女とハリウッドで出会い、すぐに恋に落ちた。彼女は晩年の彼がアルコールと闘い、1939年10月から書き始めた『最後の大君』（*The Last Tycoon*）に最後の力を打ち込むのを精神的に支えた。フィッツジェラルドは生前、メリーランド州にある一家の墓地に葬られることを望んでいたけれども、シーラのことが原因でカトリック教会から断られ、近くの共同墓地に埋められた。

『最後の大君』は第6章まで書かれ作者の死によって中断されたものを、フィッツジェラルドの友人で批評家のエドマンド・ウィルスンが整理・編集し、残りの部分の梗概と作者の手紙やノートからの抜粋を添えて、1941年に出版された。これはハリウッドで独裁者的な影響力を持つ映画プロデューサー、モンロー・スターの物語である。ハリウッドの映画も分業化が進み、何事もビジネスライクに、機械的に運ばれる。そんな中にあって、彼はすべてを個人の責任で一身に背負い、人間同士の絆を大事にするハリウッドの「最後の大君」である。この物語の中で、語りの視点が一人称から三人称へ突然移行したり、まだ未完成のぎこちなさが残っている。

1940年に亡くなったとき、フィッツジェラルドは一般にはほとんど忘れられた存在だった。彼の私生活は乱れに乱れ、作品の評価も頼りないものだった。かっては"ジャズ・エイジの寵児"ともてはやしたにもかかわらず、新聞の死亡記事は彼の私生活の乱れをあげつらい、散々なものだった。当時彼の作品はすべて絶版になっていて、彼の名前が人々の記憶から消え去るのは確実だった。

しかし第2次世界大戦後、彼の作品への関心が次第に高まり、1960年代までにフィッツジェラルドは20世紀アメリカ文学の中に確固とした地位を占めるようになった。彼の人気は現在も衰えず、ゼルダと彼の私生活は、1920年代に起

きた青春の氾濫と切っても切れないものとなり、アメリカ的風景の一部となった。彼の作品は、野心や正義、公正、アメリカの夢といった、現在でも少しも色あせないテーマを探究するための貴重な題材を提供している。

　初めに挙げた英文は、『偉大なギャツビー』第1章の最初と最後の部分を引用したものである。この小説の特徴の一つは、第1人称の語り手ニック・キャラウェイ（Nick Carraway）の視点から、ギャツビーの悲劇が物語られている点である。この手法を用いることで、この小説はギャツビーの物語に、奥行きと劇的効果をもたらすことに成功している。最初の部分はニックが自分を読者に紹介しているところで、重要である。というのはこの部分を読むことで、われわれ読者は、語り手の物の見方に問題がないかどうか、語り手が信頼できるかどうかを判断するからである。それによって、ギャツビーの悲劇の意味も変わってくる。
　第1章の最後の部分は、ニックが初めてギャツビーの姿を目にする場面で、ここではこの小説に一貫して流れるシンボリズムが働いている。ギャツビーは遠くの小さな「緑色の灯」に向かって両手を差しのべ、祈るようにしている。この「緑色の灯」は、この小説の一番最後に描かれる「緑色の灯」と呼応していて、ギャツビーの夢と希望を象徴し、ひいてはアメリカという存在が表わす夢と希望、再生と可能性を象徴している。このようなシンボリズムはこの小説のいたるところにちりばめられている。

2

　She turned her head as there was a light dignified knocking at the front door. I went out and opened it. Gatsby, pale as death, with his hands plunged like weights in his coat pockets, was standing in a puddle of water glaring tragically into my eyes.
　With his hands still in his coat pockets he stalked by me into the hall, turned sharply as if he were on a wire, and disappeared into the living-room. It wasn't a bit funny. Aware of the loud beating of my own heart I pulled the

door to against the increasing rain.

 For half a minute there wasn't a sound. Then from the living-room I heard a sort of choking murmur and part of a laugh, followed by Daisy's voice on a clear artificial note:

 'I certainly am awfully glad to see you again.'

 A pause; it endured horribly. I had nothing to do in the hall, so I went into the room.

 Gatsby, his hands still in his pockets, was reclining against the mantelpiece in a strained counterfeit of perfect ease, even of boredom. His head leaned back so far that it rested against the face of a defunct mantelpiece clock, and from this position his distraught eyes stared down at Daisy, who was sitting, frightened but graceful, on the edge of a stiff chair.

 'We've met before,' muttered Gatsby. His eyes glanced momentarily at me, and his lips parted with an abortive attempt at a laugh. Luckily the clock took this moment to tilt dangerously at the pressure of his head, whereupon he turned and caught it with trembling fingers, and set it back in place. Then he sat down, rigidly, his elbow on the arm of the sofa and his chin in his hand.

 'I'm sorry about the clock,' he said.

 My own face had now assumed a deep tropical burn. I couldn't muster up a single commonplace out of the thousand in my head.

 'It's an old clock,' I told them idiotically.

 I think we all believed for a moment that it had smashed in pieces on the floor.

 'We haven't met for many years,' said Daisy, her voice as matter-of-fact as it could ever be.

 'Five years next November.'

 The automatic quality of Gatsby's answer set us all back at least another minute. I had them both on their feet with the desperate suggestion that they help me make tea in the kitchen when the demoniac Finn brought it in on a tray.

Amid the welcome confusion of cups and cakes a certain physical decency established itself. Gatsby got himself into a shadow and, while Daisy and I talked, looked conscientiously from one to the other of us with tense, unhappy eyes. However, as calmness wasn't an end in itself, I made an excuse at the first possible moment, and got to my feet.

'Where are you going?' demanded Gatsby in immediate alarm.

'I'll be back.'

'I've got to speak to you about something before you go.'

He followed me wildly into the kitchen, closed the door, and whispered: 'Oh, God!' in a miserable way.

'What's the matter?'

'This is a terrible mistake,' he said, shaking his head from side to side, 'a terrible, terrible mistake.'

'You're just embarrassed, that's all,' and luckily I added: 'Daisy's embarrassed too.'

'She's embarrassed?' he repeated incredulously.

'Just as much as you are.'

'Don't talk so loud.'

'You're acting like a little boy,' I broke out impatiently. 'Not only that, but you're rude. Daisy's sitting in there all alone.'

He raised his hand to stop my words, looked at me with unforgettable reproach, and, opening the door cautiously, went back into the other room.

As I went over to say good-bye I saw that the expression of bewilderment had come back into Gatsby's face, as though a faint doubt had occurred to him as to the quality of his present happiness. Almost five years! There must have been moments even that afternoon when Daisy tumbled short of his dreams — not through her own fault, but because of the colossal vitality of his illusion. It had gone beyond her, beyond everything. He had thrown himself into it with a creative passion, adding to it all the time, decking it out with every bright feather that drifted his way. No amount of fire or freshness can challenge what a man can store up in his ghostly heart.

　As I watched him he adjusted himself a little, visibly. His hand took hold of hers, and as she said something low in his ear he turned toward her with a rush of emotion. I think that voice held him most, with its fluctuating, feverish warmth, because it couldn't be over-dreamed — that voice was a deathless song.

　They had forgotten me, but Daisy glanced up and held out her hand; Gatsby didn't know me now at all. I looked once more at them and they looked back at me, remotely, possessed by intense life. Then I went out of the room and down the marble steps into the rain, leaving them there together.

　1925年に出版された『偉大なギャツビー』はその時代を最もよく表わしている作品だと言われている。このギャツビーの勝利と悲劇の物語は、驚くべき仕方でアメリカ社会の一断面を捉えている。この小説はいわば社会を映す鏡の働きをしている。これは現在ではアメリカ文学の古典となっているが、出版当初は作者が期待した成果をあげられなかった。それでもそれは、「ジャズ・エイジ」と呼ばれる第1次世界大戦後の狂乱した社会を見事に写し取っていた。この作品の魅力の一つは、アメリカ史上、政治的にも経済的にもきわめて混沌とした時代を生きたある世代の雰囲気を活写している点にある。したがって、この小説を完全に理解するには、この小説の背景にある時代と社会についてある程度の知識が必要である。

　一般に「ジャズ・エイジ」と呼ばれる時代は、1919年の第1次世界大戦の終結から1929年の株価の大暴落にいたる、戦後アメリカの繁栄の時代で、「狂乱の20年代」('Roaring 20s') とも呼ばれる。〈ジャズ〉という言葉は、第1次世界大戦前は、シカゴの暗黒街の隠語で「セックス」を意味していたが、ある種の音楽とダンスを表わすようになった。ニューオーリンズの黒人音楽から生まれたジャズはこの20年代、トランペッターのルイ・アームストロング、ブルーズ・シンガーのベシィー・スミス、バンド・リーダーのデューク・エリント

ンなどの黒人天才音楽家の活躍により人気を博し、禁酒法時代のシカゴやニューヨークの〈もぐり酒場〉やダンス・ホールで盛んに演奏された。フィッツジェラルドは第1次大戦後のこの時代の享楽的、シニカルな雰囲気を、この音楽の持つ神経的興奮になぞらえ、「ジャズ・エイジ」と名づけたのだった。

この10年間はアメリカの成長と繁栄の時代だった。同時にそれは腐敗にまみれた10年でもあった。第1次世界大戦のアメリカ経済に及ぼした影響は大きかった。戦争期間中、戦禍をまぬがれたアメリカは、ヨーロッパの生活物資、軍事物資の供給国となり、政治による統制下で経済は拡大した。戦後もこの政治と経済の提携は続いた。1921年にウォレン・ハーディングが、そして彼の死の1923年にカルヴィン・クーリッジがそれぞれ大統領に就任すると、彼らは大企業と金持ちに有利な政策を展開し、クーリッジは「アメリカの仕事はビジネスだ」とまで言い放った。

この時代はアメリカ近代化の時期で、新しいテクノロジーが飛躍的な発展をみせた。自動車、ラジオ、飛行機が大量生産されるようになり、宣伝広告の発達と月賦販売の始まりと相まって、一般大衆の自動車とラジオへの需要は高まった。高速道路が建設され、ホテルやオフィスビルがどの街にも建ち並び、住宅が建設され、郊外が拡大した。ドラッグ・ストアや食料品のチェーンが登場し、合併によって巨大な銀行も出現した。

しかし、こうしたアメリカの繁栄の恩恵にあずかれない人びともいた。中西部や南部の農業地帯は、戦争が終わると、輸出の伸び悩みと、戦争中の過剰投資で重い負債を背負っていた。炭鉱労働者は安い賃金に苦しみ、ストライキを決行しては警官隊に鎮圧されていた。南部の黒人はまだ差別の状態に置かれたままだった。アメリカの繁栄の外にいたこのような人びとは、住み慣れた土地を離れ、よりよい生活を夢みて西部や北東部の都市部へ流れ込み、スラムを形成した。『偉大なギャツビー』のなかでも、この貧富の格差が広がった社会の断面が、明瞭に写し取られている。この小説の第2章には「灰の谷」('the valley of ashes')と呼ばれるスラム街が登場し、よりよい生活を得ようと夢みながら、なかなかそこから抜け出せない人びとが印象深く描かれている。

この時代の狂躁的な雰囲気を最もよく表わしているのは、何といっても、一般の人びとの株取引への興味の高まりである。第1次世界大戦以前に株式や債

券に関係のあるアメリカ人はほんの一握りの人びとだった。特にポピュリズム意識の強い南部や西部の人びとの間には、国の経済を操るウォール街の人間に対する警戒感が強くあった。しかし戦争中政府の売り出した「自由公債」('Liberty Bond')を買った人びとには、戦後、株取引に対する恐怖心が薄らいでいった。株式ブローカーも都市の真ん中にオフィスを開くようになり、配当とか信用取引口座などの株取引に関する知識も、人びとの間に広まった。U.S. スティール、ジェネラル・エレクトリック、ジェネラル・モーターズ、AT＆Tといった大企業が、一般株式を売り出した。

　1929年までに、アメリカのどの街の、どの床屋、どの食堂、どの駅の待合い室でも、人びとの話題は株式のことであった。医者や弁護士、引退した教師だけでなく、執事やメイド、ウェイター、タクシーの運転手までもが、株のゲームに参加した。というのは、彼らにとってこれが安全で、確実な金もうけの方法であったからである。彼らにとって、株式市場はアメリカ経済を表わしていて、そしてアメリカ経済は好景気にわいていた。そこで、住宅や自動車、その他の生活用品を買うための金が、株式に投資された。しかし悪夢は突然やってくる。1929年10月24日に始まった株価の下落は、29日（「暗黒の火曜日」）に最大の下げ幅を記録し、11月中旬には最低の水準まで落ち込んだ。株式につぎ込まれた金は、文字どおり紙クズとなって消え、信用取引をしていた人には借金だけが残った。翌年には、失業者の数が600万を数えるまでになり、それ以降アメリカ社会は史上最悪の大不況に沈んでゆくのである。

　『偉大なギャツビー』のなかでも株式市場の活況は触れられている。語り手のニック・キャラウェイは第1次世界大戦から戻ってきた後、「証券の仕事」を学ぶために中西部から東部へ出てくる。そして彼の知り合いもほとんどすべて株取引に関わっているという。この設定も、したがって、あながち根拠がないわけではないのである。この小説は1925年に発表されているから、フィッツジェラルドが4年後の株価の大暴落を予見できたはずはない。しかしこのギャツビーの悲劇は、ある意味で、自らの欲望の消費に浮かれ騒ぐ社会の末路を暗示している。

　この20年代の未曾有の繁栄はアメリカ社会に際限のない物質主義的風潮をもたらした。宣伝広告や新しい月賦販売の登場に刺激されて、アメリカ人は自動

車、ラジオ、電話、冷蔵庫、不動産、株などを次から次へと買うようになり、国民の多くが以前と比較にならないほどの生活水準を楽しむことができるようになった。また人びとは、レクリエーションやレジャーに時間と金を費やすようになった。彼らは"ベーブ"・ルースのホームラン記録に熱狂し、デンプシー対ターニーのボクシングの試合を観るためにスタジアムへ足を運んだ。映画産業はアメリカで最大規模の産業に成長していた。セシル・B・デミル監督のスペクタクル映画『十戒』(1923)が人気を博し、ハロルド・ロイド、バスター・キートン、チャーリー・チャップリンなどの喜劇役者に人気が集まった。ジャズ・エイジを象徴するこの新しい消費主義文化が人びとの日常生活を支配し、彼らの習慣や価値観を変えていった。

　確かに1920年代はテクノロジーの進歩を謳歌するアメリカの繁栄の時代だったが、一方で保守主義の台頭の時代でもあった。第1次世界大戦中の1917年、ロシアでボルシェヴィキ革命が成功すると、共産主義勢力の国内への浸透に怯えるアメリカ社会は、社会の改革者や労働組合の指導者、平和主義者、社会主義者などに「赤」のレッテルをはり、排斥した。1919年から翌年にかけて政府は約6,000人の共産党員嫌疑者を逮捕令状なしで逮捕し、過激な外国人を国外に追放し、労働運動を弾圧した。この〈赤の恐怖〉は一つの象徴的な事件を引き起こした。イタリアからの移民で無政府主義者のニコラ・サッコとバルトロメオ・ヴァンゼッティが、ボストンで十分な証拠もないまま強盗殺人容疑で逮捕され、1921年一方的な検察側の主張に基づき、2人に死刑が宣告された。彼らはイタリアからの移民という経歴と、その政治思想ゆえに有罪になったと考えられ、国の内外で大きな抗議運動が行われた。しかしそれも実らず、1927年2人は処刑された。

　この〈サッコ＝ヴァンゼッティ事件〉はアメリカ社会の共産主義への恐怖を物語っているとともに、他方で移民への強い嫌悪感をも表わしている。19世紀末から20世紀初めにかけてピークに達したアメリカへの移民の流入は、第1次大戦中一時おさまったが、1920年には戦前のレヴェルに戻り、年80万を数えるまでになった。しかし彼らは、イギリスやアイルランド、ドイツといった北西ヨーロッパ諸国から来た、いわゆるアングロ・サクソン系プロテスタントの「旧移民」とは異なり、東ヨーロッパのハンガリー、チェコ、ロシア、南ヨーロ

ッパのカトリックのイタリア、スペイン、ギリシャ、アジアの中国、日本などからの、雑多で、貧しい移民が多かった。これら「新移民」は英語が話せず、姿格好や習慣も異国的だった。したがって、彼らはすぐにはアメリカ社会に同化できず、都市のスラムに移民だけの独自のコミュニティを形成した。

こうした新移民の大規模な流入に対して、旧移民たちは、彼らへの人種的な嫌悪感と、彼らのために賃金が下がり、あるいは職を奪われる警戒感から、移民制限を声高に訴えるようになった。その結果、政府は1924年に16万4,000人、1927年以降は15万人までに移民の数を制限した。こうした移民への反感は『偉大なギャツビー』のなかにも表われている。第1章で上流階級のトム・ブキャナンは、有色人種が北欧人種の文明を破壊すると、外国人への嫌悪感をあらわにする。

人びとの外国人と移民への嫌悪感を助長するのに大きな役割をはたしたのが、クー・クラックス・クランの復活である。彼らは1920年代の反動的な運動のなかでもっとも邪悪なものだった。クー・クラックス・クランは南北戦争後の南部再建時代(1865–77)、奴隷から解放された黒人に反感を抱き、彼らを襲撃した白覆面の白人テロリスト集団である。彼らの勢力は一時衰えた。しかし1920年代、今度はアメリカ生まれの白人でプロテスタントの人びとの優位を叫び、移民、特にカトリックとユダヤ人への反対を主張した。人びとの恐怖心に訴える彼らのやり方は大きな効果をあげ、国民に反移民、反共産主義、反カトリック、反ユダヤ人感情、すなわち不寛容の精神を浸透させるのに役立った。

外国人から自分たちの純粋さを守ろうとする運動は、伝統的価値観が動揺するなかで宗教に拠りどころを求める人々に刺激をあたえた。何百万という人びとが、プロテスタントのなかでも聖書を字義通りに解釈しようとするファンダメンタリストの宗派に惹かれ、その時代の物質万能主義と快楽主義がまん延した社会のなかで自らのアイデンティティを守ろうとした。それを象徴する事件が1925年テネシー州で起きた。その年の初めテネシー州議会は、人類はアダムとイヴを祖先として神によって造られたのではなく、単純な原始形態から次第に変化・発達したという進化論を、公立学校で教えることを禁止する法律を制定していた。まもなくジョン・スコープスという高校の生物の教師がこの法律を破った罪で逮捕された。その年の夏、検察側と弁護側はアメリカでもっとも

著名な論者をたて、法廷で科学と宗教の問題について激論を闘わせ、マスコミはそれを国中に報じた。結局スコープスは有罪になったが、この問題は国民の間に大きな関心を呼び起こした。その後もこの宗教的ファンダメンタリズムは、急速に都市化し近代化が進むアメリカ社会のなかで、伝統的価値観を維持しようとする人びとを惹きつけ、現在にいたるまで生き残っている。

　いま一つ、アメリカ社会の保守化の傾向で『偉大なギャツビー』に大いに関係のあるのが、禁酒法である。アルコール飲料の戦争意欲をおびやかす恐れから、戦時禁酒法が1917年に制定されていたが、それをさらに永久的なものにする憲法修正第18条が1919年1月までに4分の3以上の州議会で承認され、1920年1月から実施された。この法律は0.5％以上アルコール分を含む飲料水の製造、販売、運搬を違法としたもので、事実上ビールを含むすべてのアルコール飲料を禁止するものであった。アメリカにはもともと、ピューリタンの伝統である勤勉や節約を重んじ、浪費や飲酒をいましめる価値観が根強くあった。また第1次世界大戦で敵として戦ったドイツ人への反感から生じた、国内のドイツ系のビール製造会社への反感も、この法律の制定に貢献した。

　これは国民の不道徳へはしる傾向と飲酒に伴う悪徳を抑える道徳的進歩だとして、多くのアメリカ人はこの法律の制定を歓迎した。しかし他方で、この法律を破り、非合法のアルコールを公然と飲むアメリカ人もたくさんいたのも事実である。当然のことながら、この違法な商売が大きな儲けをもたらすことを知った犯罪組織が、間もなくこの分野に進出した。そのなかでもっとも悪名高いのがアル・カポネの組織である。彼はシカゴの違法酒と悪の組織をまとめ、賄賂、脅迫、暴力によって勢力を拡大した。1931年に連邦政府に脱税容疑で逮捕、投獄されるまで、彼はシカゴの暗黒街を支配した。この禁酒法時代、違法なアルコールの製造と運搬で大きな財産をこしらえる新興成金が生まれたが、彼らはフィッツジェラルドのこの小説にも登場する。ギャツビーその人と、犯罪組織に関係のあるマイヤー・ウルフシームがそれである。『偉大なギャツビー』のなかでやたらと頻繁に飲酒の場面が描かれるのを理解するには、禁酒法時代という背景知識が欠かせないのである。

　政治的問題と同様に、社会的問題もこの小説の背景にはある。この小説の登場人物は、この時代の若い世代の雰囲気をかなり忠実に再現している。この小

説に登場する男性の多くは第1次世界大戦に出征し、現実の帰還兵と同じように、多かれ少なかれ戦争の影響を受けて帰還している。故国に戻ってみると、彼らを待ち受けていた観念や思考法が古めかしいものに映り、それらに反抗するのである。女性にもまた、戦後のアメリカ社会が自分たちの自由を制限するように思えた。戦争が始まり、男たちがヨーロッパの戦場へ向かったとき、工場やその他の職場で労働力を補ったのは彼女たちだった。そして男たちが戦争から戻ってきても、女性たちは戦争中に得た社会的、経済的自由を手放したくなかった。さらに1920年に施行された、女性に選挙権を認める憲法修正第19条が追い風となって、女性の自立を促す雰囲気が強まった。1920年代、若者たちは現状を維持することに満足するのを拒絶し、古い価値観に公然と反乱を起こした。

　1920年代のアメリカ社会のもっとも著しい変化は若い女性の風俗で起きた。女性の解放を象徴するように、伝統的な女性らしさの指標であった長い髪を切り落とし、断髪が流行した。女性はまた、ボーイッシュで、ほっそりとしたスタイルを強調しようとして、女性らしさを強調するために作られ女性の体の自由を束縛していたコルセットの使用を止めた。1920年代にはスカートの裾は膝まで上がり、若い世代の親たちを驚かせた頬紅や口紅が、この10年間にへんぴな村にまで急速に広まった。戦後の2、3年の間に数百万のあらゆる年齢層のアメリカ女性がたばこを喫いはじめ、女性が男性といっしょに酒を飲むようになった。また精神分析学者のジークムント・フロイトの学説の流布のおかげで、セックスに対する考え方が開放的になり、抑制されない性生活は精神衛生によいと考えられた。こうした因襲や伝統から解放された1920年代の「新しい女性」は〈フラッパー〉と呼ばれた。彼女たちは、飲酒であれ、喫煙であれ、セックスであれ、因襲に縛られずに行動する権利を主張し、社会生活におけるより大きな個人の自由と平等を求めた。

　フィッツジェラルドはこうした「新しい女性」の社会への反乱を『偉大なギャツビー』のなかに取り入れている。彼は社会の各層で自分を押さえつけている束縛から自由になろうとする女性を描いている。たとえば、トム・ブキャナンの情婦マートルは、社会の階段を登ってゆくことを夢みていて、どんな犠牲を払ってでもそれを成し遂げようとする。トムの妻デイジィは自分が育った抑

圧的な環境から自由になろうと試みるが、束縛から完全には逃れることはできず、結局、金という自分の知っている唯一の確実なものに拠りどころを求める。プロゴルファーのジョーダン・ベイカーも「新しい女性」である。プロゴルファーというのは1920年代の社会的、経済的進歩があって初めて可能となった職業なのである。

　フィッツジェラルドのこの小説を魅力的なものにしている理由の一つは、彼自身が生きた時代と社会を分析している点にある。彼は登場人物を通して1920年代のアメリカ社会の中流、上流階級の生活を活写するだけでなく、それらへの一連の批判をも試みている。『偉大なギャツビー』の人物造形を通して、フィッツジェラルドは、歴史的根拠に基づき、社会的変動と不安に彩られた世界における人間状況を探究するのである。トムやデイズィ、ジョーダンらが社会の階段の一番上にいて、下から登ってくる者の邪魔をしようとするとき、この小説に描かれた「ジャズ・エイジ」の社会は、崩壊の道程を歩みだすことになる。ギャツビーを通してフィッツジェラルドは、活気にみちた「ジャズ・エイジ」に社会の欲求にすなおに耳を傾け、それに応えることで成功した若者を描く。しかしその成功にもかかわらず、不幸にも、彼はそのはかない夢を叶えることはできないのである。フィッツジェラルドのこの物語は、フィクションではあるが、歴史的事実に裏打ちされていて、この点がこの物語を20世紀アメリカ小説の重要な作品の一つにしている。

　上に掲げた英文は『偉大なギャツビー』の第5章から引用したもので、この物語の一つの頂点をなしている。主人公ギャツビーが5年ぶりに、夢にみていたかっての恋人デイズィとの再会をはたす場面である。5年前ギャツビーはデイズィと恋に落ち、結婚を申し込んだが、彼の貧しさゆえに断られていた。この5年の間にギャツビーは酒の密売で財を蓄え、デイズィへの愛をはぐんでいたが、デイズィの方は上流階級のトム・ブキャナンと結婚していた。それゆえ、5年ぶりの2人の再会はぎこちないものにならざるを得ない。この場面でギャツビーは、それまでの自信にあふれた態度とは違って、顔は青ざめ、不安げで、そわそわと落ちつきがない。彼はマントルピースに寄りかかったはずみで、その上にあった「止まった置き時計」を落としそうになる。ここでもフ

ィッツジェラルド一流のシンボリズムが働いている。時計が止まっていたということは、この5年間ギャツビーの時間が止まっていて、彼のデイズィへの思いが少しも変わらなかったことを象徴的に表わしている。また、その時計が落ちて壊れそうになることは、彼の夢、ひいては彼自身の崩壊を暗示している。ギャツビーはデイズィへの思いの烈しさゆえに、自分の夢を大きく育みすぎ、現実のデイズィとの溝を大きくしてしまった。デイズィは彼が思い描いていたような女性ではなかった。彼はデイズィと会ってすぐ、自分の誤りを悟る。そしてここから、彼の崩壊が始まるのである。

　この物語は夢や理想を達成することが、必ずしも幸せに結びつかないことを示している。しかし、それでも人は夢みることを止めない存在であり、特にあらゆる可能性が開かれているアメリカという国に人びとを惹きつけるゆえんでもある。この小説は「アメリカの夢」の矛盾とともに、その魔力をも見事に表わす作品である。

3

　At two o'clock Gatsby put on his bathing-suit and left word with the butler that if anyone phoned word was to be brought to him at the pool. He stopped at the garage for a pneumatic mattress that had amused his guests during the summer, and the chauffeur helped him to pump it up. Then he gave instructions that the open car wasn't to be taken out under any circumstances — and this was strange, because the front right fender needed repair.

　Gatsby shouldered the mattress and started for the pool. Once he stopped and shifted it a little, and the chauffeur asked him if he needed help, but he shook his head and in a moment disappeared among the yellowing trees.

　No telephone message arrived, but the butler went without his sleep and waited for it until four o'clock — until long after there was anyone to give it to if it came. I have an idea that Gatsby himself didn't believe it would come, and perhaps he no longer cared. If that was true he must have felt that he had lost the old warm world, paid a high price for living too long with a single dream. He must have looked up at an unfamiliar sky through frightening leaves and shivered as he found what a grotesque thing a rose is and how raw the sunlight was upon the scarcely created grass. A new world, material without being real, where poor ghosts, breathing dreams like air, drifted fortuitously about... like that ashen, fantastic figure gliding toward him through the amorphous trees.

The chauffeur — he was one of Wolfshiem's protégé — heard the shots — afterwards he could only say that he hadn't thought anything much about them. I drove from the station directly to Gatsby's house and my rushing anxiously up the front steps was the first thing that alarmed anyone. But they knew then, I firmly believe. With scarcely a word said, four of us, the chauffeur, butler, gardener, and I hurried down to the pool.

There was a faint, barely perceptible movement of the water as the fresh flow from one end urged its way toward the drain at the other. With little ripples that were hardly the shadows of waves, the laden mattress moved irregularly down the pool. A small gust of wind that scarcely corrugated the surface was enough to disturb its accidental course with its accidental burden. The touch of a cluster of leaves revolved it slowly, tracing, like the leg of transit, a thin red circle in the water.

It was after we started with Gatsby toward the house that the gardener saw Wilson's body a little way off in the grass, and the holocaust was complete.

Gatsby's house was still empty when I left — the grass on his lawn had grown as long as mine. One of the taxi drivers in the village never took a fare past the entrance gate without stopping for a minute and pointing inside; perhaps it was he who drove Daisy and Gatsby over to East Egg the night of the accident, and perhaps he had made a story about it all his own. I didn't want to hear it and I avoided him when I got off the train.

I spent my Saturday nights in New York because those gleaming, dazzling parties of his were with me so vividly that I could still hear the music and the laughter, faint and incessant, from his garden, and the cars going up and down his drive. One night I did hear a material car there, and saw its lights stop at his front steps. But I didn't investigate. Probably it was some final guest who had been away at the ends of the earth and didn't know that the party was over.

On the last night, with my trunk packed and my car sold to the grocer, I went over and looked at that huge incoherent failure of a house once more. On the white steps an obscene word, scrawled by some boy with a piece of brick, stood out clearly in the moonlight, and I erased it, drawing my shoe raspingly along the stone. Then I wandered down to the beach and sprawled out on the sand.

Most of the big shore places were closed now and there were hardly any lights except the shadowy, moving glow of a ferry-boat across the Sound. And as the moon rose higher the inessential houses began to melt away until gradually I became aware of the old island here that flowered once for Dutch sailors' eyes — a fresh, green breast of the new world. Its vanished trees, the trees that had made way for Gatsby's house, had once pandered in whispers to the last and greatest of all human dreams; for a transitory enchanted moment man must have held his breath in the presence of this continent, compelled into an aesthetic contemplation he neither understood nor desired, face to face for the last time in history with something commensurate to his capacity for wonder.

And as I sat there brooding on the old, unknown world, I thought of Gatsby's wonder when he first picked out the green light at the end of Daisy's dock. He had come a long way to this blue lawn, and his dream must have seemed so close that he could hardly fail to grasp it. He did not know that it was already behind him, somewhere back in that vast obscurity beyond the city, where the dark fields of the republic rolled on under the night.

Gatsby believed in the green light, the orgastic future that year by year recedes before us. It eluded us then, but that's no matter — tomorrow we will run faster, stretch out our arms further... And one fine morning —

　So we beat on, boats against the current, borne back ceaselessly into the past.

　今回は『偉大なギャツビー』のストーリーとこの小説の特徴について述べたい。この物語はニック・キャラウェイ（Nick Carraway）という青年の回想録という形を取っている。彼は1915年にイェール大学を卒業し、第1次世界大戦に従軍する。戦争から戻った後、彼は中西部の故郷の街で退屈な日々を送っていた。そこで都会の活気のある生活に憧れ、1922年の春、東部の大都会ニューヨークへ出て、当時活況を呈していた証券会社に就職する。そこで上流階級の堕落した生活を眼の当たりにするが、一方でそれとは対照的なジェイ・ギャツビー（Jay Gatsby）の一途に自分の夢を追求する真摯な生き方と、彼の悲劇的な死に遭遇する。ギャツビーを死に至らせた東部の世界に幻滅し、中西部の故郷に戻ってこのギャツビーの物語を語る、というのが大まかな概略である。
　物語はニックが中西部の親元を離れ、マンハッタンの南に位置する高級住宅地区、ロング・アイランドのウェスト・エッグの借家にやってくるところから始まる。彼の家は周りの巨大な邸宅と較べると貧弱な建物で、右手には大理石のプールと40エーカー以上もある庭が広がる豪勢な屋敷がある。それがギャツビーという男の邸宅だった。引っ越して間もなくニックは、ロング・アイランド海峡を挟んだ向かい側にあるイースト・エッグ——ウェスト・エッグよりも由緒ある高級住宅がならぶ地区——に住むまたいとこのデイズィ（Daisy）を訪ねる。彼女は社交界の華やかさと女性のか弱さを兼ね備えた蠱惑（こわく）的な女性で、ニックの大学時代の友人トム・ブキャナン（Tom Buchannan）と結婚していた。トムもシカゴの出身で、大学時代フットボールの選手として活躍した、大柄な、堂々とした体格の男である。彼はいわゆる特権階級の息子で、大学時代から金使いが荒く、現在もこれといった定職につかず、ジョージ王朝時代のコロニアル様式の館に住んでいる。彼の言う言葉はすべて高圧的で、横柄な態度は大学時代からいやがられていた。そこにもう1人、デイズィの少女時代からの友人でプロゴルファーのジョーダン・ベイカー（Jordan Baker)という女性が招かれ

ていた。彼女はゴルフのトーナメントでも活躍し、社交界とマスコミで名前を賑わせている人物だ。

　4人はヴェランダで夕食を取りながら夏の予定を話し合っている。トムが人種差別的な有色人種脅威論を軽薄な調子でまくしたてていると、電話が鳴り、執事が用件をトムに伝える。トムが席を立ち、デイジィも後を追うようにいなくなると、ジョーダンはニックに、トムにはニューヨークに「女」がいて、それが夫婦のいさかいの原因になっていると話す。中西部の田舎から出てきたばかりの素朴なニックには、このような込み入った世界がなじめず、「混乱し、少し不愉快」になってトムの館を後にする。自宅に戻り、内にはいる前に月夜の庭でたたずんでいると、隣の屋敷でも誰かが星空を仰いで立っていた。ギャツビーとおぼしき人物は、それから暗い海の向こうに見える桟橋の先端にある「緑色の灯」に両手を差し出すのが見えたが、すぐに闇夜に消えてしまった。

　それから数日後、ニックはトムの「女」に会う羽目になった。トムといっしょにニューヨークへ列車でゆく途中、郊外の〈灰の谷〉(valley of ashes) と呼ばれるスラム街でむりやり降ろされ、ジョージ・ウィルスン (George Wilson) の経営するガソリンスタンド兼自動車修理場へ連れてゆかれたのである。その街は都会のゴミ捨て場のような街で、荒涼として、人間も物も灰色をおびている。そしてそこに、「エクルバーグ博士の眼」がその街を見おろすように立っている。それは半ば朽ちかけた眼医者の広告看板にすぎないのだが、人間の欲望のうごめきを冷ややかな眼差しで見つめているようである。ウィルスンは典型的なこの街の住人で、「生気のない」「青ざめた」男で、トムの車を買いたがっていた。トムの「女」というのはウィルスンの女房マートル (Myrtle) だった。マートルは肉感的な30代中頃の女性で、夫とは異なり、内に秘めた野心を表わすように活気にあふれていた。

　トムとマートルはウィルスンの目を盗んで駅で待ち合わせる手はずを整え、トムとニックは先に出発する。ニューヨークの秘密のアパートに着いたマートルは、彼女の妹と友人を呼びだし、酒盛りを始める。場所も変わり、衣服も着替えると、マートルの人格も一変し、態度が尊大になる。彼女がトムの情婦になったのも、結局トムの階級が持つ金と力が目当てだったようだ。酒の勢いもあって、彼女の口調はトムと同じように、人を見下すような調子になる。しま

いに彼女がトムの妻デイジィのことを言い出すに及んで、トムはマートルに癇癪をおこす。トムは彼女の顔に平手打ちをくらわせ、マートルの鼻の骨を折ってしまう。鮮血が飛び散り、女性の悲鳴が鳴り響く混乱のなか、泥酔したニックはひとりアパートを後にした。

　ニックの隣人ギャツビーの屋敷では、週末になるときまって派手なパーティが催されていた。大勢のきらびやかな服装の人々が集まり、オーケストラがダンス音楽をかなで、酒と食物が思う存分に振る舞われ、乱痴気騒ぎが朝まで続いた。まさに「ジャズ・エイジ」の喧噪を象徴するようなパーティである。あるときニックはギャツビーのパーティに招かれる。行ってみると、彼は招待された数少ない客の1人だった。他の人々は、ただパーティがあると聞いてやってきて、後は「遊園地」の規則に従って楽しみ、ホストのギャツビーに会わずに帰ることもあるという、そんな不思議なパーティだった。客にギャツビーの居場所を尋ねても、誰も分からない。それよりギャツビーが何者かさえも分からないのだ。「かって彼は人を殺したことがある」とか、あるいは「彼はドイツのスパイだった」という噂を言う者もいるが、誰も本当のことは知らない謎の人物であった。

　このような派手なパーティに慣れないニックも、シャンペンを2杯空けるとくつろいだ気分になり、見知らぬ男に親しげに話しかけられる。それが偶然にも、その屋敷の主ギャツビーその人だった。彼は「一生のうち4、5回ぐらいしかでくわすことのないような、永遠の安心感を感じさせる、たぐいまれな微笑」をたたえた30過ぎの青年で、周りの軽薄なパーティ客とは異なり、慎重に言葉を選んで話す印象をニックは受ける。ギャツビーはパーティ客とは交わらず、精神的にも超然としていた。

　しだいにギャツビーと親しくなっていった7月終わりのある朝、ニックはギャツビーに昼食に誘われ、ギャツビーの豪勢なクリーム色の車でニューヨークへ向かう。車のなかでギャツビーはニックに、噂で自分を誤解されたくないと言って、自分の過去を語り始める。それによれば、彼は中西部（「サンフランシスコ」と彼は言う）の裕福な家庭に生まれ、オックスフォード大学で教育を受けた。家族がみな死んでしまい、大きな財産が転がり込んできて、ヨーロッパを大名旅行をしていると、戦争が勃発した。戦争で死ぬものと思っていたら、

大きな戦功をあげ、勲章までもらったという。サンフランシスコを中西部というギャツビーの話をどこまで信用したらいいのか迷っているニックに、ギャツビーは、折り入ってお願いがある、今日の午後ミス・ベイカーがそれを君に伝えてくれるはずだ、と奇妙なことを言う。

　ニューヨークの42丁目のレストランに着くと、マイヤー・ウルフシーム（Meyer Wolfshiem）という男が2人を待っていた。彼はギャツビーの仕事仲間のユダヤ人で、ギャツビーによれば、1919年に行われた大リーグのワールド・シリーズで八百長試合を仕組んだ男だという。ギャツビーと犯罪組織との関わりを連想させる男である。勘定を払おうとすると、ニックはトム・ブキャナンを見つけ、彼をギャツビーに紹介する。するとギャツビーは顔色を変え、突然何も言わずに姿を消してしまった。

　その日の午後ニックはプラザ・ホテルの喫茶室でジョーダン・ベイカーに会った。すると彼女はトムの妻デイズィとギャツビーの昔のいきさつについて話を始める。それによると、結婚前に住んでいたケンタッキー州ルイヴィルの少女時代、デイズィはそこに駐屯していた陸軍の中尉と恋に落ちた。その相手がジェイ・ギャツビーという若者だという。彼女の両親は一介の陸軍士官にすぎない男と娘のつきあいを止めさせ、2年後シカゴの大金持ちトム・ブキャナンと娘を結婚させた。結婚式の前の晩、デイズィはギャツビーからの手紙を握りしめ、泣き暴れたという。しかし式当日は、トムから贈られた35万ドルの真珠の首飾りをつけ、「身ぶるいひとつ見せないで」結婚した。翌年には娘が生まれたが、しかし結婚したときからトムの女遊びは始まり、デイズィは必ずしも幸せではないとジョーダンは言う。また彼女は、ギャツビーが入江をはさんでデイズィの住むイースト・エッグの向かい側に豪勢な屋敷を買ったのも、偶然ではないと言う。毎週週末に豪華なパーティを開いたのも、ひとえにデイズィの関心を自分に向けさせるためだった。自分の富を誇示することで、デイズィと再会をはたそうとしたのだった。そこでジョーダンは、ギャツビーから託された彼の願いをニックに告げる。それは、ニックがデイズィを自宅に招いて、自分とデイズィの再会の仲立ちをして欲しいというものだった。

　その日は土砂降りの雨だった。ギャツビーは人をやってニックの家の庭の芝を刈らせ、「温室」ほどの花をニックの家へ運ばせた。彼は1時間前にニックの

家へやってきたが、少年のようにそわそわとして落ち着かない。しかも、デイズィがドアをノックして家のなかに入ってくると、姿を隠してしまう。しかし30分ほどふたりだけで過ごすと、彼はまったく別人になっていた。ふたりは昔の愛を確かめ合い、「幸福感が彼の体から放射」している。ギャツビーは夢を実現させたのだ。それから3人は隣のギャツビーの屋敷に移り、デイズィは一部屋、一部屋の豪華さに感嘆する。寝室でギャツビーはイギリスから取り寄せたという多様な色彩のシャツの山を見せ、テーブルの上にいくつかを広げてみせる。するとデイズィは、感激のあまりシャツの山に顔を押しつけ、激しく泣き出してしまう。ニックはそんな現実のデイズィと、ギャツビーが5年間温めてきた彼女の理想像のギャップの大きさを想像し、ふたりの前途について一抹の不安がニックの胸をよぎるのだった。

　ここでニックは読者にギャツビーの過去について多少の情報を提供する。ギャツビーはノース・ダコタ州の農家に生まれたときはジェイムズ・ギャッツという名前だった。それが17歳のときスーペリオル湖でダン・コウディという人物に出会ったときから、彼は新たな人生を創造し始める。名前をジェイ・ギャツビーと改め、コウディを人生の師として付き従い、アメリカ大陸をくまなく旅して歩いたという。ここに、貧しい身分から身を起こし、たゆまぬ努力によって成功を築くという、「アメリカの成功の夢」の神話のパターンが表われている。

　その後ギャツビーとデイズィはニックのいないところで頻繁に会っていたらしい。そしてトムも妻デイズィの単独行動がだんだん気になり始めたらしく、ある時デイズィに付いてギャツビーの派手なパーティにやってきた。そこでギャツビーはデイズィとダンスを踊り、その後ふたりはニックの家の玄関先の石段に30分ほど腰を落ちつけていた。パーティの客がすべて帰った後で、ギャツビーはニックに、デイズィにトムと別れて5年前に戻り、自分とやり直して欲しいと言っても、彼女は聞き入れてくれない、と不満を述べる。それは無茶な要求で、「過去はやり直せないよ」というニックに対し、ギャツビーは「もちろん、やり直せるさ！」と言い張るのだった。ギャツビーの時間は5年前で止まっていて、彼は現在ではなく、過去に生きているのだ。

　その後ブキャナン夫妻の間に何かあったらしく、ある日ニックはギャツビーとジョーダンともにデイズィの館に昼食に招待される。その日は異常に暑い日

で、そうでなくても気まずいギャツビーとトム、デイズィの関係をより不愉快なものにした。トムが電話をかけているすきを盗んで、デイズィはギャツビーにキスをし、「愛しているわ」と彼を安心させる。しかししばらくたつと、夫とギャツビーの間の息苦しさにたえかねて、これからみんなでマンハッタンへ行こうと言い出した。トムは自分の妻とギャツビーの間で交わされる熱い視線に愕然として、あわてて妻の提案に同意する。

　トムはギャツビーと車を交換し、ウイスキーのビンをつかんでデイズィといっしょにギャツビーのクリーム色のでかい車に乗り込もうとするが、妻は彼の腕をすり抜け、ギャツビーと2人でトムの青いクーペに乗り込んでしまう。仕方なく、トムはニックとジョーダンを乗せてマンハッタンへ向かった。途中給油のためにウィルスンのガソリンスタンドに立ち寄ったトムは、ウィルスンが女房のマートルの情事に気づき、彼女を連れて西部へ行こうとしているのを知る。妻と情婦の両方を失う可能性に怯えたトムは、プラザ・ホテルに着くなり、ギャツビーに悪態をつき始める。それに対してギャツビーは、「奥さんはあなたを愛していないし、これまでも愛したことがなかった」と告げ、デイズィに同意を求める。いまギャツビーを愛していることは認めるデイズィだが、これまでのトムとの過去の生活までも否定するギャツビーの過大な要求に泣き崩れた。トムは妻とは別れないと宣言し、ギャツビーの暗い素性を暴き始める。こいつは犯罪組織と関係があり、違法な酒の密売で財を築き、恐喝まがいの行為を平気でやる男だ、と暴露する。怒号の飛び交う混乱のなか、ギャツビーは自分のクリーム色の車でデイズィと自宅へ戻っていった。

　少し遅れてジョーダンとトムの車でイースト・エッグへ戻る途中、ニックは交通事故の現場に遭遇した。被害者はウィルスンの妻マートルで、夫の手から逃げようとして高速道路に飛び出し、黄色の車にひき逃げされたという。目撃者の話から、3人はそれがギャツビーの車であると確信した。イースト・エッグに戻ったニックは、その日の混乱と、上流社会の道徳的堕落にうんざりし、ひとりで自宅へ帰ろうとする。そこでギャツビーに出会い、車を運転していたのがデイズィだったこと、しかし彼が責任を取るつもりであることを知った。

　次の日の朝ニックはギャツビーを訪ね、すぐに車は発見されるから、1週間ほどニューヨークを離れるよう勧める。しかし、ギャツビーはデイズィのもと

を離れるつもりは少しもない。彼は自分の過去とデイズィとのいきさつをニックに語った。ギャツビーのデイズィへの愛の純粋さに感動したニックは、別れ際に、デイズィからの電話を待っているというギャツビーに、「あいつらは腐ったやつらだよ。……あなたは、あいつらをみんないっしょにしただけの値打ちがある」と言い残し、マンハッタンの会社へ向かった。一方、妻をひき殺されたウィルスンは、気が動転している。復讐にとり憑かれた彼は、その日の午後、トムから車の持ち主を聞き出した。そして自宅のプールでマットの上に浮かんでいるギャツビーを射殺し、後に彼自身も死体で発見された。

ギャツビーの葬式はさびしいものだった。すべてニックが手はずを整え、参列したのはニックと、ミネソタ州からやってきたヘンリー・ギャッツというギャツビーの父親だけだった。トムとデイズィはギャツビーが亡くなった当日、行き先も告げずに旅立っていた。ウルフシームもギャツビーと関わりを持つのを拒んだ。ニックはそれまでのギャツビーとデイズィ、トム、ジョーダン、自分のいきさつを思い浮かべ、「この話は、けっきょく、西部の物語だった」という思いに打たれる。東部の世界には何か歪んだ要素があって、自分たち西部の人間を東部の生活に適合させないのだ。そう考えたニックは、故郷へ帰ろうと決意するのだった。

東部を離れる前夜、ニックはいま一度ギャツビーの屋敷を訪ねた。そして誰もいない砂浜に寝そべり、ギャツビーが夢を抱いてここまでたどり着いた長い旅路を、初めて新大陸を眼にしたオランダ人の感動と重ね合わせて考える。そして、人は一刻、一刻と過去へ流されて行くが、それにあらがうように絶えず未来に向かって人は夢を見つづける、というアメリカの夢の宿命に、ニックはたどり着くのだった。

　以上が、この小説のストーリーである。
　つぎに、この小説のいくつかの特色について解説を試みたい。前にも述べたように、この小説の大きな特徴の1つは、ニック・キャラウェイという第1人称の語り手がいることである。この事実の意味は、他の形式の小説と比較してみれば容易に理解できる。たとえば、作者が全能の語り手となって、小説内で起きる出来事の理由や登場人物の心理をすべて解説する、ホーソーンの『緋文

字』(1850) のような小説がある。他方、小説の主人公が「私」('I') となって自分についての物語を語る、トウェインの『ハックルベリー・フィンの冒険』(1885) のような小説がある。それに対してこの『偉大なギャツビー』は、語り手のニックがこの物語の参加者となり、主人公ジェイ・ギャツビーについて見聞したことを語るという形式を取る。この語りの形式（narrative mode）の利点は、推理小説の形式に似ていることからも分かるように、劇的効果を生みやすく、読者の興味をつなぎ止めることができる。この小説でいえば、ギャツビーに関する知識はニックの経験をとおして、間接的に読者に少しずつ伝えられるので、最後まで読まないと、読者にはギャツビーの本当の正体は分からない仕掛けになっている。それとは逆に、この技法の弱点は、語り手が物語の参加者であるために、彼が経験しないことは読者に伝えられないという、作者の側にもどかしさが生まれる点である。この小説でいうと、第8章で妻をひき殺された後、気が動転したジョージ・ウィルスンの様子が語られるが、ここでフッツジェラルドの語りは破綻している。ニックはその場にはいなかったのだから、ウィルスンの様子を彼が語られるはずもないのだ。ここではやむを得ず、作者が顔をだしている。しかしながら、大体において、ニック・キャラウェイという語り手を取ったことは、ギャツビーの物語を客観的に読者に伝えるという点で、成功しているといえる。

　つぎに、「アメリカの夢／アメリカン・ドリーム」というこの小説のテーマである。この言葉は一般によく耳にするが、「ジャパニーズ・ドリーム」とか「フレンチ・ドリーム」などという言葉は聞いたことがない。それはどうしてだろうか。それはアメリカが移民の国であることに、大いに関係があるように思う。1492年のコロンブスから、現代の中南米からの不法移民にいたるまで、アメリカへ渡ってくる者はすべて、故国でさまざまな理由で才能の発揮を阻まれ、アメリカでの可能性に夢を託し、危険を冒して海を渡ったのである。この可能性を提供できることが、アメリカの力の源泉であり、それが多くの移民をアメリカへ惹きつけた理由でもある。19世紀にはホレイショー・アルジャー（Horatio Alger 1834–99）が『ボロ着のディック』（*Ragged Dick* 1868）を初めとする一連の成功物語でその夢に表現をあたえ、公式化した。それ以来、この「アメリカの夢」は重要なテーマとなったのだが、『偉大なギャツビー』の特色は、こ

のテーマの光の面ではなく、陰の面を描いている点にある。ジェイムズ・ギャッツというノース・ダコタの貧しい農家の息子が、不正な手段にせよ、自らの才覚で大きな富を築き、夢だった昔の恋人の愛を取り戻すことに成功する。しかし、まさにその夢の崇高な純粋さゆえに、ギャツビーは恋人の俗悪さを見抜けず、最後に彼女に裏切られ、悲劇的な死を迎える。それから、この小説にはもう1人、アメリカの夢を追求する人間がいる。それはトムの情婦となるマートルで、彼女は自らの肉体を武器に社会の階段を登って行こうとする。しかし彼女も、最後には、自分の追求するアメリカの夢の象徴である、豪華なクリーム色の車にはねられ、自分の夢に裏切られるのである。このように、この小説は「アメリカの夢」の負の面を描き、アメリカ社会の物質主義的傾向への見事な社会批評となっているのである。

　この小説のもう1つの重要なテーマは、アメリカの「東部」と「西／中西部」の対立である。これは「都会」対「自然」というテーマや、ヘンリー・ジェイムズが得意とした「新大陸」対「旧大陸」というテーマを変奏したものであり、またヨーロッパの小説にみられる「文明」対「野蛮」というテーマの裏返しでもある。このテーマは、単純化して言えば、文明と伝統が染み込んだ東部よりも、自由と無垢にあふれた西／中西部に、アメリカ的価値があることを強調するものである。たとえば、ヘミングウェイがこの小説とともにアメリカ文学は始まる、と言った『ハックルベリー・フィンの冒険』がそのいい例である。浮浪児のハックは文明社会の束縛を逃れ、大自然のミシシッピ河の筏（いかだ）の上で人間の尊厳とか自由といった価値を見いだすのである。『偉大なギャツビー』では、語り手のニックが「これは結局、西部の物語だった」と言っているように、西部の価値を身につけた若者たちが、東部の世界の道徳的腐敗に汚染され、身を滅ぼしてゆく、というのがこの小説の基調となっている。アメリカ小説が自由とか無垢という価値を重要視する理由は、おそらくこの国が移民の国であることに関係があるのだろう。伝統に縛られず、たえず自己を新たに革新したいという、移民の先祖から受け継いだ習い性が、アメリカ人の心のなかに深く染み込んでいるのであろう。

　初めに引用した英文は、前半が第8章の終わりの部分で、後半が第9章の終

わり、つまりこの小説の一番最後の部分である。最初の場面は、ギャツビーが射殺される直前の光景を語り手のニックが想像した場面である。ギャツビーは長く夢を見すぎたために、大きな代償を払わなければならなかった。そして、彼の崇高な夢も、グロテスクなものに変質してしまった、というニックの認識を示している。

　この小説の最後の場面は、ニックが東部を離れる前夜、ギャツビーの屋敷の砂浜に寝そべり、ギャツビーの人生を振り返る場面である。「オランダ人」とあるのは、ニューヨークをオランダ人が最初に植民したという歴史に言及したものである。現在のマンハッタンを先住民マナハッタ族から24ドル相当の品物でオランダ人が買い取り、そこをニュー・アムステルダムと命名した。ここでは、「緑色の灯」という希望や夢を表わす象徴を用いて、ギャツビーの夢とオランダからの最初の移住者の夢を重ね合わせ、ギャツビーの夢が最初のアメリカ人から普遍的に流れている夢であることを示唆している。

使用テキスト：

F. Scott Fitzgerald, *The Great Gatsby*, Penguin Books 1974

参考文献：

フィッツジェラルド『グレート・ギャツビー』新潮文庫　昭和49年
野崎孝編『フィッツジェラルド』(20世紀英米文学案内7) 研究社　1966年
刈田元司編『フィッツジェラルドの文学　"アメリカの夢"とその死』荒地出版　1982年
F・L・アレン『オンリー・イエスタデイ　1920年代・アメリカ』研究社　昭和50年
Judith S. Baughman ed., *American Decades 1920–1929*, Gale Research Inc. 1996
Gary B. Nash, et al. ed., *The American People : Creating a Nation and a Society, Vol.2 : Since 1865*, Harper Collins College Publishers 1994

第4章 公民権運動とキング牧師の説教

1. A Knock at Midnight

Martin Luther King, Jr.

Which of you who has a friend will go to him at midnight and say to him, " Friend, lend me three loaves ; for a friend of mine has arrived on a journey, and I have nothing to set before him " ? (Luke 11 : 5–6, rsv)

Although this parable is concerned with the power of persistent prayer, it may also serve as a basis for our thought concerning many contemporary problems and the role of the church in grappling with them. It is midnight in the parable ; it is also midnight in our world, and the darkness is so deep that we can hardly see which way to turn.

It is midnight within the social order. On the international horizon nations are engaged in a colossal and bitter contest for supremacy. Two world wars have been fought within a generation, and the clouds of another war are dangerously low. Man now has atomic and nuclear weapons that could within seconds completely destroy the major cities of the world. Yet the arms race continues and nuclear tests still explode in the atmosphere, with the grim prospect that the very air we breathe will be poisoned by radioactive fallout. Will these circumstances and weapons bring the annihilation of the human race ?

When confronted by midnight in the social order we have in the past turned to science for help. And little wonder ! On so many occasions science has saved us. When we were in the midnight of physical limitation and material inconvenience, science lifted us to the bright morning of physical and material comfort. When we were in the midnight of crippling ignorance and superstition, science brought us to the daybreak of the free and open mind. When we were in the midnight of dread plagues and diseases, science, through surgery, sanitation, and the wonder drugs, ushered in the bright day of physical health, thereby prolonging our lives and making for greater security and physical well-being. How naturally we turn to science in a day when the problems of the world are so ghastly and ominous.

But alas! science cannot now rescue us, for even the scientist is lost in the terrible midnight of our age. Indeed, science gave us the very instruments that threaten to bring universal suicide. So modern man faces a dreary and frightening midnight in the social order.

This midnight in man's external collective is paralleled by midnight in his internal individual life. It is midnight within the psychological order. Everywhere paralyzing fears harrow people by day and haunt them by night. Deep clouds of anxiety and depression are suspended in our mental skies. More people are emotionally disturbed today than at any other time of human history. The psychopathic wards of our hospitals are crowded, and the most popular psychologists today are the psychoanalysts. Bestsellers in psychology are books such as *Man Against Himself, The Neurotic Personality of Our Times, and Modern Man in Search of a Soul*. Bestsellers in religion are such books as *Peace of Mind* and *Peace of Soul*. The popular clergyman preaches soothing sermons on " How to Be Happy " and " How to Relax." Some have been tempted to revise Jesus' command to read, " Go ye into all the world, keep your blood pressure down, and, lo, I will make you a well-adjusted personality." All of this is indicative that it is midnight within the inner lives of men and women.

It is also midnight within the moral order. At midnight colours lose their distinctiveness and become a sullen shade of grey. Moral principles have lost their distinctiveness. For modern man, absolute right and wrong are a matter of what the majority is doing. Right and wrong are relative to likes and dislikes and the customs of a particular community. We have unconsciously applied Einstein's theory of relativity, which properly described the physical universe, to the moral and ethical realm.

Midnight is the hour when men desperately seek to obey the eleventh commandment, "Thou shalt not get caught." According to the ethic of midnight, the cardinal sin is to be caught and the cardinal virtue is to get by. It is all right to lie, but one must lie with real finesse. It is all right to steal, if one is so dignified that, if caught, the charge becomes embezzlement, not robbery. It is permissible even to hate, if one so dresses his hating in the garments of love that hating appears to be loving. The Darwinian concept of the survival of the fittest has been substituted by a philosophy of the survival of the slickest. This mentality has brought a tragic breakdown of moral standards, and the midnight of moral degeneration deepens.

As in the parable, so in our world today, the deep darkness of midnight is interrupted by the sound of a knock. On the door of the church millions of people knock. In this country the roll of church members is longer than ever before. More than one hundred and fifteen million people are at least paper members of some church or synagogue. This represents an increase of 100 per cent since 1929, although the population has increased by only 31 per cent.

Visitors to Soviet Russia, whose official policy is atheistic, report that the churches in that nation not only are crowded, but that attendance continues to grow. Harrison Salisbury, in an article in *The New York Times*, states that Communist officials are disturbed that so many young people express a growing interest in the church and religion. After forty years of the most vigorous efforts to suppress religion, the hierarchy of the Communist party now faces the inescapable fact that millions of people are knocking on the door of the church.

This numerical growth should not be overemphasized. We must not be tempted to confuse spiritual power and large numbers. Jumboism, as someone has called it, is an utterly fallacious standard for measuring positive power. An increase in quantity does not automatically bring an increase in quality. A larger membership does not necessarily represent a correspondingly increased commitment to Christ. Almost always the creative, dedicated minority has made the world better. But although a numerical growth in church membership does not necessarily reflect a concomitant increase in ethical commitment, millions of people do feel that the church provides an answer to the deep confusion that encompasses their lives. It is still the one familiar landmark where the weary traveller by midnight comes. It is the one house which stands where it has always stood, the house to which the man travelling at midnight either comes or refuses to come. Some decide not to come. But the many who come and knock are desperately seeking a little bread to tide them over.

The traveller asks for three loaves of bread. He wants the bread of faith. In a generation of so many colossal disappointments, men have lost faith in God, faith in man, and faith in the future. Many feel as did William Wilberforce, who in 1801 said, "I dare not marry-the future is so unsettled," or as did William Pitt, who in 1806 said, "There is scarcely anything round us but ruin and despair." In the midst of staggering disillusionment, many cry for the bread of faith.

There is also a deep longing for the bread of hope. In the early years of this century many people did not hunger for this bread. The days of the first telephones, automobiles, and aeroplanes gave them a radiant optimism. They worshipped at the shrine of inevitable progress. They believed that every new scientific achievement lifted man to higher levels of perfection. But then a series of tragic developments, revealing the selfishness and corruption of man, illustrated with frightening clarity the truth of Lord Acton's dictum, "Power tends to corrupt and absolute power corrupts absolutely." This awful discovery led to one of the most colossal breakdowns of optimism in history.

For so many people, young and old, the light of hope went out, and they roamed wearily in the dark chambers of pessimism. Many concluded that life has no meaning. Some agreed with the philosopher Schopenhauer that life is an endless pain with a painful end, and that life is a tragicomedy played over and over again with only slight changes in costume and scenery. Others cried out with Shakespeare's Macbeth that life

is a tale

Told by an idiot, full of sound and fury,

Signifying nothing.

But even in the inevitable moments when all seems hopeless, men know that without hope they cannot really live, and in agonizing desperation they cry for the bread of hope.

And there is the deep longing for the bread of love. Everybody wishes to love and be loved. He who feels that he is not loved feels that he does not count. Much has happened in the modern world to make men feel that they do not belong. Living in a world which has become oppressively impersonal, many of us have come to feel that we are little more than numbers. Ralph Borsodi in an arresting picture of a world wherein numbers have replaced persons writes that the modern mother is often maternity case No.8434 and her child, after being fingerprinted and footprinted, becomes No.8003, and that a funeral in a large city is an event in Parlour B with Class B flowers and decorations at which Preacher No.14 officiates and Musician No.84 sings Selection No.174. Bewildered by this tendency to reduce man to a card in a vast index, man desperately searches for the bread of love.

When the man in the parable knocked on his friend's door and asked for the three loaves of bread, he received the impatient retort, "Do not bother me ; the door is now shut, and my children are with me in bed ; I cannot get up and give you anything." How often have men experienced a similar disappointment when at midnight they knock on the door of the church. Millions of Africans, patiently knocking on the door of the Christian church where they seek the bread of social justice, have either been altogether ignored or told to wait until later, which almost always means never. Millions of American Negroes, starving for the want of the bread of freedom, have knocked again and again on the door of so-called white churches, but they have usually been greeted by a cold indifference or a blatant hypocrisy. Even the white religious leaders, who have a heartfelt desire to open the door and provide the bread, are often more cautious than courageous and more prone to follow the expedient than the ethical path. One of the shameful tragedies of history is that the very institution which should remove man from the midnight of racial segregation participates in creating and perpetuating the midnight.

In the terrible midnight of war men have knocked on the door of the church to ask for the bread of peace, but the church has often disappointed them. What more pathetically reveals the irrelevancy of the church in present-day world affairs than its witness regarding war? In a world gone mad with arms buildups, chauvinistic passions, and imperialistic exploitation, the church has either endorsed these activities or remained appallingly silent. During the last two world wars, national churches even functioned as the ready lackeys of the state, sprinkling holy water upon the battleships and joining the mighty armies in singing, "Praise the Lord and pass the ammunition." A weary world, pleading desperately for peace, has often found the church morally sanctioning war.

And those who have gone to the church to seek the bread of economic justice have been left in the frustrating midnight of economic privation. In many instances the church has so aligned itself with the privileged classes and so defended the status quo that it has been unwilling to answer the knock at midnight. The Greek Church in Russia allied itself with the status quo and became so inextricably bound to the despotic czarist regime that it became impossible to be rid of the corrupt political and social system without being rid of the church. Such is the fate of every ecclesiastical organization that allies itself with things-as-they-are.

The church must be reminded that it is not the master or the servant of the state, but rather the conscience of the state. It must be the guide and the critic of the state, and never its tool. If the church does not recapture its prophetic zeal, it will become an irrelevant social club without moral or spiritual authority. If the church does not participate actively in the struggle for peace and for economic and racial justice, it will forfeit the loyalty of millions and cause men everywhere to say that it has atrophied its will. But if the church will free itself from the shackles of a deadening status quo, and, recovering its great historic mission, will speak and act fearlessly and insistently in terms of justice and peace, it will enkindle the imagination of mankind and fire the souls of men, imbuing them with a glowing and ardent love for truth, justice, and peace. Men far and near will know the church as a great fellowship of love that provides light and bread for lonely travellers at midnight.

While speaking of the laxity of the church, I must not overlook the fact that the so-called Negro church has also left men disappointed at midnight. I say so-called Negro church because ideally there can be no Negro or white church. It is to their everlasting shame that white Christians developed a system of racial segregation within the church, and inflicted so many indignities upon its Negro worshippers that they had to organize their own churches.

Two types of Negro churches have failed to provide bread. One burns with emotionalism, and the other freezes with classism. The former, reducing worship to entertainment, places more emphasis on volume than on content and confuses spirituality with muscularity. The danger in such a church is that the members may have more religion in their hands and feet than in their hearts and souls. At midnight this type of church has neither the vitality nor the relevant gospel to feed hungry souls.

The other type of Negro church that feeds no midnight traveller has developed a class system and boasts of its dignity, its membership of professional people, and its exclusiveness. In such a church the worship service is cold and meaningless, the music dull and uninspiring, and the sermon little more than a homily on current events. If the pastor says too much about Jesus Christ, the members feel that he is robbing the pulpit of dignity. If the choir sings a Negro spiritual, the members claim an affront to their class status. This type of church tragically fails to recognize that worship at its best is a social experience in which people from all levels of life come together to affirm their oneness and unity under God. At midnight men are altogether ignored because of their limited education, or they are given bread that has been hardened by the winter of morbid class consciousness.

In the parable we notice that after the man's initial disappointment, he continued to knock on his friend's door. Because of his importunity — his persistence — he finally persuaded his friend to open the door. Many men continue to knock on the door of the church at midnight, even after the church has so bitterly disappointed them, because they know the bread of life is there. The church today is challenged to proclaim God's Son, Jesus Christ, to be the hope of men in all of their complex personal and social problems. Many will continue to come in quest of answers to life's problems. Many young people who knock on the door are perplexed by the uncertainties of life, confused by daily disappointments, and disillusioned by the ambiguities of history. Some who come have been taken from their schools and careers and cast in the role of soldiers. We must provide them with the fresh bread of hope and imbue them with the conviction that God has the power to bring good out of evil. Some who come are tortured by a nagging guilt resulting from their wandering in the midnight of ethical relativism and their surrender to the doctrine of self-expression. We must lead them to Christ who will offer them the fresh bread of forgiveness. Some who knock are tormented by the fear of death as they move toward the evening of life. We must provide them with the bread of faith in immortality, so that they may realize that this earthly life is merely an embryonic prelude to a new awakening.

Midnight is a confusing hour when it is difficult to be faithful. The most inspiring word that the church must speak is that no midnight long remains. The weary traveller by midnight who asks for bread is really seeking the dawn. Our eternal message of hope is that dawn will come. Our slave foreparents realized this. They were never unmindful of the fact of midnight, for always there was the rawhide whip of the overseer and the auction block where families were torn asunder to remind them of its reality. When they thought of the agonizing darkness of midnight, they sang:

Oh, nobody knows de trouble I've seen,

Glory Hallelujah!

Sometimes I'm up, sometimes I'm down,

Oh, yes, Lord,

Sometimes I'm almost to de groun',

Oh, yes, Lord,

Oh, nobody knows de trouble I've seen,

Glory Hallelujah!

Encompassed by a staggering midnight but believing that morning would come, they sang:

I'm so glad trouble don't last alway.

O my Lord, O my Lord, what shall I do?

Their positive belief in the dawn was the growing edge of hope that kept the slaves faithful amid the most barren and tragic circumstances.

Faith in the dawn arises from the faith that God is good and just. When one believes this, he knows that the contradictions of life are neither final nor ultimate. He can walk through the dark night with the radiant conviction that all things work together for good for those that love God. Even the most starless midnight may herald the dawn of some great fulfillment.

At the beginning of the bus boycott in Montgomery, Alabama, we set up a voluntary car pool to get the people to and from their jobs. For eleven long months our car pool functioned extraordinarily well. Then Mayor Gayle introduced a resolution instructing the city's legal department to file such proceedings as it might deem proper to stop the operation of the car pool or any transportation system growing out of the bus boycott. A hearing was set for Tuesday, November 13, 1956.

At our regular weekly mass meeting, scheduled the night before the hearing, I had the responsibility of warning the people that the car pool would probably be enjoined. I knew that they had willingly suffered for nearly twelve months, but could we now ask them to walk back and forth to their jobs? And if not, would we be forced to admit that the protest had failed? For the first time I almost shrank from appearing before them.

When the evening came, I mustered sufficient courage to tell them the truth. I tried, however, to conclude on a note of hope. "We have moved all of these months," I said, "in the daring faith that God is with us in our struggle. The many experiences of days gone by have vindicated that faith in a marvellous way. Tonight we must believe that a way will be made out of no way." Yet I could feel the cold breeze of pessimism pass over the audience. The night was darker than a thousand midnights. The light of hope was about to fade and the lamp of faith to flicker.

A few hours later, before Judge Carter, the city argued that we were operating a "private enterprise" without a franchise. Our lawyers argued brilliantly that the car pool was a voluntary "share-a-ride" plan provided without profit as a service by Negro churches. It became obvious that Judge Carter would rule in favour of the city.

At noon, during a brief recess, I noticed an unusual commotion in the courtroom. Mayor Gayle was called to the back room. Several reporters moved excitedly in and out of the room. Momentarily a reporter came to the table where, as chief defendent, I sat with the lawyers. "Here is the decision that you have been waiting for," he said. "Read this release."

In anxiety and hope, I read these words: "The United States Supreme Court today unanimously ruled bus segregation unconstitutional in Montgomery, Alabama." My heart throbbed with an inexpressible joy. The darkest hour of our struggle had become the first hour of victory. Someone shouted from the back of the courtroom, " God Almighty has spoken from Washington."

The dawn will come. Disappointment, sorrow, and despair are born at midnight, but morning follows. " Weeping may endure for a night," says the Psalmist, " but joy cometh in the morning." This faith adjourns the assemblies of hopelessness and brings new light into the dark chambers of pessimism.

2. "A Knock at Midnight" を読む

はじめに

　A Knock at Midnight はマーティン・ルーサー・キング・ジュニア（Martin Luther King, JR. 1929-68）の著書 *The Strength to Love*[1] に収められた説教のひとつである。ここでは *A Knock at Midnight* の分析を通して、1950年代のアメリカ合衆国南部における公民権運動と教会の関係を考察していきたい。周知のように、1950年代のアメリカ合衆国南部社会では、1954年のブラウン判決と1年後のブラウンⅡ判決を受け、NAACPを代表とする団体が黒人のための公民権獲得を求めて活動を繰り広げていた。その典型とも言えるのが1955年12月1日に起きたローザ・パークス（Rosa Parks）事件に端を発する、アラバマ州モントゴメリーのバス・ボイコット運動である。運動そのものの経緯は同じキングの *Stride Toward Freedom*[2] に詳しく述べられているが、ここでは信仰面からバス・ボイコット運動に言及した説教 *A Knock at Midnight* を取り上げ、人種差別問題と取り組む教会をキングが神学的にどのように理解していたのかを見ていきたい。

Ⅰ

　説教、*A Knock at Midnight* の聖書テキストは『ルカによる福音書』11：5-6 である。本章ではキングの説教分析の前提として、この箇所の新約的使信をキングの解釈に基づいて、確認しておきたい。テキストとして選ばれているのは 5-6 の 2 節にすぎないが、キングの説教は少なく見積もっても 8 節までの内容を含んでいる。また、編集者ルカが譬話として構成したのも 11：5-8 の箇所である。そこで、ここでは該当箇所を含む譬話全体を対象として考察を行う。

⁵Which of you who has a friend will go to him at midnight and say to him, 'Friend, lend me three loaves; ⁶for a friend of mine has arrived on a journey, and I have nothing to set before him'; ⁷and he will answer from within, 'Do not bother me; the door is now shut, and my children are with me in bed; I cannot get up and give you anything'? ⁸I tell you, though he will not get up and give him anything because he is his friend, yet because of his importunity he will rise and give him whatever he needs. (rsv)

キングも述べているように、これは絶え間のない祈りの必要性についての譬話である。実際には9節以下（13節まで）に、譬話の思想を強調するメッセージが組み合わされて全体が構成されている。[3] 一方で、9節以下の後半部とほとんど同内容のメッセージがマタイによる福音書7:7-11にも存在する。それに着目すると、キングは、マタイとは重複しない、ルカ独自の部分をあえてテキストとして用いる意図があったことが分かる。具体的には、説教タイトルの一部にもなっている"midnight"をキーワードとして用いることを前提に、説教の対象である南部の黒人キリスト者たちの社会的現状を十分に認識した上で、祈りの必要性に関する説教を行おうとしたことが理解できる。

さらに、キング自身このテキストを the power of persistent prayer と語っているように、キングはこのテキストが先行する「主の祈り」と内容的関連性を有していることを意識している。それは、編集者ルカ自身の意図するところでもあったが、ルカ11:9-13に相当するマタイ7:7-11もまた「主の祈り」と密接に関係を持って構成されていることを考えると、ルカにはあえてマタイには存在しない特殊資料として11:5-8の挿話を加えた特別の理由があると想像される。おそらく、それはルカが祈りの重要性（「主の祈り」の重要性）を理解させるのに際し、譬話を挿入することで、"読者に興味を引き起こさせるような一回的出来事、往々にして躓きを与えさえする特殊な物語"[4] としての効果を期待したと考えられる。このルカの姿勢はこの箇所をテキストとして用いるキングにもそのまま当てはまる。キングは聴衆の興味を喚起した上で、ルカが"この譬話の比較点を、後の文脈にイエスの「ロギア」（ルカ11:9-13）を置くことによって提示"[5]したように、自らの説教を通して1950年代後半のアメリカ南

部に相応しい形で提示していくのである。すなわち、南部社会の人種差別に苦しみ、それと闘いつつも、祈りを継続することの意義をキングは語るのである。敬虔な祈りこそが確かな黒人の未来の前提であるとキングはテキストを通して語りかけているのである。[6]

さて、ルカ 11 : 5-8 の譬話は同じルカの特殊資料 18 : 1-8（寡婦の願いの話）としばしば関連をもって考察される。キング自身は説教、*A Knock at Midnight* の中でこの譬話に言及していないが、ここで 2 つの譬話を比較しておくことは、キングの信仰に基づく公民権運動を考察する上で重要だと思われるので、簡単に論じておきたい。ルカ 11 : 5-6 で客を迎えた男が真夜中にドアを叩いたのは友人の家である。彼は誰彼かまわず真夜中にドアを叩いたわけではない。助けてくれそうな友人を選び、ドアを叩いたのである。一方、ルカ 18 : 1-8 に登場する寡婦は"神を畏れず人を人とも思わない裁判官にすがったのである"。ここには大きな差異がある。18 : 1 に"イエスは、気を落とさずに絶えず祈らなければならないことを教えるために、弟子たちにたとえを話された"と書かれていることからも明らかなように、18 : 1-8 の譬話もまた、望みを失わずに常に祈り続けなければならないことを教える物語である。このように、両方の譬話の使信とするところは同じであるが、キングが後者ではなく、前者を聖書テキストとして用いたことには重要な意味がある。次章で詳しく論じるが、前者に登場する"友人"は白人教会、および黒人教会を含む広い意味での教会としてキングには理解されている。ルカの文脈でこの"友人"が批判的に言及されているように、キングもまた白人教会、黒人教会の双方を批判した上で、真夜中における教会の役割を論じる。たとえ批判の対象であるにしても、"友人"が"神を畏れず人を人とも思わない裁判官"とは異なるように、教会は助けてくれそうな可能性をとりあえず与えてくれる存在なのである。キングがこのような説教を行うのも、多くの問題をかかえる 1950 年代の南部社会にあって、共同体としての教会がそれだけ重要な存在であったからである。後者の「寡婦の願いの話」は教会の概念を全く含まない。教会ないしは教会的なものに対する批判ではなく、祈りの継続性の意義を神への信頼との関係から力強く語ることに譬話の主目的があるからである。

II

　本章では『ルカによる福音書』11：5-6 で用いられている "midnight" "friend" "three loaves" 等のキーワードが 1950 年代のアメリカ社会を背景に、キングによってどのように解釈されているかを、説教 *A Knock at Midnight* の最初の 3 部を中心に見ていきたい。

　A Knock at Midnight は説教原稿のため、各部にタイトルは付されていない。全体の構成は、第 1 部〜第 3 部が上記のキーワードの解釈を核としてそれぞれ連関し合うように工夫され、第 4 部が説教全体の結論としての機能を果たしている。まず第 1 部では "midnight" の説明がなされる。キングは "midnight" を「人間の外的な集団生活における真夜中（midnight in man's external collective life）」と「人間の内的な個人生活における真夜中（midnight in his internal individual life）」の二極性から解釈する。前者は社会的秩序の中の真夜中（midnight within the social order）であると表現され、具体的には 1950 年代に始まった米ソ間の冷戦を背景にした国際的な緊張状況が恐怖の真夜中であると説明される。核兵器開発による、とどまるところを知らない軍備拡張競争を、キングはパワーポリティクスの生み出した真夜中と考えるのである。後者に関しては、心理学的秩序の中の真夜中（midnight within the psychological order）および、道徳的秩序の中の真夜中（midnight within the moral order）と説明される。心理学的秩序の真夜中とは、現代人の不安神経症的な精神状況を指し、一方、道徳的秩序の中の真夜中とは、現代人が相対主義に陥り、道徳原理が明確さを失ってしまい、道徳的退廃が深まった状況を指している。ここで強調されているのは、それが外的であろうと内的であろうと、具体的な真夜中の現象そのものではない。真夜中という状況におかれた人間の心的状態（心象）が問題なのである。キングの言葉を借りれば、人間にとって真夜中はまさに "闇が非常に深いため、進むべき方向が（自分では）分からない" 状態なのである。

　第 2 部のキーワードは "three loaves" である。しかし、まず注目したいのは、聖書テキストに "友よ、パンを三つ貸してください（11：5）" とあるように、この 3 つのパンは「友よ」とドアを叩かれる教会に対して望まれているものであるということである。キングによれば、この時期、アメリカ合衆国にお

ける教会員の数は飛躍的に増加している。キングは会堂（シナゴグ）も含めて1億1,500万人が教会に出席していると述べているが、ユダヤ教会の教会員登録数はともかくとして、実際に1955年から58年にかけて、ギャラップ世論調査によれば、ピーク時で49パーセントのアメリカ人が教会に通っていたと報告されている。すなわち約2人に1人のアメリカ人が教会の礼拝に出席していたことになる。[7] もっともキング自身はこの現象をジャンボイズム（Jumboism）という言葉を用いて、キリスト教的に質が向上したわけではないと批判している。キングの関心は専ら、多くの人々をして教会へ向かわせようとする、その心的状態にある。

　キングは人々が教会に求める"three loaves"を信仰のパン（the bread of faith）、希望のパン（the bread of hope）、愛のパン（the bread of love）であると言う。つまり、人々が真夜中にあってこれらのパンを見いだせずに途方に暮れ、教会のドアを叩いていると見ている。これらの3つのパンは先に言及した"midnight"の状況に対応する形で説明される。

　まず最初に、信仰のパンが語られる。2つの世界大戦を経験し、また、新たな戦争の暗雲が立ちこめる社会で、人々は失望し、神や人間や未来を信じる気持ちを失ってしまった。絶望に包まれた社会的秩序の真夜中から人間は信仰のパンを求めているとキングは語る。次に、希望のパンが語られる。科学が進歩し、人間の生活だけでなく人間そのものを高い水準へ引き上げると信じられていたのが、科学的業績が人間の利己主義や腐敗と結びつき、人間を悲観主義者に変えてしまった。多くの人間が精神不安に陥り、心理学的真夜中から人生に対する希望のパンを求めていると語られる。最後に、愛のパンが語られる。キングは現代の状況を過酷で非人格的な世界（a world which has become oppressively impersonal）であると言う。それは社会制度がある程度整い、すべてが数字に置き換えられるような社会であると同時に、一方で、自分は所属するところがどこにもないと感じさせる社会でもある。愛されていないと感じる人間が、自分は取るに足らない存在であると感じる社会である。究極の内的真夜中とも言える非人格的世界から人間は愛のパンを求めていると語られる。

　第1部と第2部が、どちらかと言えば、レトリックを駆使した抽象的な展開であったのに対し、第3部はキーワード"friend"の分析を軸に"midnight"や

"loaves"の概念が急速に現実味を帯びてくる。キングは聖書テキストを引用し、平易な言葉で訴えようとする。

When the man in the parable knocked on his friend's door and asked for the three loaves of bread, he received the impatient retort, "Do not bother me ; the door is now shut, and my children are with me in bed ; I cannot get up and give you anything." How often have men experienced a similar disappointment when at midnight they knock on the door of the church.

キングは第3部で改めて"midnight"の正体に言及し、"friend"と表現される教会の対応を批判する。キングはまず、"midnight"が人種差別であること (the midnight of racial segregation) を明確にし、多くの黒人がパンとしての自由 (the bread of freedom) を求めてきたにもかかわらず、白人教会が無関心と偽善で答えてきたことを批判する。次に、キングは"midnight"としての戦争 (the terrible midnight of war) を俎上に載せ、人々が平和のパン (the bread of peace) を教会に求めても、教会が見て見ぬ振りをし、沈黙を守り、時に積極的かつ道徳的に戦争に加担してきたことを批判する。さらに、キングは"midnight"としての経済的剥奪 (the frustrating midnight of economic deprivation) に触れ、教会が特権階級と結びつき、経済的正義というパン (the bread of economic justice) を求めた人々を無視してきたことを批判する。ここで重要なのは、文脈の中でキングが単にアメリカ合衆国の現状だけでなく世界各国の歴史的展開を視野に入れて、"midnight"における教会の対応を批判している点である。人種差別に関してはアフリカにおける各教派の対応を、戦争に関しては各国の国教会の対応を、経済的剥奪に関してはロシア正教会の対応を批判している。これは、教会の役割は一国一地域に限ったものでなく、普遍化されなければならないとするキングの神学的立場を表していると同時に、アメリカ国民の運命を、世界との連関の中で捉えようとするキングのアメリカ観の表明でもあるのである。

キングは教会の役割に関して、次のように述べる。

The church must be reminded that it is not the master or the servant of the state, but rather the conscience of the state. It must be the guide and the critic of the state, and never its tool. If the church does not recapture its prophetic zeal, it will become an irrelevant social club without moral or spiritual authority.

キングはここで、"the conscience of the state"、"the guide and the critic of the state"等の表現を用いることで教会の社会的使命を強調している。国家の良心であると同時に、国家の案内者・批判者であろうとする教会は必然的に民主主義的な意味での社会正義の監視人、および推進者としての機能を果たすことになる。キングの文脈で言えば、先に明確化した、人種差別・戦争・経済的剥奪といった "midnight" 的状況に対して、教会が民主主義の代弁者として積極的に関与し、社会正義実現のための抗議を繰り返すことこそ、友人として人々にパンを与えることになるのである。キングがここで "prophetic zeal" という表現を使用していることは注目に値する。この言葉こそ、説教、*A Knock at Midnight* の聖書テキストであるルカ 11:5-6 の究極的使信である、絶え間のない祈りの必要性——キングの言葉で言えば the power of persistent prayer ——を示すものだからである。単に民主主義的な法的正当性を盾に抗議するだけでなく、キリスト者としての自らを常に確認しつつ、抗議することがここでは重要であると訴えられている。

一方、キングの批判は一般的な教会に対してだけではない。批判の対象は自らも所属している黒人教会へも向かう。キングは言う。

While speaking of the laxity of the church, I must not overlook the fact that the so-called Negro church has also left men disappointed at midnight... Two types of Negro churches have failed to provide bread. One burns with emotionalism, and the other freezes with classism.

キングも指摘しているように、教会までが白人教会と黒人教会に人種分離されていることはアメリカ合衆国にとって最も恥ずべきことの1つであるが、と

りあえずここで問題になるのは"midnight"と闘わなければならないはずの黒人教会の姿勢である。感情主義に熱心な黒人教会は礼拝をエンターテイメントと錯覚し、真夜中にパンを与えるどころか、語るべき福音も持ち得ていないとキングは言う。また、階級主義的な黒人教会は専門職についている教会員が多いことを誇り、排他主義的であり、冷淡である。キングがあえて黒人教会の例を挙げたのは、黒人教会といえども例外ではないということを伝えたかったからである。しかし、それ以上に重要なのは、真夜中という状況の中で祈りの継続を怠っている教会の、その錯覚した共同体としての姿を批判の対象としたかったからである。

キングは説教、*A Knock at Midnight* の第1部〜第3部で、聖書テキストのキーワードを当時のアメリカ合衆国の状況に絡めて解釈した。その際に、キングは新約的使信の適用をアメリカ合衆国だけにとどめず、あえて世界と歴史の2つの方向軸に展開させ、アメリカ南部の一地域の問題を、世界、および世界史と積極的にリンクさせようとした。こうした方法を取ることで、アラバマ州モントゴメリーという1地域の問題が人類共通の問題として理解されるようになるだけでなく、おそらくはアメリカ合衆国南部の1教会で語られたであろう説教が人類の普遍的な使信ともなる可能性が生じるからである。

Ⅲ

キングが *A Knock at Midnight* で実際にアラバマ州モントゴメリーのバス・ボイコット運動に言及するのは、説教の結論とも言える第4部のみである。こうした結論で終わる *A Knock at Midnight* 自体、通常の説教とは若干異なった構成になっている。本節では、この説教の構造が提起する問題を中心に考えていきたい。

一般に、説教では聖書テキストの使信を宣べ伝えるのにイラストレーション（実例）を用いることがある。まず、テキストを理解させるために、聴衆にとって分かりやすいイラストレーションが描かれ、その後に、使信の信仰的・神学的要点を理解させるといった手法が取られる。*A Knock at Midnight* を見る限りでは、この順序が逆転している。最初に使信の信仰的・神学的要点が語られ、そ

の後にイラストレーションが続くのである。ここではバス・ボイコット運動がイラストレーションとして採用され、その叙述をもって説教が終了する形式が取られている。この間の事情を解明するためには、説教におけるキングの神学的結論を前もって確認しておく必要がある。

　第4部で、キングは改めて真夜中の際の絶え間のない祈りの必要性を強調する。同時に、複雑な個人的・社会的問題に苦しむ人々にとって、イエス・キリストこそが人々の希望であり、それこそが教会の与え得る命のパン（the bread of life）であることを、教会は認識すべきであると語る。続けて、キングは真夜中の希望としてのイエス・キリストを3つのパンになぞらえて説明する。第1のパンは神が悪から善をもたらすことを人々に知らしめる新鮮な希望のパン（the fresh bread of hope）である。第2のパンは倫理的相対主義という真夜中でさまよい、罪悪感にさいなまれる人々をキリストへと導く新鮮な赦しのパン（the fresh bread of forgiveness）である。第3のパンは死に向かいつつある人間を恐怖から救い出す、不死を信じる信仰のパン（the bread of faith in immortality）である。

　キングが述べるこの3つのパンはいずれもが希望へと人々を導くパンである。真夜中という状況において希望が存在するとすれば、それは夜明けの存在である。
　キングは言う。

　　The weary traveler by midnight who asks for bread is really seeking the dawn. Our eternal message of hope is that dawn will come.

　このように見てくると、キングが説教、*A Knock at Midnight* で宣べ伝えようとしたことは夜明けを信じる信仰（faith in the dawn）を持つことの意義であることが分かる。夜明けを信じる信仰は神への絶対的な信頼によっている。真夜中は人間が試される時でもあるのだ。先に、本稿 I で *A Knock at Midnight* の聖書テキストが「主の祈り」と内容的関連性を有していることに言及した。その「主の祈り」はまた、ルカ福音書において「荒野の誘惑物語（4：1-13）」と対応している。それに着目すると、ルカ 11：5-6 で求められたパンは、そもそもイエスが荒野で悪魔の誘惑を退けた試練のパン（ルカ 4：3-4）であり、それ

ゆえに、人間が「わたしたちに必要な糧を毎日与えてください（ルカ11:3)」と祈る、「主の祈り」のパンであると解釈することが可能になる。夜明けを信じる信仰を持つとき、人間は試練に打ち勝ち、確信を持って暗闇の夜を歩むことができると語るキングは、明らかにルカ福音書の文脈を意識して発言していると思われる。

このように考えると、キングの説教、*A Knock at Midnight* もまた、その構造がパンを基調に置くルカ福音書の構造に似ていることに気づく。すなわち、ルカは「試練のパン」「祈りのパン」「譬話のパン」の配列で一連のパンに関して扱い、イラストレーションとも言える11:5-8の譬話の部分で、日常生活に基づいて、パンを求める絶え間のない祈りの必要性をその使信として伝える。キングもまた、第1部～第3部を経て、第4部になって始めて、1950年代後半のアメリカ南部社会を舞台にした、極めて日常的で具体的なイラストレーションを置き、夜明けのパンを求める絶え間のない祈りの必要性を語るのである。

イラストレーションとして描かれたバス・ボイコット運動のエピソードは運動最終期に起きた自動車プール制（the car pool）に関するモントゴメリー市の告訴事件に関してである。実際には、公判が開かれる直前に、合衆国最高裁判所から"アラバマ州モントゴメリーのバス乗車における人種隔離は合衆国憲法違反である"との判決が下り、バス・ボイコット運動はキングたちの勝利に終わった。モントゴメリー市にしてみれば自動車プール制そのものを告訴する意義が失われたわけだが、キング側から見れば、大逆転とも言える最高裁の判定が勝ち取れない限り、たとえ自分たちに誤りがなくても、人種分離を是とする市当局の告訴に勝てる見込みはなかったのである。自動車プール制はモントゴメリーの黒人教会がボランティアで行う自動車乗り合い運動であったが、これが公判で市当局の許可を受けない私的営業と認められれば、キングたちが今後バス・ボイコット運動を継続するのは不可能な状況であった。この告訴事件は、運動が約1年間にわたって続き、黒人たちの苦しみがピークに達しつつあるときだっただけに、キングを代表とする指導者たちには脅威であり、この状況こそが真夜中の最も暗いときであった。

それだけに、このバス・ボイコット運動の勝利はキングが "God Almighty has spoken from Washington" と語るように、キングの予想を越えたものであった。

神の奇跡と呼ぶべきものであった。キングが第1部〜第4部前半まで、理論に理論を重ねて展開させてきた説教、*A Knock at Midnight* の最後に、このような人知を超えたエピソードをイラストレーションとして挿入したことの意義は大きい。それは、キングの説教の学問的・理論的要素をよい意味で薄め、説教の現場である地域社会に、説教の内容を引き戻す作用を果たした。説教の最後の部分で、キングは生活の場に向けてメッセージを送ることに成功したのである。その点ではバス・ボイコット運動の回想は聴衆にとって極めて日常的な話題でもあった。

しかし、それ以上に、このエピソードが挿入されたことで、真夜中における教会の福音的役割が明瞭に示唆されることになった。人によっては、モントゴメリーの黒人諸教会が自動車プール制を積極的に推進したことを困難時の教会の役割だと言うかもしれない。そのような社会的活動は真夜中における教会の現実的活動として十分に重要であり、おそらく欠くべからざるものであると思われる。しかし、最も重要なのは、キングが語る "The darkest hour of our struggle had become the first hour of victory" という表現にも象徴されるように、教会は最も暗いと思われるときにさえも、夜明けが来るということを人々に宣べ伝え続ける必要があるということである。その根拠となるのが希望としてのイエス・キリストの存在である。先に、キングが言及したように、イエス・キリストになぞらえた3つのパン、すなわち、希望のパン、赦しのパン、不死を信じる信仰のパンを教会が与え続けることこそ、人間を夜明けへと向かわせるのであり、それこそが、真夜中における教会の福音的使命と呼べるものなのである。

注:

1. King, JR, Martin Luther. *Strength to Love*. New York: Harper & Row, 1963
   なお、本稿では Washington, James M. (ed.) *A Testament of Hope: The Essential Writings And Speeches of Martin Luther King, JR*. New York: HarperCollins Publishers 1991 を底本として用いている。
2. King, JR, Martin Luther. *Stride Toward Freedom*. New York: Marie Rodell & Joan Daves, Inc., 1958

なお、本稿では *Strength to Love* と同様に、Washington, James M. (ed.) *A Testament of Hope : The Essential Writings And Speeches of Martin Luther King, JR.* New York : HarperCollins Publishers 1991 を底本として用いている。
3. Schweizer, Eduard. The Good News According to Luke. Atlanta : John Knox Press. 1984. p.190
4. 荒井　献『イエス・キリスト』講談社、1979年、131頁から引用。
5. *Ibid.*, p.132 から引用。
6. Rengstorf, K.H. Das Evangelium nach Lukas. Göttingen : Vandenhoeck & Ruprecht 1968
　　泉　治典、渋谷　浩訳『ルカによる福音書（NTD新約聖書註解3）』NTD新約聖書註解刊行会、1976年、309頁
7. 古屋安雄『激動するアメリカ教会』ヨルダン社、1978年、10-11頁

3. Antidotes for Fear

There is no fear in love ; but perfect love casteth out fear : because fear hath torment. He that feareth is not made perfect in love. (1 John 4:18)

In these days of catastrophic change and calamitous uncertainty, is there any man who does not experience the depression and bewilderment of crippling fear, which, like a nagging hound of hell, pursues our every footstep?

Everywhere men and women are confronted by fears that often appear in strange disguises and a variety of wardrobes. Haunted by the possibility of bad health, we detect in every meaningless symptom an evidence of disease. Troubled by the fact that days and years pass so quickly, we dose ourselves with drugs which promise eternal youth. If we are physically vigorous, we become so concerned by the prospect that our personalities may collapse that we develop an inferiority complex and stumble through life with a feeling of insecurity, a lack of self-confidence, and a sense of impending failure. A fear of what life may bring encourages some persons to wander aimlessly along the frittering road of excessive drink and sexual promiscuity. Almost without being aware of the change, many people have permitted fear to transform the sunrise of love and peace into a sunset of inner depression.

When unchecked, fear spawns a whole brood of phobias — fbar of water, high places, closed rooms, darkness, loneliness, among others — and such an accumulation culminates in phobiaphobia or the fear of fear itself.

Especially common in our highly competitive society are economic fears, from which, Karen Horney says, come most of the psychological problems of our age. Captains of industry are tormented by the possible failure of their business and the capriciousness of the stock market. Employees are plagued by the prospect of unemployment and the consequences of an ever-increasing automation.

And consider, too, the multiplication in our day of religious and ontological fears, which include the fear of death and racial annihilation. The advent of the atomic age, which should have ushered ill all era of plenty and of prosperity, has lifted the fear of death to morbid proportions. The terrifying spectacle of nuclear warfare has put Hamlet's words, "To be or not to be," on millions of trembling lips. Witness our frenzied efforts to construct fallout shelters. As though even these offer sanctuary from an H-bomb attack! Witness the agonizing desperation of our petitions that our government increase the nuclear stockpile. But our fanatical quest to maintain " a balance of terror" only increases our fear and leaves nations on tiptoes lest some diplomatic *faux pas* ignite a frightful holocaust.

Realizing that fear drains a man's energy and depletes his resources, Emerson wrote, "He has not learned the lesson of life who does not every day surmount a fear."

But I do not mean to suggest that we should seek to eliminate fear altogether from human life. Were this humanly possible, it would be practically undesirable. Fear is the elemental alarm system of the human organism which warns of approaching dangers and without which man could not have survived in either the primitive or modern worlds. Fear, moreover, is a powerftllly creative force. Every great invention and intellectual advance represents a desire to escape from some dreaded circumstance or condition. The fear of darkness led to the discovery of the secret of electricity. The fear of pain led to the marvelous advances of medical science. The fear of ignorance was one reason that man built great institutions of learning. The fear of war was one of the forces behind the birth of the United Nations. Angelo Patri has rightly said, "Education consists in being afraid at the right time." If man were to lose his capacity to fear, he would be deprived of his capacity to grow, invent, and create. So in a sense fear is normal, necessary, and creative.

But we must remember that abnormal fears are emotionally ruinous and psychologically destructive. To illustrate the difference between normal and abnormal fear, Sigmund Freud spoke of a person who was quite properly afraid of snakes in the heart of an African jungle and of another person who neurotically feared that snakes were under the carpet in his city apartment. Psychologists say that normal children are born with only two fears — the fear of falling and the fear of loud noises — and that all others are environmentally acquired. Most of these acquired fears are snakes under the carpet.

It is to such fears that we usually refer when we speak of getting rid of fear. But this is only a part of the story. Normal fear protects us., abnormal fear paralyzes us. Normal fear motivates us to improve our individual and collective welfare ; abnormal fear constantly poisons and distorts our inner lives. Our problem is not to be rid of fear but rather to harness and master it. How may it be mastered?

I

First, we must unflinchingly face our fears and honestly ask ourselves why we are afraid. This confrontation will, to some measure, grant us power. We shall never be cured of fear by escapism or repression, for the more we attempt to ignore and repress our fears, the more we multiply our inner conflicts.

By looking squarely and honestly at our fears we learn that many of them are residues of some childhood need or apprehension. Here, for instance, is a person haunted by a fear of death or the thought of punishment in the afterlife, who discovers that he has unconsciously projected into the whole of reality the childhood experience of being punished by parents, locked in a room, and seemingly deserted. Or here is a man plagued by the fear of inferiority and social rejection, who discovers that rejection in childhood by a self-centered mother and a preoccupied father left him with a self-defeating sense of inadequacy and a repressed bitterness toward life.

By bringing our fears to the forefront of consciousness, we may find them to be more imaginary than real. Some of them will turn out to be snakes under the carpet.

And let us also remember that, more often than not, fear involves the misuse of the imagination. When we get our fears into the open, we may laugh at some of them, and this is good. One psychiatrist said, "Ridicule is the master cure for fear and anxiety."

II

Second, we can master fear through one of the supreme virtues known to man: courage. Plato considered courage to be an element of the soul which bridges the cleavage between reason and desire. Aristotle thought of courage as the affirmation of man's essential nature. Thomas Aquinas said that courage is the strength of mind capable of conquering whatever threatens the attainment of the highest good.

Courage, therefore, is the power of the mind to overcome fear. Unlike anxiety, fear has a definite object which may be faced, analyzed, attacked, and, if need be, endured. How often the object of our fear is fear itself! In his *Journal* Henry David Thoreau wrote, "Nothing is so much to be feared as fear." Centuries earlier, Epictetus wrote, "For it is not death or hardship that is a fearful thing, but the fear of hardship and death." Courage takes the fear produced by a definite object into itself and thereby conquers the fear involved, Paul Tillich has written, " Courage is self-affirmation ' in spite of '... that which tends to hinder the self from affirming itself." It is self-affirmation in spite of death and nonbeing, and he who is courageous takes the fear of death into his selfaffirmation and acts upon it. This courageous self-affirmation, which is surely a remedy for fear, is not selfishness, for self-affirmation includes both a proper self-love and a properly propsitioned love of others. Erich Fromm has shown in convincing terms that the right kind of self-love and the right kind of love of others are interdependent.

Courage, the determination not to be overwhelmed by any object, however frightful, enables us to stand up to any fear. Many of our fears are not mere snakes under the carpet. Trouble is a reality in this strange medley of life, dangers lurk within the circumference of every action, accidents do occur, bad health is an ever-threatening possibility, and death is a stark, grim, and inevitable fact of human experience. Evil and pain in this conundrum of life are close to each of us, and we do both ourselves and our neighbors a great disservice when we attempt to prove that there is nothing in this world of which we should be frightened. These forces that threaten to negate life must be challenged by courage, which is the power of life to affirm itself in spite of life's ambiguities. This requires the exercise of a creative will that enables us to hew out a stone of hope from a mountain of despair.

Courage and cowardice are antithetical. Courage is an inner resolution to go forward in spite of obstacles and frightening situations; cowardice is a submissive surrender to circumstance. Courage breeds creative self-affirmation; cowardice produces destructive self-abnegation. Courage faces fear and thereby masters it; cowardice represses fear and is thereby mastered by it. Courageous men never lose the zest for living even though their life situation is zestless; cowardly men, overwhelmed by the uncertainties of life, lose the will to live. We must constantly build dykes of courage to hold back the flood of fear.

III

Third, fear is mastered through love. The New Testament affirms, " There is no fear in love; but perfect love casteth out fear." The kind of love which led Christ to a cross and kept Paul unembittered amid the angry torrents of persecution is not soft, anemic, and sentimental. Such love confronts evil without flinching and shows in our popular parlance an infinite capacity " to take it." Such love overcomes the world even from a rough-hewn cross against the skyline.

But does love have a relationship to our modern fear of war, economic displacement, and racial injustice? Hate is rooted in fear, and the only cure for fear-hate is love. Our deteriorating international situation is shot through with the lethal darts of fear. Russia fears America, and America fears Russia. Likewise China and India, and the Israelis and the Arabs. These fears include another nation's aggression, scientific and technological supremacy, and economic power, and our own loss of status and power. Is not fear one of the major causes of war? We say that war is a consequence of hate, but close scrutiny reveals this sequence: first fear, then hate, then war, and finally deeper hatred. Were a nightmarish nuclear war to engulf our world, the cause would be not so much that one nation hated another, but that both nations feared each other.

What method has the sophisticated ingenuity of modern man employed to deal with the fear of war? We have armed ourselves to the nth degree. The West and the East have engaged in a fever-pitched arms race. Expenditures for defense have risen to mountainous proportions, and weapons of destruction have been assigned priority over all other human endeavors. The nations have believed that greater armaments will cast out fear. But alas! they have produced greater fear. In these turbulent, panic-stricken days we are once more reminded of the judicious words of old, " Perfect love casteth out fear." Not arms, but love, understanding, and organized goodwill can cast out fear. Only disarmament, based on good faith, will make mutual trust a living reality.

Our own problem of racial injustice must be solved by the same formula. Racial segregation is buttressed by such irrational fears as loss of preferred economic privilege, altered social status, intermarriage, and adjustment to new situations. Through sleepless nights and haggard days numerous white people attempt to combat these corroding fears by diverse methods. By following the path of escape, some seek to ignore the question of race relations and to close their mind to the issues involved. Others placing their faith in such legal maneuvers as interposition and nullification, counsel massive resistance. Still others hope to drown their fear by engaging in acts of violence and meanness toward their Negro brethren. But how futile are all these remedies! Instead of eliminating fear, they instill deeper and more pathological fears that leave the victims inflicted with strange psychoses and peculiar cases of paranoia. Neither repression, massive resistance, nor aggressive violence will cast out the fear of integration; only love and goodwill can do that.

If our white brothers are to master fear, they must depend not only on their commitment to Christian love but also on the Christlike love which the Negro generates toward them. Only through our adherence to love and nonviolence will the fear in the white community be mitigated. A guilt-ridden white minority fears that if the Negro attains power, he will without restraint or pity act to revenge the accumulated injustices and brutality of the years. A parent, who has continually mistreated his son, suddenly realizes that he is now taller than the parent. Will the son use his new physical power to repay for all of the blows of the past?

Once a helpless child, the Negro has now grown politically, culturally, and economically. Many white men fear retaliation. The Negro must show them that they have nothing to fear, for the Negro forgives and is willing to forget the past. *The Negro must convince the white man that he seeks justice for both himself and the white man.* A mass movement exercising love and nonviolence and demonstrating power under discipline should convince the white community that were such a movement to attain strength its power would be used creatively and not vengefully.

What then is the cure of this morbid fear of integration? We know the cure. God help us to achieve it! Love casts out fear.

This truth is not without a bearing on our personal anxieties. We are afraid of the superiority of other people, of failure, and of the scorn or disapproval of those whose opinions we most value. Envy, jealousy, a lack of self-confidence, a feeling of insecurity, and a haunting sense of inferiority are all rooted in fear. We do not envy people and then fear them; first we fear them and subsequently we become jealous of them. Is there a cure for these annoying fears that pervert our personal lives? Yes, a deep and abiding commitment to the way of love. "Perfect love casteth out fear."

Hatred and bitterness can never cure the disease of fear; only love can do that. Hatred paralyzes life; love releases it. Hatred confuses life; love harmonizes it. Hatred darkens life; love illuminates it.

IV

Fourth, fear is mastered through faith. A common source of fear is an awareness Of deficient resources and of a consequent inadequacy for life. All too many people attempt to face the tensions of life with inadequate spiritual resources. When vacationing in Mexico, Mrs. King and I wished to go deep-sea fishing. For reasons of economy, we rented an old and poorly equipped boat. We gave this little thought until, tenmiles from shore, the clouds lowered and howling winds blew. Then we became paralyzed with fear, for we knew our boat was deficient. Multitudes of people are in a similar situation. Heavy winds and weak boats explain their fear.

Many of our abnormal fears can be dealt with by the skills of psychiatry, a relatively new discipline pioneered by Sigmund Freud, which investigates the subconscious drives of men and seeks to discover how and why fundamental energies are diverted into neurotic channels. Psychiatry helps us to look candidly at our inner selves and to search out the causes of our failures and fears. But much of our fearful living encompasses a realm where the service of psychiatry is ineffectual unless the psychiatrist is a man of religious faith.

For our trouble is simply that we attempt to confront fear without faith; we sail through the stormy seas of life without adequate spiritual boats. One of the leading physicians and psychiatrists in America has said, "The only known cure for fear is faith."

Abnormal fears and phobias that are expressed in neurotic anxiety may be cured by psychiatry; but the fear of death, nonbeing, and nothingness, expressed in existential anxiety, may be cured only by a positive religious faith.

A positive religious faith does not offer an illusion that we shall be exempt from pain and suffering, nor does it imbue us with the idea that life is a drama of unalloyed comfort and untroubled ease. Rather, it instills us with the inner equilibrium needed to face straims, burdens, and fears that inevitably come, and assures us that the universe is trustworthy and that God is concenled.

Irreligion, on the other hand, would have us believe that we are orphans cast into the terrifying immensities of space in a universe that is without purpose or intelligence. Such a view drains courage and exhausts the energies of men. In his *Confession* Tolstoi wrote concerning the aloneness and emptiness he felt before his conversion:

> There was a period in my life when everything seemed to be crumbling, the very foundations of my convictions were beginning to give way, and I felt myself going to pieces. There was no sustaining influence in my life and there was no God there, and so every night before I went to sleep, I made sure that there was no rope in my room lest I be tempted during the night to hang myself from the rafters of my room; and I stopped from going out shooting lest I be tempted to put a quick end to my life and to my misery.

Like so many people, Tolstoi at that stage of his life lacked the sustaining influence which comes from the conviction that this universe is guided by a benign Intelligence whose infinite love embraces all mankind.

Religion endows us with the conviction that we are not alone in this vast, uncertain universe. Beneath and above the shifting sands of time, the uncertainties that darken our days, and the vicissitudes that cloud our nights is a wise and loving God. This universe is not a tragic expression of meaningless chaos but a marvelous display of orderly cosmos —" The Lord by wisdom hath founded the earth; by understanding hath he established the heavens." Man is not a wisp of smoke from a limitless smoldering, but a child of God created " a little lower than the angels." Above the manyness of time stands the one eternal God, with wisdom to guide us, strength to protect us, and love to keep us. His boundless love supports and contains us as a mighty ocean contains and supports the tiny drops of every wave. With a surging fullness he is forever moving toward us, seeking to fill the little creeks and bays of our lives with unlimited resources. This is religion's everlasting diapason, its eternal answer to the enigma of existence. Any man who finds this cosmic sustenance can walk the highways of life without the fatigue of pessimism and the weight of morbid fears.

Herein lies the answer to the neurotic fear of death that plagues so many of our lives. Let us face the fear that the atomic bomb has aroused with the faith that we can never travel beyond the arms of the Divine. Death is inevitable. It is a democracy for all of the people, not an aristocracy for some of the people — kings die and beggars die; young men die and old men die; learned men die and ignorant men die. We need not fear it. The God who brought our whirling planet from primal vapor and has led the human pilgrimage for lo these many centuries can most assuredly lead us through death's dark night into the bright daybreak of eternal life. His will is too perfect and his purposes are too extensive to be contained in the limited receptacle of time and the narrow walls of earth. Death is not the ultimate evil; the ultimate evil is to be outside God's love. We need not join the mad rush to purchase an earthly fallout shelter. God is our eternal fallout shelter.

Jesus knew that nothing could separate man from the love of God. Listen to his majestic words :

> Fear them not therefore ; for there is nothing covered, that shall not be revealed ; and hid, that shall not be known. . . . And fear not them which kill the body, but are not able to kill the soul : but rather fear him which is able to destroy both soul and body in hell. Are not two sparrows sold for a farthing ? and one of them shall not fall on the ground without your Father. But the very hairs of your head are all numbered. Fear ye not therefore, ye are of more value than many sparrows.

Man, for Jesus, is not mere flotsam and jetsam in the river of life, but he is a child of God. Is it not unreasonable to assume that God, whose creative activity is expressed in an awareness of a sparrow's fall and the number of hairs on a man's head, excludes from his encompassing love the life of man itself ? The confidence that God is mindful of the individual is of tremendous value in dealing with the disease of fear, for it gives us a sense of worth, of belonging, and of at-homeness in the universe.

One of the most dedicated participants in the bus protest in Montgomery, Alabama, was an elderly Negro whom we affectionately called Mother Pollard. Although poverty-stricken and uneducated, she was amazingly intelligent and possessed a deep understanding of the meaning of the movement. After having walked for several weeks, she was asked if she were tired. With ungrammatical profundity, she answered, "My feels is tired, but my soul is rested."

On a particular Monday evening, following a tension-packed week which included being arrested and receiving numerous threatening telephone calls, I spoke at a mass meeting. I attempted to convey an overt impression of strength and courage, although I was inwardly depressed and fear-stricken. At the end of the meeting, Mother Pollard came to the front of the church and said, "Come here, son." I immediately went to her and hugged her affectionately. "Something is wrong with you," she said. "You didn't talk strong tonight." Seeking further to disguise my fears, I retorted, "Oh, no, Mother. Pollard, nothing is wrong. I am feeling as fine as ever." But her insight was discerning. "Now you can't fool me," she said. "I knows something is wrong. Is it that we ain't doing things to please you? Or is it that the white folks is bothering you?" Before I could respond, she looked directly into my eyes and said, "I don told you we is with you all the way." Then her face became radiant and she said in words of quiet certainty, "But even if we ain't with you, God's gonna take care of you." As she spoke these consoling words, everything in me quivered and quickened with the pulsing tremor of raw energy.

Since that dreary night in 1956, Mother Pollard has passed on to glory and I have known very few quiet days. I have been tortured without and tormented within by the raging fires of tribulation. I have been forced to muster what strength and courage I have to withstand howling winds of pain and jostling storms of adversity. But as the years have unfolded the eloquently simple words of Mother Pollard have come back agaiII and again to give light and peace and guidance to my troublbd soul. "God's gonna take care of you."

This faith transforms the whirlwind of despair into a warm and reviving breeze of hope. The words of a motto which a generation ago were commonly found on the wall in the homes of devout persons need to be etched on our hearts:

> Fear knocked at the door.
> Faith answered.
> There was no one there.

4. "Antidotes for Fear" を読む

はじめに

　先の *A Knock at Midnight* とともに *Antidotes for Fear* もまたマーティン・ルーサー・キング・ジュニアの *The Strength to Love* (1963)[1] に収められた説教のひとつである。ここでは *Antidotes for Fear* の分析を通して、公民権運動期におけるアメリカ合衆国南部社会を覆う恐怖を、キングが新約聖書神学の立場から、いかに捉え、征服しようとしたかを考察していきたい。周知のように、公民権運動期の南部社会における恐怖とは、それ以前の時代から引き継がれてきた人種差別に関連する社会的恐怖である。具体的に言えば、白人にとっては人種差別を引き起こし、長く継続させることになった恐怖であり、黒人にとっては人種差別によって引き起こされた恐怖である。キングは *Antidotes for Fear* の中で、両人種が恐怖にあえて直面することを提案し、その上で、主な思想史上の"恐怖"概念の分析に言及し、最終的にはそれが新約聖書に基づく神への信仰によって克服され得るものであると結んでいる。通常、キングを中心とする公民権運動はきわめて社会的な運動であったがゆえに、ラインホールド・ニーバー (Reinhold Niebuhr 1892-1971) やヘンリー・デビッド・ソロー (Henry David Thoreau 1817-62) 等の思想的影響もあり、その政治的側面（政治的方法論）に焦点が当たりやすい。しかし、ここでは、キングが同時に伝統的な聖書解釈の立場から公民権運動に臨んでいたことを説教使信から確認することで、公民権運動そのものが合衆国南部黒人たちの信仰告白としての要素を持つものであることを示していきたい。

I

　説教 *Antidotes for Fear* のペリコーペとしてキングが選んでいるのは『ヨハネ第一書簡』の以下の箇所である。

　There is no fear in love; but perfect love casteth out fear: because fear hath torment. He that feareth is not made perfect in love. (I John 4:18)[2]

　キングは公民権運動における恐怖の克服を4ステージに分けて考察している。第1ステージでは心理学的な立場から恐怖の克服方法を示唆し、第2ステージでは、勇気（courage）をキーワードとして、思想史的な観点から恐怖克服の方法に言及する。特に、第2ステージではエピグラムのように哲学者、神学者の言葉を羅列する手法が用いられている。それぞれの引用の内容および連関は充分に論理的であり、妥当性を有するものではあるが、キング独自の言葉が少ないために説教としてのインパクトは弱く、続く第3、第4ステージの導入部としての役割を果たすにすぎない。さらに言えば、第1、第2ステージで語られる恐怖はあくまでも一般的な語義の枠内の説明にとどまっている。それでも、第1、第2ステージを通して、恐怖の概念そのものは聴衆に対して明瞭に定義されることから、この部分が説教の中心部を形成する第3、第4ステージで語られる説教使信の前提部として意図的に構成されていることは明白である。第3、第4ステージでは上記ペリコーペを中心とする新約聖書テキストが具体的に分析されると同時に、時代的・社会的な背景が引用され、テキスト使信の時代への適応性が考察される。上記のペリコーペは第3ステージで集中して扱われ、第4ステージではその発展として、さらに、新たなテキストである、『マタイ福音書』10:26, 28-30 が追加される。本節では、キングのペリコーペ解釈を中心に、恐怖克服の第3ステージを見ていきたい。

　『第1ヨハネ』4:18 に描かれる"恐怖"は、本来的には終末論的な神の審判に対する恐怖であるが、キングはあえて新約的文脈には触れずに、国内外の現実の社会問題を例示し、キリスト教的な愛によって近代的恐怖の克服が可能かどうかを問う。同時に、ここで、キングの説教の対象となる聴衆（読者）は、

黒人はもとより、白人を中心とする広義のアメリカ合衆国市民でもある。そのため、聴衆自らの国民的アイデンティティの確認もあり、国際問題、国内問題の順に話が進められる。まず、国際社会の問題としては、当時の典型的な国際政治トピックである冷戦構造下の東西両陣営の軍備拡張競争をキングは取り上げ、恐怖の存在が国際情勢の悪化を促していることを指摘する。

キングは国際情勢における具体的な対立の構図を示した上で、軍備を増強すれば恐怖が取り除けるとするのは誤った考えであり、愛と理解と組織化された善意志（love, understanding and organized goodwill）こそが恐怖を取り除くことを可能にすると、ペリコーペを引用して語りかける。

次にキングは国内社会に目を向け、具体的にアメリカ合衆国の人種差別の問題を取り上げる。黒人に対する人種差別が白人側の経済的特権の喪失（loss of preferred economic privilege）、社会的地位の変動（altered social status）、異人種間結婚（intermarriage）等に対する非合理的な恐怖により生じていることを指摘する。

ここでも、キングは先の国際社会における軍備拡張競争の例と同じく、愛と善意（love and goodwill）だけが人種統合に対する白人の恐怖を解消し得ると語りかける。このように、全く同じ構造と論理のもとに、キングはペリコーペの使信を当時の国内外の時代的・社会的背景に適応させているが、これは彼がキリスト教的理想主義の立場から、単に恐怖を取り除くものとして、信仰の必然性を短絡的に語ろうとしたからだろうか。キングは *Antidotes for Fear* の中で、直接ペリコーペの文脈に言及してはいないが、ペリコーペの新約的背景から考えて、彼が単純なメッセージを発しているとは考えにくい。また、ニーバーを範とする政治的方法論を実践するキングが、単に道徳的説教を公民権運動の最中に行うとも思えない。

ペリコーペとの関連から、ここでキングが語る愛とは人間の愛ではなく、神の人間に対する愛、換言すれば、神から人間に贈られた愛のことを意味すると考えられる。その意味ではキングは充分にテキストの終末的背景を理解している。おそらくキングは『第１ヨハネ』4：18が示唆する終末論的文脈を説教に持ち込む煩雑性を避ける目的で、あえて「神の愛」という言葉を使用せずに、新約の語義を変えずに「完全な愛（perfect love）」という表現を用いたと想像さ

れる。逆に言えば、新約の表現をそのまま加工せずに利用したことで、キングがペリコーペの終末論的文脈を充分に意識していたと判断し得る。そのことを我々に強く示唆するのが、以下の文章である。

If our white brothers are to master fear, they must depend not only on their commitment to Christian love but also on the Christlike love which the Negro generates toward them. Only through our adherence to love and non-violence will the fear in the white community be mitigated.

ここで、キングは白人に対して、恐怖を克服するためには、自らのキリスト教徒的愛（Christian love）にのみ頼るのではなく、黒人の白人に対するキリストのような愛（the Christlike love）にも依存しなければならないと語る。この場合、黒人の白人に対する愛とは実体のない抽象的なものではない。具体的な非暴力運動という形でアメリカ合衆国において実現されているものである。重要なのは、上記引用文中の the Christlike love の語である。この語は黒人側の愛の姿勢を表していると同時に、白人側の愛である Christian love と対比して用いられている。キングが Christian love と呼ぶとき、それはたとえ信仰に基づく愛ではあっても、人間主体の愛と考えられる。というのは、「恐怖」←→「愛」という図式において、恐怖に立ち向かうものとして容易に考えつくのは、人間の主体的な愛の行動だからである。それはペリコーペの最初の部分「愛には恐れがない（There is no fear in love）」の表面上の意味とも合致する。

それに対して、the Christlike love はペリコーペの終末論的文脈に置いて、初めて理解されるものである。第1ヨハネ4：18は前節と合わせて、神による救いの確信と愛について語る箇所である。[3] その際に、ブルトマン（Rudolf Bultmann 1884-1976）のように、当該パッセージの本来の主題は「愛」ではなく「確信」であると断言する神学者もいるが、終末論的審判に際して、救いの「確信」を持つための前提は神の人間に対する「愛」の存在であると容易に理解できることから、必ずしも異質な意見ではないと思われる。[4] いずれにしても、終末における不安を克服する愛とは完成された愛である。『第1ヨハネ』4：17に "Herein is our love made perfect, that we may have boldness in the day of judgment"

第4章　公民権運動とキング牧師の説教　*161*

とあるように、神の愛は人間に救いの確信を与えることにより完成されたものとなる。それは唯一キリストによって実現された愛である。道徳的目標としての愛などでは決してなく、キリストと同質の愛である。[5] ここでは"神との交わりによってキリストと同質の者とされることが、キリスト者の救いの確信と最後の審判に関する信頼の基礎であることが論じられている。"[6] このような愛こそ神から人間に贈られた愛であり、人間を恐怖から解放し、自由を与える愛でもある。キングは白人の恐怖を解消するためにこのような愛を黒人に求めている。

キングは *Antidotes for Fear* の中で終末論的文脈を引き合いに出すことはない。しかし、キングが "the Christlike love which the Negro generates toward them（them = white brothers 筆者注）" と語るとき、彼は黒人たちにキリストとの同質性を求めている。具体的には、先にも述べた、白人に対する愛に満ちた非暴力での対応こそがキリストとの同質性を具現するものである。白人が白人の信仰や力だけで恐怖を克服できるとはキングは考えていない。同じアメリカ合衆国市民としての黒人の協力があって初めて、白人の恐怖が解消すると彼は考えている。そのような意味で、キングは人種差別を、白人だけでなく黒人も背負わなければならない合衆国の運命、すなわち十字架であると理解している。キングは "The Negro must convince the white man that he seeks justice for both himself and the white man" と述べることで、被差別者である黒人もまたアメリカ市民として、白人と共にこの十字架を担うべきであると訴えている。このようなキングのアメリカ観は『バーミングハムの獄中からの手紙』の中で展開されたアメリカ観とまさに一致するものである。

　Abused and scorned through we may be, our destiny is tied up with the destiny of America. Before the Pilgrims landed at Plymouth we were here. Before the pen of Jefferson etched across the page of history the majestic words of the Declaration of Independence, we were here.[7]

さらに言えば、第3ステージにはアメリカ合衆国特有のきわめて伝統的な思考様式が暗示されている。それは、キングが公民権運動期のアメリカ合衆国を

新約聖書の終末論的背景と重ね合わせて理解しているからである。かつて建国期のピューリタンたちが、自らの運命を旧約の古代イスラエルと並置したように、また、19世紀、20世紀を代表する幾多の作家たちが小説の中で聖書的背景を視野に入れてアメリカ合衆国やアメリカ人を描こうとしたように、キングもまた自ら確信する公民権運動の成功を、白人に対する終末論的審判として捉えようとしている。換言すれば、キングは公民権運動期のアメリカ南部を終末的状況と捉えている。差別主義者たちによって教会を爆破され、黒人の子供たちが消火栓の放水に吹き飛ばされ、罵声と激しい暴力が浴びせられる日常を終末的状況と捉えている。[8] 例によって、キングは聖書の終末論的世界については直接言及することはないが、ペリコーペの罰の概念を、終末論的審判の刑罰を示唆する表現を用いて説明していることからもそれは明らかである。

　ペリコーペの"fear hath torment"の"torment"は『マタイ』25:46等の関連箇所では"punishment"と表現されていることから、少なくともキングが白人の恐れる「苦しみ」を単なる「苦しみ」ではなく、終末論的状況における有罪の「刑罰」として理解していたことは間違いのないことだと思われる。[9] その意味からも、キングは恐怖を克服できない白人の存在を予想して、[10] 黒人に対し白人を救うべくキリストと同質の愛を要求するのである。

Ⅱ

　本節では *Antidotes for Fear* における、恐怖克服の第4ステージを見ていく。ここでは、ペリコーペの第1ヨハネ4:18を念頭に置いた上で、新たな新約テクストとして、『マタイ福音書10:26, 28-31』が引用されている。

　[26]Fear them not therefore ; for there is nothing covered, that shall not be revealed ; and hid, that shall not be known ... [28]And fear not them which kill the body, but are not able to kill the soul : but rather fear him which is able to destroy both soul and body in hell.　[29]Are not two sparrows sold for a farthing ?　and one of them shall not fall on the ground without your Father. [30]But the very hairs of your head are all numbered.　[31]Fear ye not therefore,

ye are of more value than many sparrows. (Matthew 10:26, 28-31)[11]

　第4ステージは、聴衆（読者）対象を黒人に置いていると想定される。より厳密に言えば、上記のテキストが引用されていることから、人種差別に限らず、あらゆる意味で迫害を受けている人間が対象であると考えられる。文頭で"(Fourth,) fear is mastered through faith" と語られているように、ここでの命題は、迫害を受け、恐怖に身を置く者の信仰のあり方である。そこで本節では、キングの神理解を視野に入れ、彼が人種差別の迫害の下での信仰をどのように理解しているかを中心に考察してみたい。

　キングはこの命題を考察するに当たり、本来のテキストを再編集している。とは言っても、イエスが弟子たちに語ったとされる、『マタイ』10：26-31の段落から、単に27節だけを削除したにすぎない。それでも、説教を耳で聴く立場からは、この編集によって、大きな効果が認められる。まず、最も顕著な効果として、「恐れるな（Fear them not…／fear not them…／Fear ye not…）」という命令形の強調が挙げられる。この言葉が整理された文脈の中で、間を空けずに3回繰り返されることにより（26、28、31節）、聴衆は神から、救いを前提にした力強い慰めの言葉を受けていることを強く意識する。[12] ここでは、「恐れるな」という表現が、人間に対する神の加護を表す言葉として機能している。その一方で、28、29節で語られるきわめて厳しい思想もまた相対的に強調されることになる。E.シュヴァイツァーの言葉を借りて言えば、"雀は地に落ち、イエスの弟子たちは殺される"[13] とあえて語られる不幸も強調されるのである。つまり、キングの編集によって、上記の新約テキストは、テキストが元来含有していた「救い」と「滅び」を支配する神の像を、よりいっそう強固にした形で聴衆に提示することになる。このような編集目的が意図されたものであることを裏付けるのがキングの次の言葉である。

　A positive religious faith does not offer an illusion that we shall be exempt from pain and suffering, nor does it imbue us with the idea that life is a drama of unalloyed comfort and untroubled ease. Rather, it instills us with the inner equilibrium needed to face strains, burdens, and fears that inevitably come, and assures us that the universe is trustworthy and that God is concerned.

　再編集された新約テキストと合わせ、まず、ここで明らかになるのは、キングが信仰を、人間を苦痛から救うものとは考えていないということである。同時に、キングは"親切な神様という幻想的な像"[14]もまた描いてはいない。キングは第1ステージと第2ステージで、勇気を持って冷静に恐怖と直面することの意義を語ったが、その姿勢はここでも一貫している。どれほど強い信仰を持っていようとも、黒人に対する迫害は阻止できないとキングは考えている。積極的な宗教信仰（a positive religious faith）と人種差別のような社会問題を解決することとは別問題であるとキングは認識しているのだ。彼は決して現実の問題から目をそらすことはない。人種差別を乗り越えるのは、現実的・物理的な政治行為にのみ可能なことであると彼は理解している。この点において、キングはニーバーと同じ地平に立っている。黒人聴衆はこのキングの言葉と再編集された『マタイ』10:26, 28-31を聴くことで、改めて自分たちの置かれている不快な現実を意識し、自分たちが、実存的な不安（existential anxiety）の中から生れてくる恐怖に直面していることを実感する。

　それにもかかわらず、新約テキストと同様に、キングの言葉が非常に力強く響くのは、神がすべての宇宙——救いと滅びのすべて——を支配しているという、神に対する信頼の表現がそこに聴き取れるからである。

　キングは言う。

　　Religion endows us with the conviction that we are not alone in this vast, uncertain universe. Beneath and above the shifting sands of time, the uncertainties that darken our days, and the vicissitudes that cloud our nights is a wise and loving God. This universe is not a tragic expression of meaningless chaos but a marvelous display of orderly cosmos...

　このような宗教観の背景には、『マタイ』10:26, 28-31の中で3回にわたって繰り返される「恐れるな」の表現に対応する、まったく逆の「恐れなさい（28節）」で始まる使信に関してのキングの積極的な理解がある。具体的には、"fear him which is able to destroy both soul and body in hell" と語られる部分である。『マタイ』10：26-31 では「恐れ」の語がキーワードになっているが、それは「恐れるな」の表現が3回にわたって繰り返されているからではない。反対のベクトルを表す「恐れなさい」で始まる使信が語られることで、「恐れ」が「恐れ」によって克服されているからである。すなわち、人間が引き起こす迫害に対する「恐れ（人間に対する恐れ）」が、"魂も体も地獄で滅ぼすことのできる"[15] 神に対する「恐れ」によって克服されているからである。[16] キングが "Death is not the ultimate evil; the ultimate evil is to be outside God's love." と言うとき、彼は何を本当に恐れなければならないかを理解している。また同時に、自らにとって、神への「恐れ」が神の愛に対する「信頼」であることも明らかにしている。新約神学的に言えば、ペリコーペの『第1ヨハネ』4：18 の下で『マタイ』10：26, 28-31 を引用することによって、キングは「恐れ」を「愛」へと高めている。[17] その際に、キングのペリコーペ理解の前提となっているのが、『マタイ』10：29-31 に関するキングのストレートとも言える解釈である。

Man, for Jesus, is not mere flotsam and jetsam in the river of life, but he is a child of God. Is it not unreasonable to assume that God, whose creative activity is expressed in an awareness of a sparrow's fall and the number of hairs on a man's head, excludes from his encompassing love the life of man itself? The confidence that God is mindful of the individual is of tremendous value in dealing with the disease of fear, for it gives us a sense of worth, of belonging, and of at-homeness in the universe.

ここには、すべてを包括する神に対するキングの強い信頼と確信が表明されている。この信頼と確信は決して大げさなものではない。迫害の最中にあって、人々に神の下での穏やかなアイデンティティを与えるものである。上記引用文中の "for it gives us a sense of worth, of belonging, and of at-homeness in the universe" と語られている部分、とりわけ「世界の中でくつろいだ感覚（a sense of at-homeness in the universe）」と表現される言葉が聴衆に与える響き

は、これまでの引用文中の「心の平静（the inner equilibrium）」や「秩序あるコスモス（orderly cosmos）」などの言葉と並んで、キングの神理解を示唆するものであると同時に、迫害下における信仰のあり方を述べたものと受け取ることができる。それゆえに、Antidotes for Fear の最後に置かれたアラバマ州モントゴメリーにおけるバスボイコット運動の際のエピソードは、キングの信仰者としての迫害へのスタンスを例示したものにほかならない。

　以上のように見てくると、キングが引用した『マタイ』10:26, 28-31 の部分は、『マタイ』の続く段落（10:32-33）[18]も含めることで、本来の使信が完成すると考えることができる。こうした観点からキングの編集を見た場合、彼の編集によって除かれた部分（10:27）[19]と引用テキストに続く部分（10:32-33）には共通項があることに気づく。両箇所とも信仰告白をテーマとしている点である。ここで語られるのは信仰を公言せよとの使信である。同様に、編集（ペリコーペ選択）の観点から『第1ヨハネ』4:18 を見た場合、続く 4:19-21[20]は愛と恐怖についての小論の完結部に当たり、[21]直前の 4:18 を受けて、隣人を愛する行為を要請する言葉で結ばれている。こうして見ると、キングの編集した第1ヨハネとマタイのテキストは、ともに信仰の告白（言葉による信仰の表明、および行為による信仰の表明）に関しての表現が削除されている点が類似している。このいかにも意図的な新約テキストの活用方法の背後にあるのは、削除した使信内容を、削除したと聴衆に気づかせることで、あえて強調したいとするキングの意図にほかならない。その強調したい使信内容こそが、人種差別下のアメリカ南部社会の中で日々具現化される、愛に基づく非暴力運動という信仰告白なのである。

注：
1. King, JR, Martin Luther. *Strength to Love*. New York : Harper & Row, 1963
　なお、本稿でも Washington, James M. (ed.), *A Testament of Hope : The Essential Writings and Speeches of Martin Luther King, JR*. New York : HarperCollins Publishers 1991 を底本として用いている。
2. ここでは、キングは欽定訳聖書（King James Version）を用いている。
3. 第1ヨハネ 4:17（King James Version）は以下のとおり。

第 4 章　公民権運動とキング牧師の説教　167

　　Herein is our love made perfect, that we may have boldness in the day of judgment : because as he is, so are we in this world.
4. Rudolf Bultmann, *Die drei Johannesbriefe*, Göttingen : Vandenhoeck & Ruprecht, 1967
川端純四郎訳『ヨハネの手紙』日本基督教団出版局　1987、101 頁
5. Johannes Schneider, *Die Katholischen Brief*, Göttingen : Vandenhoeck & Ruprecht, 1968
安達忠夫、他訳『合同書簡（NTD 新約聖書註解　第 10 巻）』ATD・NTD 聖書註解刊行会　1975、381 頁
6. Ibid., p.381 から引用
7. King, JR, Martin Luther. *Letter from Birmingham City Jail* 1963
なお、本稿では *Strength to Love* と同様に、Washington, James M. (ed.), *A Testament of Hope : The Essential Writings and Speeches of Martin Luther King, JR.* New York : HarperCollins Publishers 1991 を底本として用いている。p.301
8. キングの思想の終末論的側面に関しては以下の文献が有益である。
Cone, James H., *Martin and Malcolm and America : A Dream or a Nightmare*, Maryknoll, N Y : Orbis 1991
梶原　寿『マーティン＝L＝キング』清水書院 1991
9. R. ブルトマン『ヨハネの手紙』川端純四郎訳　104 頁
なお、ブルトマンはこの句の含有する終末論的審判の刑罰の意味に理解を示しつつも、ルター等にならって「恐れは苦しみを持っているから」の意をより適切であるとしている。
マタイ 25：46（King James Version）は以下のとおり。
And these shall go away into everlasting punishment : but the righteous into life eternal.
10. J. シュナイダー『合同書簡』安達忠夫、他訳　382 頁
11. ペリコーペ同様、欽定訳聖書による。
12. Julius Schniewind, *Das Evangelium nach Matthäus*, Göttingen : Vandenhoeck & Ruprecht, 1968
量　義治訳『マタイによる福音書（NTD 新約聖書註解　別巻）』ATD・NTD 聖書註解刊行会　1980、274 頁
13. Eduard Schweizer, *Das Evangelium nach Matthäus*, Göttingen : Vandenhoeck & Ruprecht, 1973
佐竹　明訳『マタイによる福音書（NTD 新約聖書註解　2 巻）』ATD・NTD 聖書註解刊行会　1978、331 頁から引用
14. E. シュヴァイツァー『マタイによる福音書』佐竹　明訳　331 頁から引用

15. 新共同訳による。なお、この場合の「魂」は「生命」と同義語であると理解される。
16. J. シュニーヴィント『マタイによる福音書』量　義治訳　275頁
    シュニーヴィントはさらに、以下のようにも言う。
    "われわれの文言（マタイ 10：28 ＝筆者注）は残酷な殉教の死に対する恐れを、神はいかなる人々よりもはるかにずっと恐れられねばならないと言うことによって克服している。" 275-276頁
17. J. シュニーヴィント『マタイによる福音書』量　義治訳　275頁
18. マタイ 10：32-33（King James Version）は以下のとおり。
    Whosoever therefore shall confess me before men, him will I confess also before my Father which is in heaven. But whosoever shall deny me before men, him will I also deny before my Father which is in heaven.
19. マタイ 10：27（King James Version）は以下のとおり。
    What I tell you in darkness, that speak ye in light : and what ye hear in the ear, that preach ye upon the housetops.
20. 第1ヨハネ 4：19-21（King James Version）は以下のとおり。
    We love him, because he first loved us. If a man say, I love God, and hateth his brother, he is a liar: for he that loveth not his brother whom he hath seen, how can he love God whom he hath not seen ? And this commandment have we from him. That he who loveth God love his brother also.
21. J. シュナイダー『合同書簡』安達忠夫、他訳　382頁

5. "Paul's Letter to American Christian" を読む

※本稿を読むに当たって、まずインターネット・サイト http://www.stanford.edu/group/King/ で上記の説教の内容を確認してください。

はじめに

　マーティン・ルーサー・キング・ジュニアは1960年の初頭にジョージア州アトランタに移転するまで、アラバマ州モントゴメリーのデクスター・アヴェニュー・バプテスト教会（Dexter Avenue Baptist Church, Montgomery, Alabama）の牧師として活動した。これまで見てきたように、この期間の前半はローザ・パークス（Rosa Parks）事件に端を発するバス・ボイコット運動が展開され、キングは一貫してその精神的・実際的指導者として運動を勝利に導いた。その際のキングのリーダーシップは周囲から高く評価され、彼は1957年2月に南部キリスト教指導者会議（SCLC = Southern Christian Leadership Conference）の議長に選出されることになる。結果的に、モントゴメリー時代の後半期は、公民権運動の指導者としての活動が中心を占めるようになり、自身の暗殺未遂事件（1958年9月20日）等もあり、教会活動を十全に行い得ないと感じたキングは1959年末に、デクスターの教会に辞任を申し出ることになる。
　ここではキングのモントゴメリー時代のターニング・ポイントとも言える、バス・ボイコット運動の勝利直前に発表された説教 *Paul's Letter to American Christians*[1] の構造分析を通して、キングのモントゴメリー時代前期のアメリカ観、およびキリスト者としてのアイデンティティの問題について考察することを目的としている。具体的には、本稿Ⅰで説教発表時のキングを取り巻く状況と説教内容の関連性を、本稿Ⅱでは、当該説教とキングがそのモデルにしたと言われる、使徒パウロによる『ローマの信徒への手紙（以下「ロマ書」と略

す)』との構造比較を行うことで、当初の目的を達成したいと考えている。[2]

I

Paul's Letter to American Christians は 1956 年 9 月 7 日の全米バプテスト会議でまず説教され、次に、同年 11 月 4 日にモントゴメリーのデクスター・アヴェニュー・バプテスト教会で説教されている。タイトルにもあるように、キングはこの説教で、使徒パウロが書簡を用いてアメリカ合衆国の教会の会衆に語りかけるという架空の状況を設定している。その結果、会衆は説教を聴くに当たり、『ロマ書』に代表される新約聖書のパウロ書簡のイメージを強く意識することになる。パウロ書簡の対象であるローマやコリント、ガラテヤ等の教会とアメリカ合衆国の教会を同次元に置くことで、キングはアメリカとアメリカのキリスト者の現状を原始キリスト教会的図式の中で描き、理解しようとしたのである。

説教の中で、キングはアメリカ合衆国の科学的進歩について肯定的に語る一方で、それに追いつかないアメリカ人の道徳的・精神的進歩を問題とする。さらに、資本主義の誤用、教会の分裂、人種差別の日常化等に代表されるアメリカ社会の現状を批判する。その上で、人種差別の非キリスト教性に言及することで、差別に苦しむ人々を励まし、現状を克服するためには愛による交わりが必要なことを力説する。

ここでは、まず、キングの現状認識と公民権活動におけるこの説教の位置づけを明確にするために、バス・ボイコット事件前後のキングの活動に関する代表的事項を時代順に列挙してみたい。

第4章　公民権運動とキング牧師の説教　171

表1　バス・ボイコット運動前後のキングの活動

西　暦	月　日	事　　項
1954年 (25歳)	10月31日	アラバマ州モントゴメリーのデクスター・アヴェニュー・バプテスト教会 (Dexter Avenue Baptist Church, Montgomery, Alabama) 第20代牧師に就任
1955年 (26歳)	12月1日	バス・ボイコット事件
	12月5日	バス・ボイコット運動開始 (1956年12月まで)
1956年 (27歳)	1月30日	キングの家に爆弾が投げ込まれる
	6月4日	連邦地裁、市バスにおける人種隔離を違憲と裁定
	6月27日	全米黒人地位向上協会 (NAACP = National Association for the Advancement of Colored People) の年次総会 (サンフランシスコ) におけるゲスト・スピーカー
	8月10日	民主党全国大会 (シカゴ) の綱領委員会における講演
	9月7日	全米バプテスト会議で "Paul's Letter to American Christians" を説教
	11月4日	モントゴメリーのデクスター・アヴェニュー・バプテスト教会で "Paul's Letter to American Christians" を説教
	11月13日	連邦最高裁、アラバマ州条例、およびモントゴメリーの市条例における人種隔離政策を違憲とする連邦地裁の判決を支持
	12月20日	連邦最高裁、アラバマ州、モントゴメリー、およびバス会社に対して人種隔離禁止命令通達
1957年 (28歳)	1月27日	キングの家で不発弾発見
	2月14日	南部キリスト教指導者会議議長に選出

　上記の事項から容易に想像し得るのは、この時期に、キングの知名度がバス・ボイコット運動における指導的活動を通して、全米的なものになったことである。若干27歳の若さで、全米における最も伝統のある公民権団体であり、すでに1930年代には人種隔離に反対する訴訟活動を開始していたNAACPのゲスト・スピーカーとして招かれたことや、民主党の全国大会で講演を行ったことは、地方の一牧師に過ぎなかったキングが早くもアメリカ合衆国の良心としての発言を求められるようになったことを示している。テレビの急速な普及もあいまって、南部のモントゴメリーという限定された地域のバス・ボイコット運動は連日全米に報道されたが、そのようなメディアの進歩もまたキングが社会指導者として認知される要因になった。

　9月7日の全米バプテスト会議における、若いキングへの説教依頼も、こうした時代の流れから理解し得ることである。また、説教のタイトルが *Paul's*

Letter to American Christians となっていることも、より広範な発言を期待されるようになった当時のキングの状況を反映している。人種問題の集中する地域のキリスト者、すなわち、「南部地域のキリスト者（Southern Christians）」ではなく、「アメリカ合衆国のキリスト者（American Christians)」という言葉が説教表題の中で使用されているのは、南部地域の人種問題を、アメリカ合衆国民の共通問題として捉え直そうとする、キングのアメリカ社会に対する新たなスタンスを表したものである。

　さらに、この説教を取り巻く状況で強調したいのは、2度にわたる爆弾騒ぎである。キングは生涯にわたって、身の危険を感じつつ宣教および公民権活動を行わなければならなかったが、クローザー神学校時代における2回のピストル事件はともかくとして、1956年1月30日の自宅への爆弾投げ込み事件は、彼への最初の目に見える形での迫害であった。また、1957年1月27日には自宅で不発弾が発見されてもいる。幸いなことに、2度ともキングや家族に被害は及ばなかったが、ここで問題なのは、爆弾事件そのものよりも、バス・ボイコット運動の背後に、敵対者の命を奪うことをも辞さない、想像を絶する憎しみの感情が存在していたことである。爆弾事件は迫害の最たるものであるが、同時にそれは迫害の象徴としての行為でもあった。つまり、ひとつの爆弾事件の陰には何十という日常的迫害が存在し、有名なKKKの迫害を例示するまでもなく、この時期のキングには記録には現れない小さな迫害が数多く待ち受けていた。ゆえに、キングが *Paul's Letter to American Christians* をアメリカ合衆国のすべてのキリスト者を対象として語ったのも、抗議せず、無言でいることが迫害を是認することになると内心では自覚しているサイレント・マジョリティに対する、パウロの名を借りた批判でもあったのである。

II

　次に、キングの *Paul's Letter to American Christians* の具体的構成について考えてみたい。先にも述べたように、当該説教はパウロの『ロマ書』をモデルにしていると言われているが、これはあくまでも、そのメッセージ性に由来してのことであり、文書分量的には『ロマ書』と比べるとはるかに短いものであ

る。分量的な問題は、キングが *Paul's Letter to American Christians* を礼拝での説教を前提として構成したために生じた結果であり、文書の長さを比較することはあまり意味のないことのように思われる。しかし、文書構成の相似性に関して言えば、『ロマ書』が導入部（冒頭のあいさつ、および主題の提示部）と終結部を除き、いわゆる本文と呼ばれている部分を全3部で構成しているのに倣い、[3] キングがこの説教全体を意識的に緩やかな3部構成としているのを容易に発見できる。

**表2　パウロの『ローマの信徒への手紙』と
キングの "Paul's Letter to American Christians" の内容構成比較 I**

パウロの『ローマの信徒への手紙』			
導入部	1:1－1:17	冒頭のあいさつと主題の提示	
第一部	1:18－8:39	救いへと導く神の力としての福音	
第二部	9:1－11:36	神による義とイスラエルの運命	
第三部	12:1－15:13	キリスト者への倫理的生活の勧め（キリスト者の倫理的生活綱領）	
終結部	15:14－16:27	伝達事項と結びのあいさつ	

キングの "Paul's Letter to American Christians"			
導入部	第1～4段落	冒頭のあいさつ	
第一部	第5～11段落	アメリカ合衆国におけるキリスト者の責任―キリスト者の二重国籍について	
第二部	第12～17段落	教会の定義と役割	
第三部	第18～25段落	人種差別の犠牲者（迫害を受ける者）への励ましと愛の意味について	
終結部	第26段落	結びのあいさつ	

　上記の表2でも明らかなように、導入部と終結部を除く各部に関して、2文書間の内容上の関連は薄いが、説教を構成する上で、文書上の分量バランスの面からもキングが『ロマ書』の3部構成を範としているのは明確である。

　一方で、『ロマ書』本文（第一部～第三部）について取り上げると、第11章と第12章の間に大きな境目があるとはよく言われていることである。[4] すなわち、第1章18節～第11章36節では福音の証が述べられ、第12章1節～第15章13節では、その福音に根ざした実践訓的な勧めが述べられている。[5]　換言すれば、『ロマ書』は組織神学的・歴史神学的展開を示す前半部と、実践訓的

なキリスト教的生活綱領の後半部に分割される。このような立場から、キングの説教を見た場合、やはり同様のことが当てはまる。3部に分ける構成比較よりも、むしろこちらの方が内容的にも蓋然性が高い。

表3　パウロの『ローマの信徒への手紙』と
キングの"Paul's Letter to American Christians"の内容構成比較Ⅱ

			パウロの『ローマの信徒への手紙』
主要部	前半	1:18 - 11:36	福音の証
	後半	12:1 - 15:13	福音に基づく実践訓的勧め (特に、愛の交わりの奨励 14:1 - 15:13)

			キングの"Paul's Letter to American Christians"
主要部	前半	第5～21段落	現代アメリカにおける福音の理解
	後半	第22～25段落	最高善(救済のキーワード)としての愛の奨励

表3は、先の表2では不明瞭であったパウロとキングの比較文書における、内容に関する類似性を明確に示している。特に、パウロ、キングともにそれぞれの所属する地域社会を背景に、福音についてのメッセージを前半で語り、その上で、福音に基づく倫理的行動を、「愛」の語句をキーワードに展開させている。さらに強調したいのは、両者とも前半と後半の接合部をほぼ同種のブリッジ構造で連結させている点である。

表4　パウロの『ローマの信徒への手紙』と
キングの"Paul's Letter to American Christians"の前・後半接合部

	パウロの『ローマの信徒への手紙』における前半・後半の接合部
前半	For of him, and through him, and to him, are all things : to whom be glory for ever. Amen. (11:36)
後半	I beseech you therefore, brethren, by the mercies of God, that ye present your bodies a living sacrifice, holy, acceptable unto god, which is your reasonable service. (12:1)

	キングの"Paul's Letter to American Christians"における前半・後半の接合部
前半	The end of life is not to be happy. The end of life is not to achieve pleasure and avoid pain. The end of life is to do the will of God, come what may.
後半	I must bring my writing to close now. Timothy is waiting to deliver this letter, and I must take leave for another church. But just before leaving, I must say to you, as I said to the church at Corinth, that I still believe that love is the most durable power in the world.

第4章　公民権運動とキング牧師の説教　175

　表4から明らかになることは、両者ともに前半部を終了するに際し、人間における神の主体性を確認する文章で結んでいる点である。パウロは「神の栄光」と言い、キングは「神の意志」と言う。前者は「神の（永遠の）栄光（のために）」と理解され、後者は「（何事が起きようとも）神の意志（に従うために）」と理解されることから、いずれも"神のみが救済史の起源であり、統括者であり、目的である"[6]との意味を含有していることは明白である。それは同時に、神の栄光が讃美され、神の意志が実現されるための、人間社会における具体的な行動指針が示唆される終わり方でもある。

　そのことをパウロの『ロマ書』で検証するならば、後半部開始の"ye present your bodies a living sacrifice"の表現に見ることができる。パウロが使用するa living sacrificeの概念には、ユダヤ教に代表される、宗教における祭儀的犠牲の意味はもはやなく、[7] 神の栄光のためには、あえて迫害をも甘受するという、犠牲についての新たな解釈がある。おそらくキング自身、パウロと同じベクトルで犠牲について理解していたと思われるのが、キングの説教における以下の記述である。

　Don't worry about persecution, America; you are going to have that if you stand up for a great principle. I can say this with some authority, because my life was a continual round of persecutions. After my conversion I was rejected by the disciples at Jerusalem. Later I was tried for heresy at Jerusalem. I was jailed at Philippi, beaten at Thessalonica, mobbed at Ephesus, and depressed at Athens. And yet I am still going. I came away from each of these experiences more persuaded than ever before that "neither death nor life, nor angels, nor principalities, nor things present, nor things to come... shall separate us from the love of God, which is in Christ Jesus our Lord." I still believe that standing up for the truth of God is the greatest thing in the world.[8]

　上記の引用文は前半部の終わりの部分（先に表4で示した箇所の直前）で語られている。あえて迫害というキーワードを用いるまでもなく、この引用部分

は、キングがパウロのキリスト者としての人生そのものを、自らの体を神への供え物として捧げた犠牲的行為であると認識していることの証左と言えよう。[9] しかも、キングは自らの言葉に加え、具体的に『ロマ書』からの引用を用いてパウロ自身に語らせてもいる（『ロマ書』8：38–39、上記引用符内の部分）[10]。キングが *Paul's Letter to American Christians* における前半・後半の接合部分を、『ロマ書』に倣って構成した背景には、アメリカ合衆国における人種差別の状況を、原始キリスト教会の、とりわけパウロを取り巻く迫害の状況と重ね合わせることにより、予型論的に強調しようとしたと見ることができるのである。

すなわち、パウロ的背景におけるユダヤ人キリスト者グループの対立と異邦人キリスト者グループの対立はそのままアメリカ合衆国における白人と黒人の対立に置き換えることができるかもしれない。こうした対立を背景にして、パウロが異邦人の福音とイスラエルの運命を結びつけたように、キングはアメリカの福音をイスラエルの約束と結びつけようとしたのではないかと思われる。[11] さらに言えば、その際に、パウロが迫害下にある自らの特定の具体的状況から福音を提示したように、キングもまた人種差別に苦しむアメリカ南部の危機的状況から語りかけているのである。[12] ゆえに、両者ともに迫害にさらされた宣教の主題として提示されるのは、キリストの愛をキーワードとする、具体的状況を視野に入れた救済論なのである。[13]

最後に注目しておきたいのは、キングは後半部に移行するに当たって、一見当面の話題とは関係のないようなコメント（テモテに関する言及）を、述べている点である。[14] その後に、キングは救済のキーワードである愛について語り始める。このテモテに関する間奏部は、説教を聴く会衆に、前半部が終了し、後半部が開始されることを自覚させるための一種の説教学的技法であることは明白である。さらに言えば、この間奏部分は、後半部開始の単なる合図としての機能だけでなく、その中で、具体的に"the church at Corinth（コリントの教会）"という言葉を用いることで、同じパウロの『コリントの信徒への手紙1、および2』を会衆に想起させ、[15] 権威ある倫理的勧告の開始を告げる後半部のプロローグとしての機能も有しているのである。

このように見てくると、*Paul's Letter to American Christians* の文書構造と使信内容を見る限り、キングがパウロの『ロマ書』をモデルに当該文書を執

第4章　公民権運動とキング牧師の説教　177

筆したことは疑いのないことのように思われる。キング自身はパウロの『ロマ書』には言及せずに、単にパウロ書簡とのみ語っているが、人種差別が続く1950年代後半のアメリカ南部の危機的状況を、パウロが長く置かれた危機的状況とオーバーラップさせて捉え、パウロと同じ福音をアメリカ合衆国においてキングが展開させようとしたことだけは間違いない。そのような意味では、必ずしも『ロマ書』のみがモデルである必要はなく、パウロの書簡すべてがモデルであるということも可能である。しかし一方で、時代の特定な具体的状況に基づいて福音を証し、その上で、実践的な倫理として愛の交わりを勧告する『ロマ書』が危機的状況の中で宣教活動を行わざるを得ないキングにとって、最も適切なテキストであったのも確かなことなのである。[16]

注

1. 本稿はウェブ・サイト "The Martin Luther King, Jr. Papers Project at Stanford University" に収蔵されている *Paul's Letter to American Christians* を底本として用いている。
2. *Paul's Letter to American Christians* は2種類の原稿が残されているが、ここでは1956年11月4日に行われたモントゴメリーのデクスター・アヴェニュー・バプテスト教会における説教を用いている。表1を参照。
3. Paul Althaus, *Der Brief an die Römer*, Göttingen: Vandenhoeck & Ruprecht, 1966 杉山好訳『ローマ人への手紙（NTD新約聖書註解　第6巻）』ATD・NTD聖書註解刊行会 1974、III-VII 頁および 8-10 頁
4. *Ibid*., pp.8-9, 306
5. *Ibid*., pp.8-9
6. *Ibid*., p.297 から引用
7. *Ibid*., p.308
8. ウェブ・サイト "The Martin Luther King, Jr. Papers Project at Stanford University"
9. P. アルトハウス『ローマ人への手紙』杉山好訳　307-308 頁
10. 『ロマ書』8：38-39（King James Version）では以下のように語られている。下線部分がキングの引用箇所。

    [38]For I am persuaded, that neither death nor life, nor angels, nor principalities, nor powers, nor things present, nor things to come,

[39]Nor height, nor depth, nor any other creature, shall be able to separate us from the love of God, which is in Christ Jesus our Lord.

11. P. アルトハウス『ローマ人への手紙』杉山好訳　4-5頁
12. *Ibid.*, p.3
13. *Ibid.*, p.3
14. キングのテモテ、およびコリントの教会への言及は以下のとおり。

    "I must bring my writing to close now. Timothy is waiting to deliver this letter, and I must take leave for another church. But just before leaving, I must say to you, as I said to the church at Corinth, that I still believe that love is the most durable power in the world."

    ウェブ・サイト "The Martin Luther King, Jr. Papers Project at Stanford University"
15. キングの使用した "the church at Corinth"、およびその背景となるパウロの『コリントの信徒への手紙1、および2』が会衆に喚起するイメージとしては、Heinz-Dietrich Wendland が述べているように、"この世における教会の状況と課題を示す最も古典的な例" という理解が適切であると思われる。コリント書はロマ書に比べて実際的であるとはよく言われることだが、おそらくキングはコリント書の一般的イメージを念頭に "the church at Corinth" の語を使用したと想像される。

    Heinz-Dietrich Wendland, *Der Brief an die Korinther*, Göttingen : Vandenhoeck & Ruprecht, 1968

    杉山好訳『コリント人への手紙（NTD 新約聖書註解　第7巻）』ATD・NTD 聖書註解刊行会 1974、4頁
16. *Ibid.*, p.3

■著者略歴

青木　敦男（あおき　あつお）
1956年生まれ。学習院大学大学院人文科学研究科イギリス文学専攻博士課程前期修了
現在、玉川大学文学部助教授。(専門) 古英語

飯村　龍一（いいむら　りゅういち）
1959年生まれ。英国ノッティンガム大学大学院言語学科修士課程修了
現在、玉川大学文学部助教授。(専門) 英語学、談話分析

佐藤　成男（さとう　しげお）
1954年生まれ。玉川大学大学院文学研究科英米文学専攻修士課程修了
現在、玉川大学経営学部助教授。(専門) 19世紀アメリカ文学

菊池　重雄（きくち　しげお）
1953年生まれ。米国南メソジスト大学大学院パーキンス神学部修士課程修了
現在、玉川大学経営学部助教授。(専門) アメリカ教会史

資料で読む欧米の社会と文化

2001年10月20日　初版第1刷発行

■編　者────菊池　重雄・佐藤　成男
■発行者────佐藤　正男
■発行所────株式会社 大学教育出版
　　　　　　　〒700-0951 岡山市田中124-101
　　　　　　　電話 (086)244-1268　FAX (086)246-0294
■印刷所────互恵印刷㈱
■製本所────日宝綜合製本㈱
■装　丁────ティー・ボーンデザイン事務所

Ⓒ 2001, Printed in Japan
検印省略　　落丁・乱丁本はお取り替えいたします
無断で本書の一部または全部の複写・複製を禁じます

ISBN4-88730-453-6